P9-ECM-861

DEADLY TIMES

Irwin, Lew.
Deadly times : the 1910
bombing of the Los Ange
[2013]
33305227844804
cu   07/22/13

DEADLY TIMES

The 1910 Bombing of the Los Angeles Times *and America's Forgotten Decade of Terror*

LEW IRWIN

LYONS PRESS
Guilford, Connecticut
An imprint of Globe Pequot Press

SANTA CLARA COUNTY LIBRARY

3 3305 22003 9444

Dwight Williams invested more than a year of his life in the research and writing of this book, and he deserves great thanks.

―～―

To buy books in quantity for corporate use
or incentives, call **(800) 962-0973**
or e-mail **premiums@GlobePequot.com.**

© 2013 Lew Irwin.

ALL RIGHTS RESERVED. No part of this book may be reproduced or transmitted in any form by any means, electronic or mechanical, including photocopying and recording, or by any information storage and retrieval system, except as may be expressly permitted in writing from the publisher. Requests for permission should be addressed to Globe Pequot Press, Attn: Rights and Permissions Department, PO Box 480, Guilford, CT 06437.

Lyons Press is an imprint of Globe Pequot Press.

Interior photos by Lew Irwin unless otherwise noted.

Project Editor: David Legere
Layout Artist: Justin Marciano and Maggie Peterson

Library of Congress Cataloging-in-Publication Data is available on file.

ISBN 978-0-7627-8354-0

Printed in the United States of America

10 9 8 7 6 5 4 3 2 1

To the memory of Barbara Sinclair Van Noy, without whose prodding, encouragement, assistance, and love this book would never have materialized. She was the first to read every word and comment on nearly every page. That she did not live to see it published is my saddest regret.

Victor Hugo, in his immortal work, Les Miserables, *sends the kind priest to reason with the old dying revolutionist, who sat on the porch of his hermit's cottage, waiting for the night and death, which were coming side by side. The priest upbraids him for the cruelty of the revolution; the old man rouses from his dying stupor and says, 'You speak of the revolution—a storm had been gathering for fifteen hundred years; it burst, you blame the thunderbolt.' ... With the land and possession of America rapidly passing into the hands of a favored few; with great corporations taking the place of individual effort; with the small shops going down before the great factories and department stores; with thousands of men and women in idleness and want; with wages constantly tending to a lower level; with the number of women and children rapidly increasing in factory and store; with the sight of thousands of children forced into involuntary slavery at the tender age that should find them at home or in the school; with courts sending men to jail without trial for daring to refuse to work; with bribery and corruption openly charged, constantly reiterated by the press, and universally believed; and above all and more than all, with the knowledge that the servants of the people, elected to correct abuses, are bought and sold in legislative halls at the bidding of corporations and individuals: with all these notorious evils sapping the foundations of popular government and destroying personal liberty, some rude awakening must come. And if it shall come in the lightning and tornado of civil war, the same as forty years ago, when you then look abroad over the ruin and desolation, remember the long years in which the storm was rising, and do not blame the thunderbolt.*

CLARENCE DARROW, 1895

I'm not cynical; don't get that impression. I go on the assumption that the great majority of the people are right, and that all that is necessary is that they have subjects presented in the proper way to them; that a campaign of education should be carried on to enlighten them as to conditions as they actually are.

J. J. McNAMARA, OCTOBER 11, 1911

Contents

PREFACE

This book was conceived nearly fifty years ago when I interviewed Irving Stone, one of the leading practitioners in his day of the art of biographical fiction. Combining fact with his imagination, he churned out absorbing accounts of the lives of Charles Darwin (*The Origin*), John and Abigail Adams (*Those Who Love*), Michelangelo (*The Agony and the Ecstasy*), Van Gogh (*Lust for Life*), Jack London (*Sailor on Horseback*), Abraham and Mary Lincoln (*Love Is Eternal*), Sigmund Freud (*The Passions of the Mind*), and others.

In preparation for my interview with Stone, I had read several of these books, but it was *Clarence Darrow for the Defense*, which he wrote in 1940, that particularly intrigued me. In it, the iconic lawyer is portrayed the way many of his disciples regarded him—as a champion of the working man who risked his career in 1910 to come to California to defend two union men, the McNamara brothers, who had been accused of bombing the *Los Angeles Times*, killing at least twenty men, and attempting to murder the newspaper's owner and the head of the city's primary business organization. While the jury was being selected, it became clear to Darrow that the evidence against the men was overwhelming and, determined not to allow them to "die for a cause," he made a plea deal that sent them to prison. But before the deal could be presented in court, Darrow was arrested for attempting to bribe two talesmen (selected members of the jury) to vote not guilty.

When I read *Clarence Darrow for the Defense*, I was not even aware that the *Los Angeles Times* had been bombed fifty years earlier. The event was not mentioned in any California history textbook that I had read in high school or college. I had worked part-time in high school for a sports columnist for the *Times* and made numerous trips to the newspaper to deliver his copy. In no hallway that I entered, no office that I visited was there a photograph or a front-page facsimile related to the bombing—which to this day remains the deadliest crime ever to go to trial in California.

How is it that this cataclysmic event, with all its detective-story intrigue, colossal characters, and historical impact, had never been recounted in book form in its entirety? I decided to write a book that would investigate the causes of the bombing, the people who ordered and carried it out, and those who tracked them down and brought them to justice.

Two people who had been alive at the time of the bombing were enormously helpful to me then. They were Oscar Lawler, a member of the prosecution team (who himself was nearly killed when a union terrorist bombed his home a few years later), and Adela Rogers St. Johns, an old newspaper hand herself, and the daughter of famed attorney Earl Rogers. She was by her father's side when he visited some of the injured and dying victims in the early morning of the attack, and she watched him in the courtroom as he defended Darrow against the jury-bribing charges a year later. Although he was ninety-one years old at the time, Lawler's memory of the case was extraordinarily vivid—he even remembered the odd weather the city was experiencing on the day of the bombing.

But as I dug more deeply into the case, I became astounded by the liberties Irving Stone had taken with the facts in his account. Stone admitted that, "In 1940, when I wrote *Clarence Darrow for the Defense,* I staged, as though they were being acted under a proscenium, all of the conversations that seemed interesting and important. . . . I feel sure they had considerably more emotional impact than if I had related at second hand what the conversations had been about." (The dialogue that appears in this book, on the other hand, is taken verbatim from contemporary court transcripts and newspaper and magazine interviews.) Stone took Darrow's side: He had been framed. But Stone's effort to portray Darrow as an untarnished, lionhearted hero of the working man crumbles in light of the facts—particularly the facts laid out in Darrow's second bribery trial in Los Angeles.

I can understand now why Stone had portrayed Darrow so. There would otherwise have been no hero/villain theme, no great man to extol and follow into the sunset. I realized that it is something of a fool's errand to try to concoct an appealing drama, based on the interactions of powerful personalities, when all of your protagonists are in the wrong. That is the problem with this story. The bombing of the *Times* was the culmination of a ten-year war in California in which one side carried a banner proclaiming "Industrial Freedom" and the other, "Power to the People," each reflecting a grand pretense in order to acquire overweening authority and influence. Employers who at the turn of the century were willing to sign modest union agreements slightly improving wages and agreeing to the six-day week banded together to prevent further advances. Labor responded with boycotts not only of the companies that insisted on the open shop but also of companies that did business with them. The city's government, an obsequious cohort of business, passed not only antiboycott legislation but also anti-picketing legislation.

The *Los Angeles Times*, in editorials often written by the newspaper's owner, Gen. Harrison Gray Otis, gave business its voice. "Employers of labor should be ready to meet and vanquish those who make unreasonable and arrogant demands upon them," he wrote. But the unions escalated their demands and by 1910 were striking one business after another.

Labor-capital turmoil in Los Angeles was reflected in the businesses of other US cities as well, particularly in the building trades. Bridges and buildings erected by nonunion workers were often blown up within days of their completion. Terrorism reigned in America. During the four years from 1906 to 1910, terrorists—they wore the label proudly—struck more than 200 construction sites.

And then the Los Angeles Times Building was bombed, killing at least twenty workers. (The actual number is in dispute. Reports at the time indicated that the remains of twenty-one or twenty-two bodies, many of them merely incinerated or mangled body parts, were removed from the wreckage. Only fourteen could be identified. The names of the others came to light only after relatives and friends reported them missing, and it appears likely that one or two who perished may not have had relatives or friends living in the city. At any rate, twenty names are listed on the monument in their honor erected on the site of a mass grave where most lie buried at a Hollywood cemetery. It is the number that the *Times* now regards as official. The dynamiters, to confuse the matter further, were charged with nineteen counts of murder.) One local weekly, the *Pacific Outlook*, editorialized following the bombing, "And on the morning when the tragedy was announced, nine men out of every ten in Los Angeles said in their thoughts: 'Well, I have long expected something to happen.'" It was later revealed that the bombing—or *bombings*, if the failed attempts on the lives of General Otis and Merchants & Manufacturers Assn. chief Felix J. Zeehandelaar on the same day are included—was to be only the opening salvo in a terror campaign funded by a major US union, the Iron Workers, aimed at bringing the city to its knees.

This story interweaves the lives of two rough-and-tumble men who came from similar humble stock and who would come to represent the opposing forces of labor and capital of the day. Eventually their fates would converge in Los Angeles—although they would never meet—where one would establish an ascendant empire and the other would attempt to demolish it.

Still, the story lacks heroes. However, look at the world around us today. It is now more than a hundred years after the bombing of the *Times,* and the forces of terrorism and suppression are still engaged. It's still a tragic story. With no heroes.

Chapter 1

And so it had come to this, as he had always feared it would. Ortie McManigal glanced down at his fettered hands and feet, then at the detectives guarding him, then out the train window at the stiff cactus and the rolling chaparral, kicked up by the concussive force of the Santa Fe Chief as it breached the natural stillness of the desert landscape rolling inexorably toward Los Angeles, California. To him the panorama must have seemed as bleak and as barren as his future had become.

He had ridden the same train in the opposite direction only a few months earlier after a botched job in Los Angeles. When he had arrived in California in the late fall of 1910, he was captivated by the city's warmth and Spanish charm. He had bought a ticket for the Tilton Trolley Trip, a sightseeing tour that included visits to the San Gabriel Mission, the soldiers' home, the orange groves, and the beaches. At the mission he had posed for a group photo that he planned to show to his wife and kids when he returned home to Chicago. Later that day he had visited Eastlake Park, stopping for a while by the placid man-made lake, tossing bread crumbs to the fish. He had strolled over to the park zoo, spending several hours watching the animals, including two lion cubs whose mother had died and were now being nursed by a large dog. He wished his children, Evelyn and Walter, could have been at his side. Indeed, he had thought that this city was a place where he might eventually bring his family to live permanently. It had been Christmastime—a time that most men spent with their families, not thousands of miles away from them, planting dynamite bombs.

He had done it all for them. He never would have planted a single stick of dynamite under a building just to serve some idealistic cause. But for his family, he would do anything. And so he had allowed himself to be recruited as a terrorist—the most prolific one this country has ever seen, then or since. In a span of just two years, he had single-handedly destroyed dozens of buildings and bridges in America. For his family. Now he was haunted by the question, what would become of them?

Perhaps he had felt so unfailingly devoted to them because as a child he had never known a real family of his own. He was four when his mother died in 1878 and twelve when he was placed in the care of his grandfather, a stern blacksmith who did not hesitate to put the boy to work at the local stone quarry in Bloomville, Ohio.

The quarry's owner, Nat France, taught Ortie how to handle all manner of explosive devices, showing him where the charges should be properly placed in order to yield granite rubble small enough so that it could be easily hauled away for processing. Placed improperly, the charges would set off an explosion that produced huge boulders that would have to be broken up by hand—miserable, backbreaking work.

But above all, his watchword had been safety. No substance then known to man was more dangerous than dynamite. And, as with anyone who has ever handled explosives, it was drilled into young Ortie that a careless moment could wreak injuries and death.

Still, blasting away rock was not the way that Ortie McManigal wanted to spend the rest of his life. He would later call his experience at the quarry "accidental training" since he had not chosen it himself. At age twenty-two, he left the quarry and moved to Chicago, where he took a job as a structural ironworker, joining a workforce of hundreds of thousands of men who, at the dawn of the twentieth century, were raising the steel for bridges and buildings that would define America's skylines. Two years later he joined the Second Ohio Regiment and was sent to Cuba, where he saw no action in the Spanish-American War—at least none that he ever cared to talk about. He returned to his job as an ironworker.

If serving the US Army in war and working with explosives in stone quarries were risky occupations, working with steel girders hundreds of feet above the earth was positively precarious. Men often lost fingers or toes to the steel or lost their lives to gravity. In 1901, Ortie's first year in

Chicago, eighteen ironworkers in Local No. 1 fell to their death, while another fifteen were permanently disabled.

In the spring of that year, Ortie married Emma Swantz, a petite and emotionally fragile young woman whose tousled chestnut hair and red-rimmed eyes betrayed her chronic state of anxiety. Her greatest fear, of course, was that her husband would be killed or injured on the job, leaving her without means and perhaps alone. Although Ortie was a good provider, her anxiety only intensified with the arrival of their two children.

Six years later, in May 1907, he moved his family to Detroit where, he had heard, a building boom had created a clamorous demand for construction workers, especially for experienced men like himself, who were being lured with the prospect of lucrative pay.

The day after arriving in town, he joined a crowd of sweaty, boisterous men—most of them like himself, Irish immigrants or the sons of Irish immigrants—who packed into Bridgemen's Hall. He had joined the queue in this smoky assembly hall, the local headquarters of the Iron Workers Union, to transfer from his previous union local in Chicago to Detroit local 25.

The printed forms that he filled out and submitted to a clerk outlined his work history. Before he joined the Iron Workers in Chicago, they indicated, he had spent three years rigging explosives in the rock quarries of north-central Ohio. The clerk scanned his papers, then excused himself. McManigal was left standing with a queue of impatient workers behind him as the clerk approached a group of grim-faced men standing at the back of the hall, saying a few words to one of them with sunken blue eyes and a graying mustache, then showing him McManigal's form. The man stared at it, then at McManigal, and nodded at the clerk, who returned a moment later, filed away the form, and handed McManigal his new union card.

McManigal was hired at once to work as a hoisting engineer at the construction site of the new Ford Motor Company headquarters in Highland Park. On his first day on the job, he locked eyes with the man he had seen standing in the rear of Bridgemen's Hall. Each day he had noticed the man talking to other workers during their lunch break.

Now, a week later, the man approached him, introducing himself as Herbert S. Hockin.

Hockin said that he was a union organizer, but that his job was not just to encourage workers to join the Iron Workers. Part of his task, he said, was also to organize "entertaining committees."

"He said he wanted a gang to get together," McManigal would later recall, "and go over to one of the nonunion jobs that was about two blocks from where we were working, and watch those fellows when they were through work, and either catch them leaving the job or catch them as they were getting on the streetcar, or get on the streetcar with them, and as they were getting off the streetcar, why, jump onto them and beat them up. . . . That is what they call an 'entertaining committee,' to go out and beat up a man, a nonunion man."

Like most other union members, McManigal was aware of the escalating violence against workers at nonunion construction sites. But this was the first time that anyone had attempted to recruit him to participate in the clandestine operation. Some union members, he knew, were not averse to committing murder to further their ends. McManigal wanted no part of such a bloody business and told Hockin so.

Hockin, however, was not done with him. At Bridgemen's Hall a few weeks later, he buttonholed McManigal again.

"I understand you have handled high explosives and worked around stone quarries in your time," Hockin said.

McManigal replied that he had.

"Well," Hockin told him, "we decided to have you do some exploding here."

McManigal balked. "I didn't come over here to do any exploding or entertaining anybody," he told Hockin. If he had to do that kind of work, he said, he'd withdraw his union card in Detroit and return to Chicago. Hockin told him that he would fix it so that he wouldn't be able to find work in Chicago. In fact, he'd be blacklisted by the Iron Workers everywhere.

The term "iron-willed" might have been thought up by a writer who had the men who ran the Iron Workers union in mind. Ortie McManigal realized well enough that to refuse to carry out the orders of a union official like Herbert Hockin could become a mortal mistake.

More to the point, Herbert Hockin was smugly confident that McManigal realized all of that as well.

Besides, Hockin was able to offer McManigal a tidy payment for the job, an offer that overwhelmed his reticence in a flash. After all, Emma's money worries had sometimes caused her to suffer what Ortie described as "nervous prostrations" that at times left her incapacitated.

But what if he were caught? he asked Hockin.

"Stand pat and keep your mouth shut," he replied. The union would provide lawyers and bail money. "Money was plenty . . . free as water."

McManigal yielded.

A few days later, Hockin called on McManigal again and gave him $20 to purchase dynamite, caps, and fuse wire and bring the bundle back to Detroit. The union, he told him, had decided to have him blow up a building in the city being constructed by the open-shop Russell Wheel and Foundry Company. It was one of Michigan's largest construction companies, responsible for producing the wheels for thousands of train cars and building the dome of the Detroit observatory, the Hillsboro Lighthouse, and countless office buildings in Detroit. If brothers George H. and Walter S. Russell signed an agreement with the Iron Workers, many other builders would follow suit, Hockin remarked.

And so McManigal headed back to Nat France's stone quarry, the place he had once thought he would never see again, where he purchased thirty-five pounds of 60 percent dynamite, plus caps and fuse from a cousin. He packed it all in a suitcase and carried the lethal luggage onto the train that carried him back to Detroit.

The next day Hockin gave McManigal his final orders.

"I am janitor at the Elks Temple and they are having a big supper there tonight, and it will be two o'clock or after before that is over, and I will be over there and I will have a fine alibi. . . . I want this to come off at about 12:30 or 1:00 [a.m.]" The strategy did not include an alibi for McManigal too.

McManigal arrived at the skeletal structure shortly after 10:00 p.m. He set three charges at key structural locations where they were likely to cause the most consumptive damage, attaching a fifty-foot fuse to each four-stick charge, long enough to burn for a half hour. As he did so, he looked up and saw the lights of a restaurant across the alleyway from the structure. A steel door leading to the kitchen was open, and McManigal could see activity inside.

Fearing that after hearing the first explosion, someone would run out of the kitchen and into the next explosion, he stealthily crept across the alley to the doorway and silently pushed the steel door partially closed, leaving it open just enough to let in outside air but not enough to let a worker pass through. He then cautiously rolled a heavy garbage barrel sitting next to the wall against the door so that it couldn't easily be pushed open.

Satisfied now that the men would not be harmed, he set the charges, left the plant, and returned to his hotel room. At about 12:30 a.m. he heard three explosions, followed instantly by the crackling of the steel beams as they collapsed. A few minutes later he could hear the clattering of horse-drawn fire wagons and the whistles of the firemen as they rushed to the scene.

An hour after sunrise he was still lying sleepless in bed when he heard the newsboys hollering the story of the bombing. He rose and skulked to the edge of a window, where he could see police officers posted at every street corner. He had been found out, he thought. Panicked, he ran to the wardrobe, retrieved his suitcase, then began cutting the remaining dynamite and fuse into small pieces and flushing them down the toilet. He placed the caps in his pockets, then checked out of the hotel, composing himself as he walked past one police officer after another on his way back to his construction job at the Ford Tower, where he buried the caps.

Two days later Ortie read in the newspapers that Hockin had been arrested on suspicion of having had a hand in the bombing. Certain that his own arrest was imminent, McManigal nevertheless reported back to work, where he noticed several strangers "prying about the building" and correctly took them to be detectives. He ascended the building's framework just as he did every morning, but this time in a cold sweat. At the third floor he heard someone on the ladder below him. Assuming it was a detective, he climbed faster.

"Why are you hurrying?" the man called up.

Ortie didn't answer but stopped to catch his breath at the eighth floor of the skeletal structure.

"Wait a minute!" the man shouted.

As he looked down, McManigal realized that the man wasn't a detective but a fellow worker, and let him approach. When he finally caught up to McManigal, he reached out to hand him a sealed envelope, remarking, "There is a little something in there for you."

The "little something" turned out to be $75 (the equivalent of $1,400 today) and a note reading, "Compliments from the executive board. More to follow."

Seventy-five dollars. To McManigal, it was a staggering windfall.

He expected to be able to return to his normal life. But in February he got word that Hockin—released from custody because of his "unshakable" alibi—wanted to see him again. They met in a private wine room of a saloon at the corner of Van Buren and Morgan Streets in Chicago. Hockin issued new orders.

"Now, I will tell you, Mac, what I want you to do. The Wisconsin Bridge Company has got a job out at Clinton, Iowa, across the Mississippi River. They have a derrick car out there, and I want you to go out there and turn that trick for me."

McManigal protested, saying, "I am out of business. I have quit it altogether. I am sorry I turned that over at Detroit."

Hockin replied, "Well, I know you can do the job. You done a good one over there for me at Detroit, and I want you to do this one."

McManigal still balked. "No, Hockin, I ain't got nothing to do with it. . . . I want to stay out of it."

To which Hockin replied—in words straight out of a dime gangster novel—"You better think it over a couple of days. . . . There is no use in laying down now. You have got to go right along with this thing. We have got to have this thing done."

It was clear to McManigal that Hockin was not about to take no for an answer—ever. His orders were like a net. McManigal was caught.

"We've got the goods on you now," Hockin told him. "You've got to do as we say or we'll jail you. Then where will your wife and children be? You can't lay down on us now. The executive board has set aside $125 and expenses for this job and for other jobs that you're going to do. You're going to do just exactly as we say, when we say it, and as often as we say it."

On February 13, 1908, McManigal again took a train to his hometown of Tiffin, Ohio, where he spent the night with his uncle, George Behm. The following day he rented a livery rig and bought caps and fuse from a hardware store and one hundred pounds of dynamite from his cousin in Bloomville. He then headed back to Chicago, where he rented another rig, loaded his recent purchases onto it, and drove 130 miles south to Clinton. The following Sunday afternoon, he pulled into the site of the job, a railroad yard. Bridge Company's derrick. That night, in biting cold weather, he waited in the yard until 1:00 a.m., then set a charge of fifteen sticks on each side of the hoist and twenty under the car of the Wisconsin Bridge Company's derrick. After setting the explosives, he walked along a road, across a cornfield, and then began dogtrotting along a railroad track. He heard an explosion go off and instantly realized that only one charge had detonated. He figured that the others had frozen.

The next day McManigal learned that while the blast had caused little damage, the Wisconsin Bridge Company had nevertheless authorized a new contract with the union local calling for a wage increase of 60 cents per day for every worker. When McManigal arrived back in Detroit, he was handed an envelope containing $125.

Although the money represented a veritable fortune to McManigal, he continued to be wracked with worry that he would be tracked down and jailed and that no one would be able to look after his wife and children. Desperate to free himself from Hockin's grip, he fled with his family to Howell, Indiana, where he signed on for a job at a site where a steel building was to be torn down and re-erected at nearby Evansville.

But he had been working in Evansville only a week when he spotted Hockin waving his hat and yelling to him from the middle of the street in front of his hotel.

"Jesus," yelled Hockin, "I never was so glad to see a man in all my life."

"What is the matter?" McManigal asked as they approached each other and shook hands.

"Didn't you hear about it? They picked a man up there at Iowa with a suitcase full of dynamite. I thought that was you."

"No, I have been here for a week now."

Hockin took his arm. "Let us go over to—where is the telegraph office? I must get busy right away. I must send a wire to international headquarters that you are safe."

They spotted the Western Union office directly across the street from them and entered. Hockin filled out a telegraph form, scratched out a few words, and handed it to the clerk. It was addressed to J. J. McNamara in Indianapolis: "The man is safe in Evansville."

Safe but still trapped. Years later, McManigal would write from his jail cell that with the end of the job in Evansville, so ended his peace of mind. Hockin and the union "now had me bound hand and foot. I had become their slave. I gave a lot of thought to the subject. I pondered ways of escaping them. I discussed the matter with my wife. I could see no end save jail or perhaps, should I even unintentionally kill someone, a worse fate. But men with strong will dominated me, and events proved that there was to be no escape."

Chapter 2

"It is the fattest land I ever was in. . . . It has all the elements of a great future," Harrison Gray Otis had written to his hometown newspaper when he first arrived in California in 1875 at the age of thirty-eight. He had come across the country intrigued by advertisements he had seen in the back pages of magazines touting the riches to be garnered from raising Angora goats, prized for their mohair wool. But after inspecting an Angora ranch on the uninviting and virtually deserted island of Guadalupe off the Baja coast, he set out on a tour of Southern California via the San Marcos stagecoach trail to see what else this balmy and halcyon land might have to offer him.

It clearly had a lot. "Just enough has been done in the way of developing the wonderful, varied and rich resources of Southern California to show what are the mighty possibilities of the section," he wrote to the *Ohio Statesman* in Columbus.

Otis was born in a log cabin in 1837 in Marietta, Ohio, the youngest of sixteen children packed into a modest farmhouse. They were, he would later write, "neither rich nor poor." His parents, Stephen, a farmer, and Sara, named him for a celebrated Massachusetts cousin who a generation earlier had served as the mayor of Boston and later as a US senator. His grandfather, James Otis, had seen battle in the Revolutionary War, and young Harrison worshipped him from his earliest days, never tiring of the tales of his heroic exploits.

Too restless for schooling and the restrictions of his rigid, Methodist parents, he left home at fourteen and took a job as an apprentice at a print shop in Sarahsville, Ohio, that published the *Sarahsville Courier*. It was a job he took to with the excitement and dedication of a teenager who had been lured into a cult. He became adept at flinging type and spacing slugs into their vice-like holders, then dumping the contents into frames and securing them for printing. He pored over the usually handwritten text of the local reporters and the editorials written by the paper's owner, enthralled by the often fiery and elaborately ornate prose.

He discovered that there was a demand for compositors in virtually every town where his itinerant impulses took him. In Rock Island, Illinois, he joined with colleagues at the *Courier* to demand that they be represented by the National Typographical Union. When the owners refused, the always-mobile printers quit the paper and moved elsewhere, the nineteen-year-old Otis among them.

He landed in Lowell, Ohio, where he enrolled at Wetherby's Academy, determined to hone his writing skills and learn about the business of business. He spent only eight months at the academy but nearly the remainder of his life with his teacher, Eliza Ann Wetherby, the daughter of the school's owner. "Lizzie," as he affectionately called her throughout their lifetime together, was nearly four years his elder and possessed a sophistication that the rough-hewn Otis—"Harry," she called him— marveled at. She wrote and recited poetry, was well read—and as ambitious for her young student as he was for himself. Her father, a wealthy businessman and sometime minister, was appalled at her romantic choice. When they were married in 1859, he granted her only a token dowry, and the couple began life together on his wages of $8 a week.

They did not "settle down," as most newlyweds did in those days. They continued moving from town to town, becoming embroiled in abolitionist politics along the way and eventually joining the nascent Republican Party. Landing in Louisville in 1860, the twenty-three-year-old Otis began work at the *Louisville Journal* and soon was appointed an apprentice delegate from Kentucky to the second Republican National Convention, which assembled in Chicago in May 1860. For the remainder of his life, he would boast that he had helped nominate Abraham Lincoln as the party's presidential candidate.

He hoped that his party work would be recognized by Republican leaders. In a letter to Lizzie, he warned her that he might "become the recipient of Presidential favors" and be assigned to some remote "Hottentot Country or to the Unexplored Region where they converse in the unknown tongue and live on dirt." If so, he said, she should be prepared to come with him. "I couldn't treat with dirt eaters without the aid of my wife," he quipped.

If Washington called, there would soon be three of them to take up stakes. On March 28, 1861, Lizzie gave birth to their first child, Harrison Gray Otis Jr. Mere weeks later, when shots were fired at Fort Sumter in April 1861, the new father was among the first to enlist, joining the Twelfth Ohio Volunteers as a private on June 25. Lizzie moved into a boardinghouse with the baby and two other women.

Otis plunged into military training with gusto. He and his volunteer unit performed their military drills wherever a vacant lot, pasture, or park could be found. And then, in late February 1862, he received devastating news. His son, not quite a year old, had died. But far from sending Otis into a state of despondency, the event seems to have actuated him. He was promoted to first sergeant on March 1. In August he arrived in Washington. He would soon find himself in a whirl of action in the campaign from Bull Run Bridge to Antietam.

In a small leather notebook, he set down an account of his unit's retreat at Bull Run Bridge, including phrases like "Bullets fly like hail. Enemy try to flank . . . Hot work for while—Again retreats, the enemy pursuing. Got behind myself—Saw enemy advance and from line of battle in open field on right of railroad. . . . Bullets fly like mad. Retreat through open fields and woods."

On May 20, 1863, he was promoted to first lieutenant, then to captain on July 1, 1864, the same day he was transferred to the consolidation of two regiments of the Twenty-third Ohio Veteran Volunteers. Three weeks later, on July 24, he suffered what he described as a "gun shot flesh wound right thigh" during a battle in Winchester, West Virginia, and was removed to the government hospital in Frederick, Maryland. There he was given a thirty-day furlough to recuperate at home in Ohio. A local doctor who examined him later submitted an affidavit declaring that his wound had not healed sufficiently to permit him to return to his unit.

His furlough was extended another thirty days, enabling him to be with Lizzie when she gave birth to their second child, Lilian, in September. He would not see them again for the duration of the war.

On March 13, 1865, as the Civil War was drawing to an end, Harrison Gray Otis was breveted Colonel Otis—an honorary rank bestowed for "gallant and meritorious service" (he continued to be paid as a captain) but one that he would retain for the next thirty-three years. He had been recommended for the honor by his commander, Rutherford B. Hayes. The war ended three weeks later, on April 9, and on July 25, after serving more than four years with the Grand Army of the Republic, he was mustered out of service.

He returned to his childhood home of Marietta, Ohio, where he invested some of his military earnings in the local newspaper, the *Washington County News,* and took a job as its editor. Lizzie composed poetry for it. But the paper failed to produce a profit. He later wrote that 1866 was a year in which he was "'stuck in the mud' on the job, with starvation even nearer than it was the year before" (when he was serving in the Union Army but, along with the rest of his unit, not receiving a paycheck). To get by, he also became the official reporter for the Ohio State House of Representatives. While in Columbus, he became familiar with the machinations of political patronage and eventually landed a job as a compositor in the Government Printing Office. He, Lizzie, Lilian, and now another child, Emma Marian, pulled up stakes once again and left for Washington, DC, shutting down the *Washington County News* in the process.

He and Lizzie lived a rather comfortable life in the nation's capital—at least compared with the one they had left in Ohio. He joined the Typographical Union local and eventually became foreman at the printing office. The following year he moved over to the US Patent office, eventually becoming division chief. At the same time, he edited a newspaper, the *Grand Army Times,* and also served as a Washington correspondent for the *Ohio State Journal.*

He might have lived comfortably as a minor functionary amid the Washington bureaucracy for the rest of his days. If he had not spotted that advertisement for an Angora goat farm in California.

Chapter 3

A blinding light. A muffled bang. A puff of smoke. The firing of the flash powder from a newspaper photographer's camera caught Ortie McManigal momentarily off guard as he looked away from the train's window.

"Say," he shouted to the photog with a wink and a smile, "these sounds remind me of something." He would use the line frequently, and it never failed to get a laugh from the men who were assigned to cover him.

After Evansville, the orders had kept coming.

McManigal would find himself at a train station, carrying another unnaturally heavy suitcase, and after planting a bomb, he would often return to the train station and be waiting there when it went off. Once, after he had followed his instructions from Hockin to plant one amid a stack of girder spans at a bridge being constructed by the McClintock-Marshall Company in the close vicinity of the train station in Buffalo, New York, he and those around him at the station flinched when they heard the blast and flinched again when the shock wave hit them.

In Boston he met a local Iron Workers official named Mike Young. He told him, "My name is Clark, and Ping sent me here. He said you had some work to be done at the new theater," referring to the nearly completed Boston Opera House. (Herb Hockin used the code name "Ping." McManigal was "Clark" or occasionally "McGraw.")

Young took "Clark" to the new opera house, where construction workers were placing a large girder over the stage.

"Put the shot there and blow hell out of her," Young said, pointing to the spot where he wanted the dynamite placed.

When McManigal asked why someone at the local couldn't perform the dynamite job, Young replied, "The boys here have not got the old-fashioned spirit they used to have. . . . They have made their wads and now they are spending it."

McManigal performed at the Boston Opera House on March 27, 1910.

From Boston he took a train to New York, where he was met by Frank Webb of the Iron Workers local. Webb was aware that McManigal had received orders to bomb a viaduct under construction in Hoboken. But he also thought that McManigal might be available for a little free-lancing. Would he be interested in a "big job" in New Jersey?

McManigal turned down the offer, telling Webb that he received orders only from Hockin at the union's international headquarters.

Webb upped the ante: "The boys here have got $5,000 to $6,000 in the treasury and want to use it up. We want you to come back East [and work] for us."

McManigal refused, and the next day, April 1, he took the ferry from New York to Hoboken, where he planted dynamite under the viaduct and lit the fuse. He was waiting among a crowd at the ferry dock when he heard the explosion.

Heading home the next day to Chicago, he found a telegraph office at a train stop in Pittsburgh and sent a message to "Ping" in Indianapolis reading: "Sold the stock."

No sooner had he arrived in Chicago than McManigal received new instructions from Hockin. Bombings in Mt. Vernon, Illinois, Cincinnati, Pittsburgh, Cleveland, and Akron soon followed. On several of these trips Hockin accompanied McManigal, helping to carry the explosives and making certain that McManigal carried out the job according to instructions.

"If ever a man had an evil genius, I had one in Hockin," McManigal would later remark.

Evil, certainly. A decade earlier Herb Hockin had become the most notorious man living in Detroit, suspected of prowling the city's streets and abducting and raping sixteen girls, ages ten to fourteen.

The *Detroit Free Press* described him this way: "Tall, of a wiry build, with sharp gray eyes, those who know Hockin describe him as a sensationalist of the deepest dye. . . . He has a pleasant and convincing manner . . . but has sought to throw a mantle of mystery about himself."

He was tried twice. In the first case, he was picked out of a lineup by one of his victims. Before his trial, however, police began receiving a series of anonymous letters from someone claiming to be the actual perpetrator. Though prosecutors suspected that the letters were fakes, at his trial Hockin testified that he had a long-lost brother who so closely resembled him that he might have been the guilty man. It was enough to deadlock the jury 12 to 1 for conviction, and Hockin was released.

When police came to arrest him to stand trial a second time, he was working on the construction of the Detroit post office building, high in the network of girders. Police shouted for him to climb down, but Hockin refused. By the end of the day eighteen detectives had gathered at the base of the building—along with assorted members of the local press and other spectators watching the stand-off: Hockin refusing to come down, the detectives unable to go up. Hockin would occasionally entertain the assembly by swinging from one beam to another. The detectives were not amused. They continued to wait, their meals brought to them by fellow officers.

Seven hours later Hockin climbed down and was promptly taken into custody and booked. The second trial also ended in a mistrial.

In July 1907 he was arrested again on charges brought by a girl living in Wayne, Michigan. The case never came to trial. He settled it by paying the girl $195.

In September 1907 his wife, Maude, sued him for divorce. Her divorce papers charged that her husband had taken a room at the Elks' temple where he "entertained women other than his wife."

None of all this appeared to faze the executives of the Iron Workers Union, who promoted him to ever-more expanding positions of authority and trust.

On his way home from the East Coast, Ortie McManigal transferred to a train bound for Bloomville. Exhausted by anxiety, he took a few days to gather his thoughts and to visit with his grandfather, his uncle, and Nat France, the man who had taught him his craft. The only person he confided in was his uncle, George Behm. Behm, a union card–carrying locomotive engineer, quietly expressed approval of his nephew's work, and even offered to drive him to the quarry himself to pick up more dynamite. McManigal accepted the offer, but his mind was hardly eased.

Back home again in Chicago, he confided in Emma his persistent fear of arrest, a long prison term, and, inexorably, a life of penury for his family. "The strain," he told her, "is killing me."

"Is it that serious?" she asked.

Ortie nodded. He shared with his wife the details of a few of the bombings—what it was like for him to sneak through the night with a suitcase of explosives, to be waiting for his train sometimes in the company of a policeman when the dynamite detonated, to feel terrifyingly convinced that he would be sent away and not see his wife and children for a very long time.

Emma held Ortie's head in her hands as she counseled him to quit. Ortie mumbled that he didn't know how.

When McManigal saw Hockin next, he again told him he wanted out. To his surprise, Hockin told him he was free to leave. It would, in fact, benefit the union leadership if he did so. As McManigal stared at him, puzzled, Hockin continued: The union would have him arrested and inform authorities that they had been actively policing their own ranks and had discovered the vigilante responsible for the terrible violence. By turning him in, they would demonstrate that they were doing their best to halt this shocking law-breaking.

McManigal left Hockin's company heartsick.

He turned his next trick on July 1, 1908, in Buffalo, New York. He was assigned to blow up the girder spans for an elevated railroad track that was being built by the McClintock-Marshall Company for the Lehigh Railroad.

He had just set the charges and was sneaking out beside a line of railroad cars when he decided to climb on top of a box car to see the shortest way out. A passing guard threw the beam from his flashlight on McManigal, whose figure was distorted by the misty air, and, thinking he was another guard, shouted, "Hello, Jack, is that you?"

When McManigal failed to reply, the guard shouted again, "Come down off there, you fellow, or I will shoot."

"All right, I will go down," McManigal shouted back. He climbed off the car and approached the guard, who immediately searched him. "What were you doing up there?" the guard asked. McManigal replied that he was a watchman assigned to a nearby bridge.

"Well, in that case, you had better get back on the bridge," the guard said.

A short time later, McManigal was standing in Union Station with his luggage. He had just purchased a one-way ticket to Chicago when he heard the explosion go off.

In mid-October he was detailed to Holyoke, Massachusetts, and assigned to blow up the derrick and material being used for the construction of an over-the-street bridge for the New York, New Haven & Hartford railroad. However, after setting the charge and returning to his hotel, McManigal heard no blast.

The next day he read in the morning papers that three guards had spotted smoke from the long fuse that he had lit and bravely put it out. McManigal would eventually pay tribute to the guards:

"They risked their lives to undo the crime I had committed. . . . But however it is looked at, the lives of three men were thus put in jeopardy. . . . This incident taught me that however careful I might be, I could not tell when an act of mine was going to lead to murder, and this added to the burden of worry the increasing number of crimes was placing on me."

Still, there was an upside to life as an industrial terrorist. The money McManigal made for a single bombing was nearly seven times what he could earn each week as an ironworker—enough to provide Emma and the children a comfortable middle-class existence in Chicago. And it gave him an opportunity to see the country. Sent to Buffalo to pull off a bombing job, he took a side trip to Niagara Falls, standing at an observation deck and marveling at the inexorable force of the plunging waters. Perhaps he saw his own life plunging over a similar precipice. He wandered into a small shop and bought a set of souvenir spoons that he mailed to Emma the next day.

Where would he be heading next?

Chapter 4

The white mists rolled above me, and the blue
    Made shining rifts only within the west,
And the sun lingered there, and smiling, threw
    Around his form a gold and crimson vest.
And lying there with arms above my head,
    And eyes far-reaching to the deep of skies,
The warm, sweet earth beneath me for my bed,
    That grain-wrought pyramid with all its rich supplies
So near me that my hand could reach
    And touch its yellow blades; with mountains near
With emerald seas of orchards at my feet,
The echoing roar of waves upon the beach
    Coming in softened whispers to my ear.
And June's soft, tender kisses on my face,
As if she were my lover, and her place
Beside me there to whisper hope and peace
And bid life's futile, vexing worries cease,
I lay in calm content so full and sweet,
While perfumed odors wrapped my head and feet.

ELIZA OTIS

One year after Harrison Gray Otis reconnoitered the land on his trip to California, he brought Eliza and the children to Santa Barbara (population about 3,000) to live more or less permanently. There Col. William Hollister, a member of Otis's Ohio company during the war, had already been building a personal fortune. But he had fallen afoul of the

Rev. Joseph A. Johnson, a fundamentalist Protestant minister who had purchased the local newspaper, the *Santa Barbara Press*. Hollister had ended Johnson's attacks on him and the local establishment by buying the newspaper, then in 1876 offered to resell it to his onetime army sidekick for $6,000—on credit. Otis jumped at the chance, seeing the newspaper as a means to promote Santa Barbara businesses and thereby boost advertising in the paper.

For Eliza, California seemed positively magical. She saw the newspaper as a way to share her muse with those living in the lovely seaside town. She would write poems for the newspaper about the flitting bees hovering over the local sage fields. Her husband would rhapsodize in editorials about how Santa Barbara beekeepers were able to take advantage of a "ranch" that was "free as air, for the busy bee can't be corralled, and is not amenable to the trespass laws, fence laws, poundmasters, or judges of the plain, thanks to his business end."

But although the Colonel had carefully examined the business possibilities of his new environs, he had spent little time at all examining the attitudes of its residents. He was a hellfire-preaching Republican. The good citizens of Santa Barbara were by and large easygoing Democrats (only half of whom could read).

Otis's florid populist rants seemed more like the rabid ravings of a loon to Santa Barbarans. He made no effort to court Democratic readers; on the contrary, he referred to Democrats as "hags, harlots, and pollutants." He referred to union leaders as "corpse defacers." And although Eliza charmed the local social set, her husband was shunned. For nearly six years the couple struggled to make the paper profitable. The *Santa Barbara Press* was being printed in red ink.

In 1879, when Otis's old Civil War field commander, Rutherford B. Hayes, was occupying the White House, Otis left Eliza in Santa Barbara to run the newspaper and crossed the country to meet with Hayes, hoping that he might again be billeted with a distinguished bureaucratic title—perhaps, even an ambassadorship. As he himself would later write, "The sledding being extremely hard in Santa Barbara, I applied for and was appointed chief US Treasury Agent in charge of the Seal Islands of Alaska at ten dollars a day." In truth, it was the only job that Hayes offered him.

He had been snubbed once again, and the ostracism stung. He returned to Santa Barbara and packed his warmest clothes for the trek to Alaska, writing tersely in his newspaper, on February 13, 1880: "On the first day of March, 1880, I will relinquish control of the *Santa Barbara Press* and transfer it to other hands. Meantime I wish to close up my business here, preparatory to leaving for the far north." The "other hands" were Lizzie and their two daughters, now teenagers. Lizzie, with some help from the children, wrote the entire paper each day, occasionally even setting the type. And always weaving the verses of her poetry. She had come to love this seaside town.

> The sky was wrapped in veil of soft white mist,
>   As if its summer bridal hour had come,
> And one sweet gleam of gold and amethyst—
> A wandering sunbeam into glory kissed
>   By the near sunset splendor—shone,
> A crown upon the fog-veiled mountain peak.
>   The west rained sunset kisses on the sea,
> Till all the dimples on its pure, fair cheek
>   Showed lovelier than sea-shell tints; in ecstasy
> Laughed the bright waves, and rushed along their way,
>   And threw white arms of foam and shining spray
> Upon the waiting sands, that, silver-white,
> Waited their coming through the day and night.

Few Santa Barbara residents shed tears upon the Colonel's departure. He had made no lasting friends among the townsfolk, and he bore a grudge against them for the rest of his life.[1]

And so he was compelled to move to a faraway and isolated "Unexplored Region," as he once imagined he would—alone. But if Santa Barbara was inhospitable to him, Alaska was downright, well, frosty. In his letters home, he wrote about the hardship of isolation, the intolerable weather, the futility of trying to apprehend seal poachers in a land nearly as large as the United States. And while some officials at home were arguing in favor of a territorial government for Alaska, Otis argued that such a government would be "a useless expense to the United States."

During a visit to California to see Lizzie and the children in December 1881, he and the family visited Los Angeles, where the *Los Angeles Daily Times* interviewed the Treasurer of the Fur Seal Islands. Asked about a proposal by California Senator John Franklin Miller, a fellow Republican, that the president appoint a governor of the territory, Otis replied, "The people who are agitating that question don't know what kind of a government Alaska wants." When the *Times* reporter asked, "What do the natives want?" Otis responded scornfully, "That's a very peculiar question. You might as well ask an Apache what kind of a government he would like to have."

Governing Alaska really amounted to a handful of functions, he indicated. "All we want is to keep liquor from the natives, protect the fur seal, and punish crime. Nothing more."

Otis had been sending nearly all of his $10-a-day earnings to Lizzie in Santa Barbara in an effort to accumulate a stockpile that would allow him to buy a stake in the *Los Angeles Times.*

In the spring of 1882, she sold the *Santa Barbara Press* and joined her husband in Los Angeles, where the Colonel bought a 25 percent interest in the paper, which at the time printed two hundred copies a day. He also became its editor at a weekly salary of $15. In his first editorial he wrote: "I enter upon my journalistic duties in Los Angeles with a profound faith in the future development and sure destiny of the city!"

The paper needed a motto, and Eliza provided it: "Stand Fast, Stand Firm, Stand Sure, Stand True." The paper would stand for whatever Harrison Gray Otis stood for. While Eliza provided articles on the refined social and religious life of the small town of twelve thousand, her husband wrote virtually every news article and rancorous editorial, focusing on the seamier life of the city—crime, prostitution, and politics. Together, with the help of their children, they also sold and wrote advertisements, set type, proofed copy, and greeted visitors. Then, before dawn each morning, they would start up their hydropowered printing press, run off the two hundred copies, fold them, and distribute them to newsboys by 6:00 a.m. If a major news event was covered by the paper, the newsboys would race through the streets, slapping folded copies of the paper on their thighs, and shouting the headline of the story.

But usually they simply shouted, "*Los Angeles Times*—paper!"

Chapter 5

Riding trains had become a routine function of Ortie McManigal's daily life. When trains were not transporting him to cities for dynamite jobs—and back again to his home base in Chicago—they were carrying him to planning meetings with Hockin or to the headquarters of the Bridge and Structural Iron Workers in the imposing American Central Life building in downtown Indianapolis.

After the bombings in Boston and Hoboken in April 1909, McManigal returned to Chicago and reported to Hockin.

"I have another man in the field now," Hockin told him. "He has got another invention to do away with that black fuse and all that smoke. The finest thing you ever saw."

Hockin explained that the device employed an alarm clock that could give the dynamiter up to eleven hours and fifty-nine minutes to get away from the scene before the explosion occurred. Crude and simple by today's standards, similar devices had been effectively used as early as the French Revolution. They would allow a bomber to get away to another city, or even another state, by the time the explosion occurred.

The one Hockin displayed for him was essentially an assembly consisting of an altered 89-cent Junior Tattoo New Haven alarm clock, a dry-cell battery, fulminate of mercury, and wire. On December 9, 1909, Hockin introduced McManigal to the device's maker, J. B. Bryce, in the lobby of the Braun Hotel. He referred to McManigal as J. W. McGraw.

That evening Bryce tried to explain to McManigal the principle of the time bomb. He improvised a demonstration, using a lead pencil for a battery and his wristwatch for the Junior Tattoo alarm clock. The infernal machine, as such a device was known, could be casually carried in a suitcase into a building and planted in an out-of-the-way nook; employees could be at work in the same building with a bomb and not even be aware of it. They would be at home asleep in their beds when it went off. To Ortie's mind, the infernal machine was "clean."

"We've also got the pure quill now," Hockin added.

The "quill" was a large batch of nitroglycerin that union operatives had recently purchased from an Indianapolis well shooter. This, too, was significant. With the device there would be no more smoldering, crudely spliced fifty-foot fuse to give the scheme away or sputter out, while the nitroglycerin produced a concussive blast so powerful that hardly a clock gear would be left behind as a clue for detectives. For McManigal it was enough that he would no longer be left standing next to a policeman in a depot when the next explosion occurred.

In early April 1910, McManigal was assigned to blow up an open-shop construction job in Mount Vernon, Illinois. He boarded a train carrying a heavy suitcase containing two four-quart varnish cans filled with nitroglycerin, two electric fulminating caps, and two infernal machines. He had been instructed to place one charge under a locomotive crane and the other under a hoisting engine in the Mount Vernon railroad yards.

But while casing the job, McManigal realized that it posed a difficult dilemma. The night watchman used the construction derrick that he had been ordered to blow up as a kind of eagle's nest. How to coax him out?

He approached the watchman, handed him two cigars, and invited him to join him in town to see a performance of the opera:

"My intention was to leave him in the show there, go out and blow up the job while he was at the show; but I couldn't induce him to go down to the show, no way," he would later relate.

Several hours went by while he watched the guard surveying the site from the derrick. He had already set the two infernal machines to go off at 10:30 p.m. He was fearful that when they did, the guard would be severely injured or killed. Suddenly, he hit on a plan. He snuck over to the hoist where he had planted the second bomb and reset the alarm so that it would go off a few minutes before the device planted at the derrick, figuring that when the first blast occurred, the guard would immediately leave his perch to investigate what had occurred.

The ruse worked as planned, and McManigal was standing in the Mount Vernon train station when he saw the brilliant flashes in the sky as each dynamite package went off one at a time.[2]

In the weeks that followed, McManigal became so adept at incorporating the infernal machine into his routine that he was able to accelerate the bombings. With no means to detect the device, open-shop (non-union) businesses, one by one, surrendered, signing closed-shop agreements with the Iron Workers Union that called for significant pay raises and safer working conditions. The accomplishments only emboldened the union's executive committee to finance more of the same. Soon orders for bombings of open-shop building contractors began pouring in from union locals across the country, and McManigal became maddeningly busy, with Hockin shadowing him, suddenly appearing like a specter with instructions, infernal machines, and envelopes of cash. Hardly a week went by without a new assignment.

The device had given the bombing campaign national notoriety, and McManigal had begun to understand the context of his role in the larger effort. In eighteen months he had become the preeminent, albeit anonymous, soldier in this shadow war of the labor movement. It has been estimated that he single-handedly pulled off at least 150 bombings before he was stopped. Indeed, McManigal's record as America's most prolific terrorist stands to this day. He was the fang and claw of an extensive covert campaign orchestrated by men he had yet to meet, a committee who held his fate in its hands, men who publicly denounced what he did while secretly paying him to do more.

Hockin, meanwhile, had been promoted to the executive post of "international organizer" in the Iron Workers Union—clearly the result of McManigal's work, which had yet to produce a single fatality while garnering dozens of much-improved contracts for the union membership. While other union men performed assignments for Hockin, they were often unreliable and erratic. Without McManigal, the campaign would stumble and Hockin's career collapse. Hockin's threats to expose him, however, were utterly convincing to McManigal—and he kept his discontent more or less to himself.

But the risk of capture increased with every bombing as law-enforcement authorities mobilized their resources to try to apprehend the perpetrator. All through the summer and fall of 1909, McManigal's work was assiduously chronicled in the newspapers, sometimes accompanied by a description of a "short, round-faced" stranger "with warm, brown eyes" who had been seen in town the night of the bombing wearing a wide-brim hat with a rounded crown, and an oil-cloth slicker. Each morning Emma would sit down at the kitchen table with a long pair of scissors, anxiously scan the news items, and neatly cut out the article about her husband's deed. McManigal would then present the clipping to Hockin as a receipt for the completion of a job in exchange for another envelope of cash, along with a new set of instructions—his work ever escalating in frequency, always expanding farther and farther afield, eventually moving westward, all the way to the Pacific.

Chapter 6

At the turn of the century, families and individuals who left their homes in the East and hauled their possessions aboard the Los Angeles–bound Southern Pacific Railroad train were mostly motivated by either of two objectives: to find the lucrative opportunities that the West seemed to hold out or to escape the often brutal weather that they were forced to endure winter after winter.

Harry Chandler found himself among the latter group. He had grown up as a robust lad, the eldest son of Moses Knight Chandler and Emma Jane Little Chandler in Landaff, New Hampshire. Landaff had only one school, the Blue School, and Harry attended it through the eighth grade. But his parents recognized that Harry had the potential to rise above their humble circumstances and in 1880 moved to Lisbon, a larger town nearby, so that Harry and a younger brother, Fred, could enroll in the local high school.

He excelled there, even while working with his father at a bobbin factory after school hours. In 1883 he was accepted for entry into Dartmouth, and that's when his life would change forever.

It was the sort of stunt strapping college youths took on in those days—and, for that matter, sometimes in our own. A friend dared him to dive into a vat of starch that had frozen over in the first cold snap of winter. He took the dare and came out of the vat blue but exultant. Within hours, however, he was overcome with a high fever and a hacking cough. He was soon coughing up blood.

He would be unable to survive the winter, his doctor told him. No known medicine would cure him. The doctor's prescription: Go to a warmer climate like Southern California.

And so Harry dropped out of Dartmouth, joined the travelers on the Southern Pacific Railroad, and headed, nearly penniless, across the country to Los Angeles. Arriving in the dusty, inhospitable town, he found a cheap hotel and checked in. He had no idea what he would do next.

Chandler's persistent cough bedeviled him. He was considered a "lunger," to use the term of the day for tuberculosis victims, a possible risk to those around him. No matter that his condition was not brought on by disease but by youthful horseplay—he sounded like, and by this time looked like, a sickly young man on the fringe of life.

He eventually took a $12-per-week job in Colonel Otis's circulation department at the *Times*. The work involved hard physical labor hauling bales of the newspaper, now eight pages long, onto the loading docks. The work toughened him. He once again regained his health and put on muscle and weight. The sickly, wheezy student who had originally come to California seeking simply to stay alive had become a strapping, six-foot-two physical presence who turned the heads of ladies and whose piercing blue eyes intimidated other young men. He also caught the eye of his supervisors at the *Times*. He was soon promoted to chief of collections, and then to mail-order manager.

More significantly, he had started running a side business. He quietly began buying up delivery routes of virtually every newspaper in Los Angeles, including the *Express, Tribune, Herald,* the *San Diego Union,* and of course the *Times*—his earnings from one route financing the purchase of the next. The newspaper distribution process of the day involved a system in which the papers' owners sold their subscriber lists to independent contractors who, in turn, organized the routes and hired and commanded the army of newsboys to deliver the papers to subscribers and hawk them on street corners. Soon Harry Chandler's subscriber list numbered more than 1,400. He was as astute, hardworking, and ambitious as they came, rising before 4:00 a.m. each day to supervise his delivery crew, then heading to the *Times* for his day job. And his plans did not stop with being clerk and chief delivery boy for the Colonel, a boss who didn't yet know his name.

Harry Chandler would later recall a turning point in his life. Unable to sleep on a hot summer night in about 1887, the twenty-three-year-old

rose before 2:00 a.m. and headed in the direction of the Times Building.
The warm air accentuated the odor of horse manure in the streets that had
yet to be cleaned up from the day before. The dimly lit streets forced him
to walk slowly and cautiously. Then, at First and Spring Streets, he noticed
in the pitch dark a strange apparition for this hour of the night—a line
of about four hundred men, seemingly standing about, doing nothing. He
soon learned that they were waiting for a land office to open, where they'd
be able to buy a subdivided empty lot in Alosta (now Glendora) the next
morning. Some of the men, he learned, had been waiting in the line for
days. One of them called him aside and told him that he had been expecting his son-in-law to relieve him for a couple of hours so he could get some
rest. He offered to pay Harry a dollar an hour to hold his place in line.
Harry informed the man that he had to be at work at 4:00 a.m. and couldn't
remain beyond that time. The man returned promptly in two hours, paid
Harry $2 and, more importantly, indirectly delivered an invaluable lesson:
People were frantically desperate to buy developed land in Los Angeles.

Cheap and bounteous, hundreds of acres could be bought up. He soon
acquired a three hundred-acre tract in Burbank, complete with a modest
farmhouse, where he installed his parents and grandfather, who tended
orchards of apricot and peach trees and a field of grape vines. If he had
come to the land of opportunity, he had realized soon enough that opportunity was land.

He made no lofty pretensions about his goals in life. He intended to
make money, lots of it, as quickly as possible. He began purchasing stock
in the *Los Angeles Times*.

By 1885 the *Los Angeles Times* was bringing in $50,000 a year, the
equivalent of $1.1 million today. It was a huge sum for the Colonel, who
had led an itinerant life, meandering aimlessly from one nondescript job
to another through most of his adult life, "a typical drifter," as one writer
later put it. In that year, he and Henry H. Boyce, a fellow Civil War colonel
and one of the five co-owners of the *Times*, agreed to buy out their three
other partners, thereby becoming fifty-fifty owners of the newspaper.

Boyce saw himself not so much as an investor but—horrors!—a newsman. He held the strong belief that the *Times* could become an influential

force for good in the city of Los Angeles. There was a significant problem for the Colonel, however. Boyce was a Democrat who favored such things as women's suffrage, allowing foreign ownership of real estate, and—most unforgivable as far as the Colonel was concerned—the right of unions to negotiate "closed shop" agreements with employers barring the hiring of nonunion workers.

At times the confrontations between the two men threatened to drift beyond the threshold of rhetoric. Matters became so dire that Boyce finally exercised an option that allowed him to sell off his interest to Otis should the Colonel be able to come up with $27,000. Otis was forced to scrounge about town, dropping by his various friends and banking allies, but managed to borrow the money, and on April 8, 1886, the *Los Angeles Daily Times* fell under the total control of the Colonel for the first time.

Two of the Colonel's first orders of business were, first, to drop "Daily" from the masthead, simply calling the newspaper the *Los Angeles Times*. He then set about financing a new building. When it opened in May 1887, he christened it "the Fortress," in keeping with his military posture. It was an imposing four-story brick-and-granite structure rigged out with state-of-the-art electric printing presses that spat out newspapers faster than the old hydropowered presses by a factor of ten. Eliza's motto greeted visitors at the doorway: "Stand Fast, Stand Firm, Stand Sure, Stand True." Four years later, Otis had a splendid eagle, cast in bronze and modeled after the one on the newspaper's masthead, mounted above the front turret of the building, where it kept a vigilant watch.

With Los Angeles enjoying its biggest growth spurt in history, the Colonel's newspaper was making money, but Harrison Otis was leveraged to such an extent that it must have seemed to him that he was buying as much red ink for his accountants as black ink for his printers. Meanwhile Henry H. Boyce had not simply taken his $27,000 and walked out of Otis's life. He had instead invested the money in the *Times*'s chief competitor, the *Los Angeles Tribune*. On the editorial pages of each paper, they savagely libeled one another and then, in turn, sued one another for libel, making for a toxic melodrama that the entire city followed. Circulations of both papers soared.

In one typical *Tribune* editorial, Boyce referred to Otis as a "brute" and the *Times's* city editor, Charles Lummis, as a "sneak" and a "little liar." Otis may have taken such language in stride and replied in kind in the *Times*. (He is "a coarse and vulgar criminal," he wrote.) Not so Lummis. As the editor recalled years later in his autobiography, he confronted Boyce in front of the Nadeau Hotel on Spring Street and "whacked him across the face with my leather cane." The encounter was duly reported in the *Times*, which maintained that it was justified by Boyce's libelous attack "to which no sober person would think of replying in words." Three days later Lummis suffered a stroke that left him paralyzed on his left side.

Thus the conflict between the two rivals continued to play out—until Harry Chandler entered Harrison Otis's life.

Chandler arranged a meeting with the Colonel and laid out a plan. He informed him that he had been able to gain control of the circulation of most of the newspapers in Southern California—if not the *Tribune*—and that he had the means to put Boyce out of business.

As Chandler, seemingly blind to his own ruthlessness, would later recall: "He said I couldn't do it. I told him I could and not only that but for the *Times'* sake I should. My scheme was to starve out the *Tribune*. With two of the three morning papers' distribution systems under my control, it would be simple to play them together against the *Tribune*. If a *Times* subscriber quit, we could swing him to the *Herald*, whereas he might have gone to the *Tribune* if left alone. If a *Herald* subscriber quit, we could swing him to the *Times*. Of course, no one but General Otis would know of my connection. The *Herald* routes were to be handled through a dummy."

It took nearly two years for Chandler's "starvation" scheme to play out. As the *Tribune's* circulation slid, local businesses began to withdraw their ads and place them with the *Times*. Boyce never figured out how he was being ruined, and he was eventually forced into bankruptcy, getting no more than 5 cents on the dollar for his presses and other assets. Otis had hoped to take over his rival's business, but someone bidding under an assumed name beat him to it. A few days later, during a meeting between

Otis and Chandler, the young circulation manager admitted that he was the new owner of the *Tribune*. Otis was impressed, to say the least.

On June 5, 1894, eighteen months after his first wife's death, Chandler was again standing at the alter with a new bride, who wore a wedding gown of pearl-gray silk. She was none other than the Colonel's daughter, Emma Marian Otis, a business office secretary at the *Times*. Harrison and Eliza were the two witnesses, and the very private ceremony took place at their home at 1948 Grand Avenue. Emma was twenty-seven and not quite a beauty, her very own father's newspaper describing her on her wedding day as "tall and handsome." Nevertheless, Harry was either in love or single-mindedly doing whatever it took to ascend to the very heights of power in his adopted home of Southern California. Twelve years after having arrived here, deathly ill and relatively impecunious, he now had accumulated a small fortune and secured for himself a place in the sun.

History is replete with tales of how two men of opposite temperament and character forged a powerful nexus. Had Harrison Gray Otis and Harry Chandler never met, they might have gone on to lead prominent but inconsequential lives. But the two Harrys together forged an epic relationship that impacted the course of Southern California history like no personal alliance before or since.

Harrison Gray Otis had found someone who would prove vital to the *Times* and its place at the center of a family dynasty. The Colonel would dream and his son-in-law would actualize the vision, guiding his father-in-law's attention away from his newspaper and to the Southern California real estate game, which was where the truly big money was.

Their bonding would make them two of the richest, most powerful men in America.

Chapter 7

After lurking in the shadows for years, taking inordinate care to avoid being identified as a potential suspect in the bombings that he single-handedly carried out, Ortie McManigal had landed on the front pages of every major newspaper in America. At every train station, photographers from the local newspapers would clamber aboard and snap photos of the most famous American terrorist who had ever lived.

Reporters elbowed for position behind them, fetching ragged note-pads from their pockets and pencil stubs from their hat bands.

"Do you have a statement to make?" he would invariably be asked.

"Nothin' stirrin'," McManigal would invariably reply.

He would have plenty to say later.

Ortie McManigal was well aware that he would not have been riding this train, with his legs and arms in heavy shackles, if J. B. McNamara had never entered his life. He was, however, unaware that at this very moment, J. B. was riding in another car of this same train, manacled too.

J. B. McNamara had courted trouble from the time he was a rowdy tyke hanging out in the Irish neighborhood of Cincinnati. Runts like J. B. would often peek through the swinging doors of the local saloons to see what the bigger and tougher kids were up to. When the saloon owners heard their voices and angrily barged out the doors, J. B. would be the last one to run—and consequently, the only one likely to be caught. He wound up spending much of his childhood in church-run correctional institutions for juvenile delinquents—or "houses of refuge," as the Catholic diocese called them.

In time he would find his place inside the saloon and make it his second home, growing into a coarse, hard-drinking chain smoker who courted prostitutes and bedded married women while he worked as an itinerant printer. J. B.'s temper was connected to a short fuse. By the time he was in his mid-twenties, he had been fired from nearly every job he had ever held, once calling his foreman at a printing plant an "old gray-haired son of a bitch," then shouting, "You can stick this job up your ass," as he walked out. After poking about central Indiana for work, he finally landed at the office of his brother, John Joseph ("Joe") McNamara, at the American Central Life Building in downtown Indianapolis. Joe—or, as he was often called, J. J.—had been elected to the prestigious job of secretary treasurer of the Iron Workers Union. And he had a job handmade for his troubled little brother.

Four years earlier, the Bridge and Structural Iron Workers Union had gone on strike against the American Bridge Company to demand a closed-shop contract—one that would not permit the company to employ non-BSIW workers. By the following year, the strike had spread across the country to other steel makers and erectors, who banded together to form the National Erectors Association to fight it. The NEA had billions of dollars at its disposal. The union had a few thousand. It lost. In every major US city, except Chicago and San Francisco, the open shop continued to prevail.

But the union did not surrender peacefully. A series of explosions mysteriously wrecked new buildings and bridges being constructed by NEA members. There was only one bombing in 1906. Three more in 1907. Then, beginning in February 1908, after Ortie McManigal was recruited by Herb Hockin, they began occurring almost every week. The solid front of the NEA began crumbling as threatened contractors began signing closed-shop agreements with the Iron Workers.

At BSIW conventions, union officials made indirect and jocular references to the bombings—and were cheered. At one convention, Thomas Slattery, a business agent for the Iron Workers in Brooklyn, moved "that no more bombs or explosives of any kind be exploded while this convention is in session." His audience howled with laughter. The officials who were clandestinely directing the bombing strategy, including President

Frank Ryan and his chief lieutenant, J. J. McNamara, were reelected without opposition.

In the spring of 1909, J. J. introduced his brother to Hockin, who instructed him on how to buy explosives, how to splice together long, slow-burning coils of fuses, how to secrete them in construction sites and light them with a cigar so as not to be noticed, and how to establish an alibi by being at a public saloon when the device went off.

On May 9, 1909, J. B. joined Ortie McManigal in the dynamite plot, blowing up a viaduct under construction by a subcontractor for McClintock-Marshall in Kenosha, Wisconsin. The subcontractor caved the moment contract negotiations resumed the following day, and the union local received a pay raise for its members. Like an addict hooked after his first fix, J. B. experienced a profound, almost overpowering exhilaration from that initial success. Not only had he enhanced the career of the older brother he worshipped, but at age twenty-eight the ne'er-do-well believed he had found his calling.

The work quickly came to consume J. B.'s waking hours. He had always been a handy tinkerer. Now he was professionally motivated for the first time in his life, and thus took it upon himself to devise new methods of striking terror in the hearts of open-shop companies across the upper Midwest. He had seen any number of diabolical weapons and explosive devices in men's magazines, and he began attempting to replicate one that particularly intrigued him, using an alarm clock, a dry-cell battery, and fulminate of mercury. A few weeks later he presented a finished device to his brother. J. J. was impressed and showed it to Hockin, who in turn wanted McManigal to examine it.

Hockin brought J. B. and McManigal together for the first time at the Braun Hotel in Muncie in December 1909. Surprisingly, McManigal got along well with the combustible McNamara. J. B. was a lively spirit, always ready for a drink, often spouting outrageous, provocative political opinions. McManigal would later note that he could be unpredictable socially and careless in his work. And, unlike McManigal, J. B. was not inspired to take precautions against injuring workers when he pulled off a dynamite job. Far from it. In December 1909 he dynamited a house in

Struthers, Ohio, occupied by nonunion men working for the American Steel Sheet and Tinplate Company. Seven persons were injured.

Moreover, J. B.'s whiskey dependence made him prone to getting into scraps with strangers over trivial matters. In July he dynamited the house of David Wheeling, a member of the Iron Workers Union. It's not known whether J. B. had simply become involved in a drunken dispute with Wheeling or suspected that the man harbored antiunion sentiments. Wheeling quit the union afterward.

McManigal and J. B. McNamara were the two principal agents of an unprecedented terrorist campaign that struck the nation in the summer of 1910. But as calls for "assistance" poured into J. J. McNamara's office from labor leaders in other parts of the country, McNamara began assigning other men to construction sites. The alternates were generally ill trained and often too agitated to pull off the jobs as directed. Some who were assigned to work with McManigal or J. B. McNamara, fearful that they would be injured by the dynamite they transported or that they would injure others, became unglued and bowed out at the last minute. Meanwhile the general public remained less than alarmed, as were the poorly paid rank and file of law enforcement who had few reservations about open-shop companies being blown into submission on behalf of poorly paid workers.

The fact that the victims of the bombings were, without exception, faceless, tight-fisted corporations who demanded cheap labor, coupled with the widely publicized statistic of a fatality-free bombing campaign, had given rise to a popular toleration, if not tacit approval, of this manner of violence. By the early spring of 1910, a vast number of union workers were engaging in industrial sabotage of one kind or another. In the eyes of many desperate working Americans, this was an imperative fight. But the damage to property was real (averaging approximately $1,000 per bombing), as was the terror it inspired in those Americans who saw corruption in the labor movement and took a stand against it, not to mention those nonunion workers who feared that the next bomb might explode under them.

To further skew perceptions in the court of public opinion, J. J. McNamara announced in *Bridgemen's Magazine,* which he edited, a $500 reward for the capture of the bombers. McManigal was impressed by J. J.'s sheer straight-faced duplicity. J. J.'s ability to assume disparate roles was impressive: By day he could pass himself off as a distinguished and admired union boss, while at night he smuggled explosives.

By the spring of 1910, McManigal had reconciled himself to his illicit life. He'd grown accustomed to the comfort that the money he made as a bomber had brought him and, to a certain extent, the excitement. "I was on the verge of what for the next two years was to be my sole occupation," he would later write. And that was fine with him. Like J. J. McNamara, he had become a chameleon, effortlessly posing as a traveling businessman by day while carrying out his secret life with a new sense of equanimity by night.

In June of 1910 J. B. McNamara came to visit him in his Chicago home for the first time. There, in an atmosphere of domestic normalcy—McManigal's wife, Emma, served refreshments; his six-year-old daughter and four-year-old son played nearby—the two men talked about their recent bombing activities. Soon McManigal had a weekly visitor to his home on Sangamon Street in Chicago. Together the two would sit around a table in McManigal's parlor on a Sunday afternoon, busily building infernal machines and testing them with wires running to the front of the house. If the device passed their test, instead of exploding it would ring the doorbell.

But McManigal and the two McNamaras had a problem: Herbert Hockin.

Things began to unravel for Hockin when McManigal and J. B. were assigned to pull off a job together in Cleveland. They were to make the trip with a stopover first at Indianapolis, where they would report to J. B.'s brother. On the train, McManigal expressed his satisfaction with the arrangement and remarked that he hoped that they would work together as partners from that time on.

"It is better for the two of us to work [together] continually," he told J. B. "Many times you run across places where another man would be a very good partner to you. While you set the explosion, the other man would be doing the watching."

J. B. wasn't at all happy about such an arrangement, however. They were only going to be paid $100 each for the Cleveland job. He told McManigal, "I would rather work alone. . . . There is more [money] in it." His hands were busy rolling cigarettes.

McManigal replied, "There is only $25 difference."

"How do you make that out?" J. B. asked, fussily placing a wad of tobacco on a thin slip of paper.

"They only pay $125 for one job and expenses when you work alone."

J. B. retorted, "Hell no, they pay $200 and expenses."

McManigal was mystified. "They have raised it, ain't they?" he asked.

"No, that has always been that."

"Well, I never got it."

"You got $200 for the Mt. Vernon job, didn't you?"

"No," replied McManigal, still confused, "I did not. I got $150."

J. B. pressed the point. "Yes, because I seen the stub, and it called for $235. You got $200 for the job and $35 for expenses."

Suddenly it all became clear to McManigal. Herbert Hockin was the one who had been paying him. And J. B. had been present at his home when Hockin had handed him the cash for his last job.

"You were up at the house when that fellow paid me, and he gave me $125 there and my expenses were $25, which made $150 . . . I never got that money [$200], and Hockin has never given me more than $125 for a job."

J. B. stopped arguing. He said, "I thought there was something wrong when he called you into the kitchen and handed you the money. You have been double-crossed."

McManigal was ready to get off the train at the next station.

"I'm not going any further," he told J. B. "I'm done."

J. B. calmly lit a cigarette, then began rolling another one.

As the train chugged on toward Indianapolis, the two men talked incessantly about the duplicitous Herbert Hockin. Not only did it appear that Hockin was skimming money off the payments made to McManigal, but he was also padding McManigal's expenses and keeping the overage.

J. B. told McManigal, "I always did think he was a crooked son of a bitch, and I know he is now. I never got a cent off him and I never will. I always got my money direct from J. J. McNamara."

When they arrived in Indianapolis, they found the Iron Workers secretary-treasurer in the executive boardroom at union headquarters. J. B. told his brother, "This fellow has been double-crossed and is pretty damn sore about it. He claims he has $475 due him."

McManigal told J. J. McNamara that Hockin had recently paid him $125 for the job he had just pulled. McNamara reached for an office checkbook bound in a blue cover and began thumbing through the stubs until he found one for $235 made out to himself as part of the stratagem of avoiding a paper trail. His fingers flicked through the stubs and found similar ones for each of the other jobs McManigal had pulled—each stub showing figures over $235.

McNamara's face reddened. "By God! This thing will never be carried on like this!" he shouted. The executive board set aside $200 and expenses for each job, and that has been drawn for every job so far. If that's the kind of business Hockin is in, I'll see about it."

If anything, J. J. McNamara was even more outraged than McManigal about Hockin's unmistakable treachery. The honor-among-thieves code had been breached by a trusted union agent. In recent years the typical union ironworker's pay had increased from $2.50 for a ten-hour workday to $4.30 for an eight-hour workday. J. J. knew he had Ortie and his brother Jim to thank for this—not Hockin. Thus he acted with purpose, summoning Hockin into his office, demoting him on the spot, and promising to pay McManigal himself for each job from that moment on. Hockin erupted in rage at his punishment, shouting that he wasn't paid enough for all he did and the risks he took. J. J. insisted that his decision was final, and Hockin bolted from the room fuming. Once he had left, Ortie asked J. J. why he hadn't just fired Hockin.

"He simply knows too much," J. J. replied.

It was a particularly inauspicious moment for a quarrel to surface among the Entertainment Committee. Requests were coming in with ever-greater frequency from union locals, and with each job J. J.'s star ascended a little higher. He had clearly become a figure to be reckoned with among the leadership of the AF of L.

In the words of McManigal, "[J. J.] thought money and destruction all the time."

The jobs were also getting bigger. While McManigal was now being paid directly by J. J. McNamara, he was still receiving bombing assignments from Hockin. One of these involved the destruction of a bridge being constructed over the Beaver River in Ohio, destined to become the longest cantilever span in the United States. Hockin instructed McManigal to take a train over the bridge, wait until it passed the halfway mark, then throw a bomb from the rear of the train onto the bridge.

McManigal responded: "You mean to tell me that the way that train travels through, you can tell when you're getting in the middle of the bridge? That train travels forty miles an hour, and you could tell when you get in the center and throw her off?"

Hockin insisted that there would be no problem doing so.

McManigal retorted that there certainly would be a problem. "You couldn't guess it within twenty feet of it," he said.

Hockin asked, "What is the difference?"

It was more than McManigal could put up with. "It makes a hell of a lot of difference," he told Hockin. "I am on that train, and that train is on the bridge."

The job did not come off. The next day Hockin received a telegram and left town. McManigal later concluded that it had been sent by J. J. McNamara. He was to learn that the charges against Hockin had come to the attention of the union's executive board, which forthwith relieved Hockin of his duties as the overall chief lieutenant in the dynamite plot.

A few days later, Hockin visited Lindsay Jewell, the construction superintendent for McClintock-Marshall, and made a deal to become a paid informer for the company. He told Jewell that the executive board of the union planned to have Beaver Bridge blown up as a loaded passenger train passed over it. He said he could not stand for murder.

With Indianapolis as his hub, Ortie McManigal followed spokes drawn on his map to small towns like Greenville, New Jersey; McKees Rocks, Pennsylvania; and Superior, Wisconsin, as well as booming cities like Pittsburgh, Omaha, Kansas City, and Peoria.

In Kansas City on August 22, 1910, he set two "infernal machines" on the girders of a bridge being built by McClintock-Marshall (the company was the union's most prominent target) across the Missouri River. The explosions were timed to go off at 9:30 p.m. McManigal sat outside his hotel that night, waiting to hear the booms. But 9:30 came and went, and not a pop was heard from the direction of the river. He listened until 11:00 p.m., then went to bed.

The next afternoon, he walked over to the construction site and, as he put it later, "casually" strolled over to one of the girders where he had set one of his machines, and duly noted that there was no trace of damage. McManigal would later relate:

"As I passed there I seen the two cans [of nitroglycerin] were still setting there, and the infernal machine still setting on them. I walked down around and came back and slipped in between the two girders and picked up the infernal machine and put it under my coat and walked down toward the river. . . . I had an electric ammeter in my pocket, and I tested the battery, and I found the battery was too weak to explode the cap. I took the battery off the board and went up in the city and got another battery, and had it tested out to be sure it was a good, live one. Went back to the river and fastened this battery on the board and tested it there by exploding a cap, and after I had . . . I retimed it for 9:30 that night, and went back and set it in these cans that were still between the two girders. Went back up in the city and was outside the hotel when the explosion took place at 9:30 that night."

Still, he had had to leave one of the duds behind at the site.

J. J. McNamara was pleased with McManigal's work. A highlight of his day would be reading news accounts of the bombings. Still, the relationship between the two men remained one of employer and employee; no friendship developed between them. When one of McManigal's jobs did not go off as planned, J. J. vented his displeasure.

The Kansas City job was a case in point. When McManigal returned to Indianapolis, he met the following day with J. J., who was livid that so little damage had occurred at the construction site. McManigal explained what had happened. He also informed J. J. that, on his return, he had stopped off in Rochester, Pennsylvania, to pick up nitroglycerin from a cache, only to discover that all sixty two quarts were missing. (Hockin had by now visited Jewell, and Jewell had arranged to have them removed.)

"That stuff costs money," McNamara yelled. His face grew red as he berated McManigal. His fist pounded his desk for punctuation.

McManigal was piqued. "Well, all right, J. J.," he said, "you ain't satisfied with me, I guess I will quit."

"No, you won't. We are going to go right through with this work," J. J. replied.

But McNamara could also be generous with his praise, and McManigal generally enjoyed his visits to Indianapolis headquarters, where he often collected nitroglycerin and infernal machines that McNamara had stored in the basement of the building—enough explosive material to bring down not only the massive building in which the union was headquartered if an accident occurred but also the entire block.

On one visit in early July, McManigal spotted a telegram lying on McNamara's desk, sent from San Francisco. It read, "Has Jim left for here? If not, have him come at once." It was signed "Gene."

The telegram had been sent by Eugene Clancy, business agent of the Iron Workers' local in San Francisco and an executive of the San Francisco Building Trades Council headed by Olaf Tveitmoe.[3] A few weeks earlier, McNamara had received a letter from Clancy saying, "The Iron Worker never had a better chance to do what they have been wanting to do in that city,"

"That city" was Los Angeles. And "Jim," of course, was J. B. McNamara. "I can give you a man who has got the nerve," J. J. had responded to Clancy's letter, "if you can get the money."

Los Angeles had been on J. J. McNamara's mind for months. In June he had received a less-cryptic message from James Lynch, president of the typographical union. He wanted the *Times* silenced. Do that, he argued, and opposition to the unions among Los Angeles businesses would topple. The labor movement in California, he argued, and perhaps in the country, hung in the balance.

Responding to Lynch, McNamara introduced a personal note: "We work with a man one week and the next we read of his falling to his death," he said. "We become so accustomed to it that I've never realized what it meant until I sat by my own [union] brother's deathbed last year."

McNamara never questioned the wisdom of making a sensational strike against the nerve center of capitalist intransigence in Los Angeles. He should have. Had he only bothered to take a closer look at what was actually occurring in the city's industrial struggle, he might have entertained second thoughts about sending his brother there.

From January 1, 1910, to September 30, 1910, the Los Angeles Central Labor Council increased in strength from sixty two unions with 6,000 members to eighty five unions with 9,500 members. Many of the city's—indeed, the country's—union leaders hailed the massive progress. Within days of the anti-picketing arrests, the Socialist Party issued a pamphlet calling them an act of desperation, brought about because "in California especially within the last two or three years, the Labor Unions and the Socialist Party have been making a steadily winning fight against the hitherto unbridled exploitation of labor by capital."

In July, after an anti-picketing ordinance went into effect—and 472 people were arrested for breaking it in an often brutal police crackdown—union members kept right on picketing. The suppression of the pickets, in fact, ignited political agitation among the unionists, who put up Socialist attorney Job Harriman as their mayoral candidate. (In the primary election that followed in the fall of 1911, Harriman won more votes than any other candidate and seemed to be a shoo-in for the runoff.)

But it is unlikely that J. J. McNamara, sequestered in his fourth-floor office in Indianapolis, was aware of any of all this.

He decided to send his brother to the West Coast at once. He told McManigal that while his brother was out West, he would be stepping up his assignments in the East and Midwest.

"You're going to be busy," McNamara told him.

He directed McManigal to pick up explosives in Portland, Indiana, to be used at a job in Peoria.

J. B. McNamara and Ortie McManigal left Indianapolis together, taking the train to Chicago. J. B. said that he was looking forward to the trip. "I'm going to give them a damn good cleaning up," he remarked.

Chapter 8

Fifteen years after leaving the Civil War battlefield, Harrison Gray Otis still often donned his old uniform, which was frequently altered by his tailors to accommodate his expanding girth, then neatly pinned his medals on his ample chest. He would fling his front door open and emerge from it as if he were stepping out of a bivouac onto a field of battle. (He would in fact name his home The Bivouac.)

At the *Times* he barked orders as if he were commanding troops. One writer said: "He was a holy terror in his newspaper plant; his natural voice was that of a game warden roaring at seal poachers."

He targeted his most belligerent adversaries almost from the day he began running the *Times*. They were the local leaders of the International Typographical Union, of which he had once been a member when he worked for the US Government Printing Office. At first he reluctantly negotiated with the union's leaders and paid the members tidy regular raises. But by his second year on the job (he took the title of editor and general manager of the *Times*), he began railing against the union's insistence on "deadheading," precipitating an implacable conflict between the *Times* and the union movement that would persist for a hundred years.

The union's deadheading requirement represented a kind of make-work strategy. Under it, every story, every advertisement, every public notice had to be completely reset for each edition. The unions justified this requirement by asserting that without it, the newspaper could repeatedly use the work of one man day after day and thereby eliminate jobs. That was precisely what Otis wanted to do, and he eventually balked at the deadheading requirement. He was not going to pay workers to repeat work that didn't need to be repeated.

As part of a strategy to counteract the encroachment of unions in Southern California, he had cofounded the Merchants and Manufacturers Association (MMA) in 1886, the same year he took over control of the *Times*, assembling into its membership all of those business leaders in Los Angeles who saw themselves threatened by the advance of organized labor. Its motto: "We will hire no union man." They installed Felix J. Zehandelaar, a former reporter and recently the MMA's publicist, as president and blacklisted all businesses that had signed closed-shop contracts with labor unions. According to the MMA's unwritten policy, open-shop businesses would be patronized by open-shop businesses; union shops would not be. The members, without exception, were Republicans.

Los Angeles then amounted to little more than a scattered collection of nondescript buildings nestled in the abyss of a vast geological basin. Only eleven thousand people lived in the dusty frontier town, but it was growing at a faster rate than any city in the world has ever grown. And with it grew Colonel Otis's *Times*. As land speculators flooded into the city, they placed ads in the newspaper, driving advertising revenues. The ads told their own story of the land boom. Lots being advertised for $150 in 1886 were being touted for $8,000 a year later. Eventually speculators began buying up land far from the city center, areas that fifty years later would still be sparsely populated. Courts were flooded with land-fraud disputes. One developer was hauled into court for selling lots in wetlands that were covered by ocean water half the year. When word spread of the worthless land deals and the original buyers were unable to resell their property, panic swept the entire basin, and L.A.'s first big real estate boom suddenly became its first bust. As advertisers bailed out of the *Times*, Otis found himself in a painfully familiar situation; he brooded that his latest crack at publishing seemed on the verge of failure.

In order not only to survive but to thrive in the grand manner he had adopted, he had to cut costs, which, in the labor-intensive business of the newspaper world, meant laying off workers or slashing their salaries. In August of 1890 the publishers of the city's four newspapers—the *Times, Herald, Express,* and *Tribune*—met with Otis's old union, the International Typographical Union, where they asked the printers to take a salary cut. The union's reaction was predictable. Not only did the printers spurn the pay cut, they demanded a guarantee from the papers that wages would remain at their current levels for the next nine months. They gave the publishers forty-eight hours to agree to their terms or face a strike.

The silence that followed the deadline ushered in the strike on August 6, 1890. The *Herald, Express,* and *Tribune* quickly caved in to the printers' demands, leaving the *Times* standing alone and casting Otis in the role of a militant crusader with an uncompromising cause—the open shop, which he promoted on the masthead of the *Times* as "industrial freedom," a political euphemism for a union-free business environment. He placed ads in national magazines proclaiming that the *Times* "is against the strike, the lockout, the boycott, and the conspiracy to injure the citizen and the country."

Like the military strategist he was, the Colonel mounted an all-out campaign against the printers who had defied him, recruiting scabs from all over the country to replace them. At the same time, Otis began increasing the wages of his nonunion employees while completely excluding unionists. Each day the editorial page of his newspaper featured an ad blazoned, "Compositors Wanted. Full Union Wages Will Be Paid." On August 14, 1890, he editorialized, "As for us, we are now independent of these people and we intend to remain so." Two days later the strike against the *Times* began to dissolve, and Otis was able to declare, "The strike is a failure and we now have a new, ample, and competent force of printers." Such boisterous editorials would become his signature. They would mobilize, inspire, and unite the young city's burgeoning business community.

And as the Colonel railed, the *Times*'s circulation mushroomed, increasing more than 10 percent in just the first ninety days following the strike. But with the strike broken, unionists throughout the country enlisted in the battle, mounting a new tactic—a boycott of the *Times* and the businesses that advertised in it. All around town hundreds of blue buttons began appearing on workers' shirts and jackets, bearing the inscription "I Don't Read the *Times*." The American Federation of Labor began organizing letter-writing committees, which sent out thinly veiled threats to the newspaper's advertisers, warning them that their products would lie unsold on their shelves if they continued to advertise in the *Times*.

But the union movement in Los Angeles had no one to match the military savvy of the Colonel. Their ragtag leadership was as capable of challenging the united members of the Merchants and Manufacturers Association as the militia of Georgia was in defying Sherman's army.

And then, just as the Colonel was about to declare categorical victory over his labor foes, a war of the traditional sort intervened.

On February 20, 1898, President William McKinley, who had been Otis's Civil War commander, serving on the staff of Rutherford Hayes, declared war on Spain. Otis immediately wrote to him, asking to be appointed Assistant Secretary of War. The appointment was opposed by the war secretary, Russell Alexander Alger, who in his book *The Spanish American War*, written after the war, condemned McKinley's attempts to surround himself with cronies.

Nevertheless, at the age of sixty-one, Otis was able to persuade McKinley to elevate him to the rank of brigadier general and return him to service. He was initially dispatched to San Francisco, where regulars and volunteers in the US Army were being assembled for duty in the Philippines. The encampments quickly became magnets for peddlers, "loose women," and other "disreputable persons of both sexes." Otis forthwith published general orders for sentries that outlined who could and who could not enter regimental campsites.

In May, Otis left for the Philippines to command an expeditionary force against Spanish troops. Or so he thought. He never laid eyes on a Spanish soldier. But as the war wound down, he set up camp to make ready for the American occupation of the land. When, to his astonishment, insurgents rose up in a willful effort to drive out the Americans, Otis, who continued to file regular dispatches to his newspaper, became infuriated, referring to the rebels in one report as "ignorant, misguided, and bumptious natives . . . [who] wantonly assailed the authority of the Republic."

He set out onto the battlefield, armed with both pen and sword. One of his staff officers would later recall noticing the general during a skirmish sitting on his horse, writing a dispatch to the *Times,* seeming to be searching for "the nicety that his superb literary workmanship demanded." A Filipino battery had spotted Otis and his men, and every few seconds a shell exploded near them, splattering them with mud. But still the general wrote. Finally, the staff officer spurred his horse to the general's. Had he noticed that the shells were coming close? "Yes, yes," the general replied, perturbed that his word search had been interrupted. "I noticed them." And he continued composing his dispatch.

In the winter of 1899, General Otis commanded a brigade against Filipino insurgents in a bloody engagement that left more than one hundred Americans dead and hundreds more wounded. But the general relentlessly drove his exhausted troops forward, pressing them past the enemy trenches. Outflanked, the insurgents finally broke and ran, eventually dispersing and waging an unyielding guerilla campaign of attrition against the American occupiers that persisted for nearly the next half century.

Interviewed by a *New York Times* reporter following the battle, Otis declared that it was necessary for the United States to remain in the Philippines because the Filipinos were incapable of governing themselves. "I do not believe they have any proper and correct appreciation of republican liberty and self-government as we in America understand those terms."

Said Philippine President Emilio Aguinaldo: "It is my duty to maintain the integrity of our national honor, and that of the army so unjustly attacked by those, who posing as our friends, attempt to dominate us in place of the Spaniards."

General Otis, now breveted major general, returned to Los Angeles. Among the war booty that he came home with: an Arabian mare.

Then on June 28, 1899, the following headline appeared in the *New York Times*:

MAY SUCCEED GEN. ALGER

The President Summons Gen. Harrison G. Otis to Washington.

TO DISCUSS THE PHILIPPINES

But It Is Also Rumored in the Capital that Gen. Otis May Have the War Secretaryship Offered to Him.

It is likely that Otis planted the rumors himself. But nothing came of them. A writer who attended the White House meeting said later that Otis "talked long and earnestly about his duty and the willingness of friends to help him [the president] out." The two did rekindle their wartime friendship, and McKinley accepted an invitation from Otis to visit him at The Bivouac. And in May of 1901, McKinley became the first president of the United States ever to come to California while in office. He and the First Lady attended a reception at The Bivouac and spent the night there. (Otis had had a presidential apartment, offices, and a patio especially constructed for the visit.) Five months later McKinley was dead, assassinated by a fanatical anarchist at the Pan Am Exposition in Buffalo.

The Los Angeles that welcomed the now–Gen. Harrison Gray Otis on his return from the Philippines was no longer the placid pueblo that he had once known. Electric streetcars were now clanging and clattering over miles of iron tracks that spread like so many surface roots over the dusty roads of the city. The general could hardly walk a block without witnessing the lumber framework of new homes and the iron skeletons of new commercial buildings that were rising up around him. Automobiles were now chugging over the dusty streets, discharging a trail of faint smoke that became trapped within the geological basin, merging with the ever-present low clouds into what would one day be referred to as smog. He could retreat from the noise and pollution to an adobe-brick country retreat that he had acquired in the Hollywood Hills, which he called The Outpost. From there he could survey the entire land—from the burgeoning business area of downtown to the shining seaside town of Santa Monica.

Yet it had become obvious to him that the city's growth could not continue at its current pace without access to an adequate supply of fresh water. Even as a smaller city, the local citizenry had had to persevere during years of drought, often at a deadly price. Another crucial matter: The city lacked a deepwater harbor to receive provisions directly from overseas and the Atlantic seaboard.

But Los Angeles was in luck. Indeed, it was nothing if not lucky in its adolescent years. What the turn of the century offered the city was an epic opportunity. Plans for the construction of a canal through the isthmus of Panama had been completed and work was about to begin. Once completed, ships from the East Coast would have their voyage to the West Coast cut by eight thousand miles.

Los Angeles business leaders began to argue loudly that the city needed to have a free deepwater harbor in place by the time the first ships set sail for Panama, and the most strident voices in that debate were those of General Otis and Harry Chandler. But a deepwater harbor would come at a cost of millions of dollars, a price that the few thousand taxpayers of Los Angeles could not afford to pay—but which the federal government could.

Otis and Chandler threw their personal support and the considerable weight of the *Times* behind the Free Harbor League, an organization that championed the construction of a deepwater harbor at San Pedro, then a small coastal settlement about twenty miles south of downtown L.A..

Otis pulled whatever strings he could in Washington, DC, and soon a trickle of US senators began arriving by rail to see whether such a radical project was worthwhile or even feasible. Otis faced powerful opposition in the person of Collis P. Huntington, president and chief architect of the Southern Pacific Railroad. Huntington appeared so confident that the United States would finance such a port in Santa Monica, where he had established the terminus of his rail line, that he set about building a $1 million pier where the arriving ships would dock.

But Huntington reckoned without taking into account the shrewdness of the General, his chief lieutenant Chandler, and the Free Harbor League. Together they mobilized an army of letter writers, who sent messages and petitions urging their representatives in Washington to vote for the $2.9 million San Pedro appropriation. The San Pedro project simply made more sense, they pointed out. It called for the development of a deep inlet into the harbor where ships could be docked, protected from the capriciousness of the weather.

No such inlet could be constructed in Santa Monica, where a granite bluff faced the sea. Otis received word that the San Pedro harbor bill had been passed by Congress just as he returned to Los Angeles from the Philippines. He had arrived twice victorious.

❧

As the tide of settlers began to swell at an exponential rate at the turn of the century, Los Angeles faced a fundamental problem that literally represented a shut-off valve on its continued growth—an unreliable source of fresh water. William Mulholland, the head of the city's Water Bureau, had designed a masterful plan to solve it—an aqueduct system to divert water from the Owens River, 250 miles to the north, directly to Los Angeles. It would be, he said, like bringing "white gold" to the city.

But such a project would cost millions of dollars—in fact, Mulholland had no idea just how many millions—money that could only be raised through a bond issue. But how to convince the citizens of Los Angeles, many of whom were striving to establish new lives here after escaping from grinding hardship, to support such a measure? The story goes that in 1905 Mulholland brought his plan to the attention of Harry Chandler, who quickly envisioned another use for such a system: Instead of bringing the water in a straight route from the Owens Valley to Los Angeles, the aqueduct could take a side trip through the arid San Fernando Valley—a sparsely populated, bone-dry area bordering the city on the northwest that was so inhospitable that acres of land could be had for a few dollars.

Anyone who has seen *Chinatown* knows what happened next (although the movie is set in the 1930s)—a massive and underhanded campaign by a land syndicate headed by Chandler and Otis to inveigle the citizens of the city to support the bond issue so that they could buy up land in the Valley cheaply and then rake in millions by turning their desert property into a garden paradise when the water from the aqueduct arrived.

The problem with that account, which first appeared in Hearst's *Los Angeles Examiner,* and has been embroidered in scores of books and articles since, is that it is as insubstantial as the *Chinatown* scenario. Chandler did indeed bring together an impressive investors group, the San Fernando Mission Land Co., to buy Valley land, but that was well before there had been any talk of constructing an aqueduct. All of the aqueduct water was pledged to the city of Los Angeles, which at the time did not include the San Fernando Valley. Not until 1916 did the Valley's residents vote to be annexed to Los Angeles, and not until the following year did they begin to get any of the water. By that time, the San Fernando Mission Land Co. had already sold off most of the land that it had acquired more than a decade earlier, none of it at inflated prices.

It seems clear that Chandler and Otis had championed the aqueduct for one reason only: It would be good for business.

It turned out to be particularly good business for the *Times*. Otis and Chandler's ability to convince a struggling population to shell out millions for a project that took five years to complete by an army of four thousand construction workers indisputably established the *Times* as the city's driving force. No one else could have done it.

~ ~

With those successes under his belt, it was now time for General Otis to renew his die-hard battle with the unions. Indeed, over the next decade the general would become the de facto commander of antiunion forces— if not nationally, then unquestionably in California.

A profile of the general, appearing in *Sunset* magazine at the time, said: "His slogan is 'You may break but shall not bend me.' Though he has won laurels in the Civil, Spanish-American, and Filipino wars, the fight of fights in his fighting life has been the fight with lawless labor unions. . . . Sufficient it is to state that when a man finds striking workmen on his hands, it is hardly human for him to sit down and consider basic principles. Action is imperative. General Otis faced this situation in 1890 [during the printers' strike]. . . . The general's loves are genuine and numerous. He loves friends, home, family, children, dogs, horses, birds, flowers, fine pictures, and good printing. . . . A tiny sleek gray creature once took up its abode in the general's desk at the old Times Building, gnawed at his valuable papers, and richly deserved extermination. He made friends with the varmint and it became so tame it ate from his hand."

Obviously the general had a way with varmints that he didn't have with unionists. On the other hand, many of Otis's critics who came in to personal contact with him often wrote about how charming and gracious he appeared to be close up compared with his notorious public persona. He would find friends and reluctant admirers among many of the people who despised his editorial pronouncements.

In his autobiography, Milton McRae, who founded the Scripps-McRae newspaper syndicate with E. R. Scripps in 1900—and who was devoutly pro-union—wrote, "I became well acquainted with General Harrison Grey [sic] Otis, owner and publisher of the *Los Angeles Times*, for many years the most bitterly hated advocate of 'The Open Shop,' as opposed to Organized Labor, in America. Although we were the very antithesis of each other, we became close friends."

One can only speculate on how history might have been disarmed if the general had invited Samuel Gompers, the founding head of the American Federation of Labor, to Los Angeles, as he had invited President McKinley. Could the two old men, over cigars and whiskey, sitting on the breezy patio of The Outpost, have put aside their past bombastic rhetoric and revived the spirit of Appomattox? Could they have reasonably discussed each other's interests and found a path to compromise? Could they at least have agreed to mediate their disagreements?

Such an encounter probably never entered either man's mind.

By 1905 the *Times* was grossing more than $1 million annually, and the general's lifestyle was ample evidence of his affluence. He traveled widely, entertained lavishly, and invested grandly, buying a one-million-acre ranch in Mexico, for example. But the general himself was slowing down. The same year, his wife, Eliza, died at age seventy-one of heart failure, and Otis began to retreat from the day-to-day business of running his newspaper.

By the end of the decade, he began to appear obsessed with all things military, wearing his medal-bedecked uniform to the *Times*'s office more regularly and keeping a stand of fifty Springfield rifles installed "at the ready" in The Fortress. Another case of sawed-off shotguns was kept next to the managing editor's desk in the third-floor editorial room. He had an ornamental cannon mounted on the hood of his brand-new six-cylinder, air-cooled Franklin. And rifles and swords hung from the ceiling of the second-floor hallway of The Bivouac.

Many thought the martial displays to be signs of senility. Others saw them as evidence of an old man's growing resolve for a decisive confrontation with the unionists.

By 1910 Los Angeles was known nationally as "Otis Town of the Open Shop." Otis had risen to become the most formidable figure in California and, among many, the most despised. Even fellow Republican Hiram Johnson, no friend of the unions himself, raged against Otis during his successful gubernatorial campaign. In a legendary speech, Johnson, who would dominate California politics for nearly the next half century, depicted Otis as an antiunion lunatic and painted a vivid rhetorical caricature of the general: "He sits there with senile dementia, with gangrened heart and rotting brain, grimacing at every reform, chattering impotently at all things that are decent, frothing and fuming, violently gibbering, going down to his grave in snarling infamy. This man Otis is the one blot on the banner of Southern California; he is the bar sinister upon your escutcheon."

But Johnson's words might have seemed like faint praise compared with those set down by W. C. Brann, editor of *The Iconoclast*, who wrote: "I can but wonder what will become of the *Times* editor when the breath leaves his feculent body and death stops the rattling of his abortive brain, for he is unfit for heaven and too foul for hell. He cannot be buried in the earth lest he provoke a pestilence, nor in the sea lest he poison the fish, nor swung in space like Mahomet's coffin lest the circling worlds, in trying to avoid contamination, crash together, wreck the universe and bring again the noisome reign of Chaos and the old Night. The damrascal seems to be a white elephant on the hands of the Deity, and I have some curiosity to know what He will do with it."

But to the general's aging mind, his own public frothing and fuming, his medal-bedecked uniforms, the stand of fifty rifles in The Fortress, the cannon mounted to the hood of his automobile, and the fortifications installed in his home may have constituted an exhibition of his vigilant preparation for the inevitable bloody showdown with the unions. Perhaps the old general was not as senile as so many had thought.

Chapter 9

At each train station en route to California, newsboys would rush aboard and race through the cars, shouting the headlines emblazoned on the local newspapers.

Ortie McManigal read every word in every paper about his case, offering his own critiques of the reports: "They got this all wrong....That fellow's got the story right." Etcetera. On one occasion he remarked to the detective sitting across from him, "I guess I'm the biggest man in the country."

The only newspaper stories that troubled McManigal were those that referred to his wife and children. Emma McManigal, he read, had told reporters: "It is all a police plot. I know Ortie is innocent. He could never have done these awful things charged against him. He was the kindest man in the world and would not harm a soul. And he never, never made that alleged confession. It is a police plot."

Standing next to her, clutching her dress as she spoke to reporters outside her home, were their children, Evelyn and Walter. When Emma mentioned that her husband's business required him to be out of town often, five-year-old Walter added, "Papa was out of town because he could make more money."

She took the children by the hand and led them into the house. When she returned, she told the reporters, "I kept them out of school today because I could not bear to expose them to the taunts of thoughtless children. I couldn't bear to have the other children point their fingers at my babies and tell them their father is a criminal."

Poor Emma! Ortie McManigal must have thought as he tried to make sense of the news items. *Poor Evelyn and Walter!* How would they survive without him now? Of course there was probably no use thinking such thoughts. He—and they—were now caught up in the eye of an epic whirlwind, and there was no escape without their being brutally battered some more. He may have taken some pleasure in his role as national celebrity. But it never left his consciousness that he was also a prisoner, facing the dismal possibility of spending the rest of his life behind bars, unable to provide for the woman and children whom he loved. As a newspaper photographer on the train attempted to snap yet another picture of him, McManigal suddenly lifted his legs in the air, pointed to his shackled ankles, and said, "Take [a picture of] these."

In truth, he had hardly felt less restrained in the years since he had been recruited by Herb Hockin. His business had indeed required him to be out of town often, but how could he have known that his fate would be sealed in a city he had never seen?

Four hundred miles to the north of Los Angeles stood another burgeoning city, one with very different civic leadership. Indeed, during the first decade of the century, labor leaders in San Francisco occupied all the major offices of government or directed political action off stage. They had succeeded in promoting wage hikes for the city's workers to the point that new businesses and those considering relocating to California were frightened off by the wage scale there and turned their sights on open-shop Los Angeles instead.

The union movement in San Francisco was enmeshed in local politics and government. The Union Labor Party was headed nominally by Patrick Henry ("Pinhead") McCarthy, president of the San Francisco Building Trades Council. But the real power was wielded by Abe Reuf, "The Little Boss." Reuf succeeded in carrying a full slate of Union Labor Party members to the highest positions at City Hall, including a mayor who was a local orchestra leader, a board of supervisors that included the local presidents of the Piano Polishers, Piano Tuners, Bakery Wagon Drivers, Hack Drivers, and Carpenters unions, as well as a saloon keeper, grocer, plumber, drummer, and machine operator.

Their opponents called them The Boodle Board. Reuf had negotiated a sweet bargain with them. They would go about using their positions to better the conditions of the San Francisco working man. He would handle the graft.

When McCarthy made the long trek to Los Angeles in 1906 to urge local labor leaders to follow the San Francisco example and form a political organization, he was greeted with a blast from the *Times,* which demanded that he be deported from the city as "an industrial excrescence ... a putrescent pustule which indicates a suppurating [festering] disease."

Indeed, a labor-sponsored candidate for mayor of Los Angeles was overwhelmingly defeated in 1906. A contributing reason: A series of graft trials had already begun to shake San Francisco as intensely as the recent earthquake, and the orchestra-leader mayor and cohorts were hoofing off to jail—along with Little Boss Reuf.

Still, union organizers in Los Angeles pressed on. Delegations of labor leaders from the Bay City arrived at regular intervals to aid and instruct the struggling local labor chiefs. Their intervention became increasingly determined and intense. The reason for their exertions was patently obvious. As the *California Journal,* a weekly newspaper published in San Francisco, observed on July 1, 1910: "Skilled labor in and around San Francisco is pretty well unionized. It is not at Portland, at Seattle, at Tacoma, or at Los Angeles. . . . This situation cannot permanently continue. Manufacturing cannot endure one-quarter unionized and three-quarters non-unionized. . . . Production costs more in San Francisco than in the other cities named. . . . Frankly in self-defense it would be good policy for San Francisco employers as well as laborers to contribute their sympathy, their influence, of their means, to aid organized labor in Los Angeles, in Portland, in Tacoma, and in Seattle."

Indeed the unionists had an imperative motive to organize Los Angeles posthaste. They had signed a labor contract with Bay Area metal trades manufacturers calling for the institution of the eight-hour day—but only on condition that the standard be agreed to statewide. Placed in charge of the campaign to bring the eight-hour day to Los Angeles was a six-foot tall, three hundred-pound Norwegian who, like many men of his day, sported a cane as a fashion accessory by day and as a defensive weapon by night.

A colleague once described Olaf A. Tveitmoe as "a dark Scandinavian, of powerful build, a gorilla." His friends and enemies alike called him "the Viking," for he possessed the defining hallmarks of his ancestors, most prominent of which was a ferocious temper. He was also a brilliant intellect who read Greek, played the violin, and had translated several Norwegian literary classics into English. During meetings, he would hang his hat on his cane and, somewhat disconcertingly, twirl the hat as he awaited his opportunity to speak. By 1910 this Scandinavian immigrant was considered the most powerful labor leader on the West Coast.[4]

Olaf Tveitmoe served as the chairman and principal architect of the Los Angeles Strike Committee and as such had frequently traveled to the southern city to issue instructions to union members to picket construction sites in defiance of the city's strict new anti-picketing ordinance, which even gave police authority to arrest anyone "speaking in public streets in loud or unusual tones." But Tveitmoe made it clear that if the union members declined to picket, they would lose their union benefits (so either way these workers would be paying a harsh penalty). The choice they solidly made was to follow the Viking's orders.

Tveitmoe's faithful lieutenant was fellow Scandinavian Anton Johannsen, the famously gregarious state organizer for the Building Trades Union. His uproarious laugh was his signature. His wife and their friends formed a very wide and notable circle that included the notorious anarchist Emma Goldman; national labor-union leaders Eugene Debs and Samuel Gompers; Mary Field, the journalist and paramour of the renowned labor attorney Clarence Darrow; and Darrow himself. Whereas Tveitmoe was "the Viking," Johannsen was "the Laugh of Labor," and together they embodied the deceptively avuncular essence of the labor movement on the West Coast.

Like nearly everyone in this circle, Johanssen was a recent transplant to San Francisco who had arrived from his home in Chicago in the first weeks of 1910 to take on the express task of unionizing Los Angeles. He brought with him his gift for public relations. He also brought with him an eccentric cohort with a glass eye, Matthew Schmidt. Schmidt would harangue anyone who would listen with his views about the cardinal necessity for a violent workers' revolution. The subject of dynamite seemed to enthrall Schmidt as much as politics. He often carried a set of grimy pamphlets about dynamiting in his pocket, and at his local saloon he could discourse at length on the relative advantages of nitrogelatin over nitroglycerin.

Whoever met Matthew Schmidt was left with a vivid memory of the encounter. From his lips flowed an endless torrent of anticapitalist tirades, which, as it happened, won him a devoted fan in anarchist agitator Emma Goldman, who would one day refer to him as "one of the finest types of American proletarians." (By contrast, she thought the trade-union movement was misguided.) Schmidt looked the part, being short and stocky, invariably wearing dusty, stained denim work clothes everywhere. His most unforgettable feature, however, was his glass eye, which he alternately claimed was the result of a dynamite explosion or of his being born without the eye. According to his contemporaries, the glass eye tended to squint and gaze off in a different direction from his seeing eye. Depending upon Schmidt's mood, the cumulative effect was either unsettlingly comic or oddly sinister.

In March he was introduced to another young man whose mindset was so similar to Schmidt's that it seemed inevitable that their paths would cross. He was David Caplan, "Cap," a Polish Jew who often wore tiny steel-rimmed spectacles and was a lover of Russian literature, Tolstoy in particular. Both he and Schmitty were loud, both gregarious, but it was their common attraction to an alloy of socialism and anarchism prevalent throughout the United States in the first decade of the twentieth century that bonded them.

Caplan had recently arrived with his wife and two children from the Home Colony, the legendary utopian commune near Tacoma, Washington. The community of about one hundred anarchists had attracted national attention a few years earlier when one of its members was convicted of obscenity under the Comstock Act for sending an article through the US mails advocating free love.[5] Now in San Francisco, Caplan quickly became caught up in the city's exhilarating political life. He formed a kind of urban home colony in his Fulton Street apartment, a gathering place for Socialists, unionists, Communists, anarchists, and free thinkers. Caplan invited Schmidt to join the group on the day they met. Even Tveitmoe eventually came to attend.

They were a small but raucous bunch, often holding sessions late into the night, disturbing other tenants and prompting complaints. Schmidt, the most bellicose of them all, relentlessly tried to dazzle the group with his exhaustive knowledge of explosives.

One night following a meeting, Tveitmoe offered to arrange a job for Caplan as a San Francisco police officer patrolling a waterfront beat. He remained on the job for only a week before quitting, explaining that the money was insufficient for a man with a family to support. Tveitmoe would soon offer him a better-paying job, this one on the other side of the law.

Meanwhile, Schmitty was falling in love. The object of his affection was Belle Lavin, a young, rail-thin widow and proprietress of a boardinghouse, who was also an acquaintance of Anton Johannsen. On occasion she was escorted to Johannsen's house for dinner by one of her boarders and fellow political activist, John Lofthouse. There she was given an open forum to argue loudly and militantly on behalf of women's suffrage and other garden-variety Socialist and feminist causes. At twenty-seven Belle was esoterically attractive, with elongated features and thin cheeks and lips that an understandably biased *Los Angeles Times* reporter would later describe as "starved looking." Her cool demeanor often lent her an emotionless aspect, that of "a typical south-of-Market-Street landlady—world-hardened and world-wise." Her softest feature was perhaps her hair, which she kept in a bun loosely bailed together with a matrix of steel pins.

Belle's boardinghouse at 2410 Mission Street in San Francisco had been (and would continue to be) the site of extraordinary personal dramas. In 1908 she had become sexually involved with one of her boarders, Wilbur Sarman, a barber. When Belle's husband, George Lavin, learned of the affair, he burst into their bedroom, shot Sarman, then slashed his own throat with a razor in the bathroom and fell dead at his wife's feet. Belle's lover died a few hours later. This was the first time Belle's name appeared in the newspapers. It wouldn't be the last.

Now, in the spring of 1910, the widowed Belle had found a lover in another boarder. But this time she was unencumbered by a jealous husband. A physical as well as an ideological chemistry drew her to Schmitty, creating a combination as volatile as the explosives that he never tired of talking about.

Oddly, he began referring to himself as F. A. Perry, although Belle Lavin and his visiting friends—and they included Tveitmoe and Johannsen—continued to call him Schmitty. He appeared to be rising in prominence among the union figures (perhaps it had something to do with the name change), and he now often accompanied Tveitmoe and Johannsen on their junkets on behalf of the union to Southern California.

The small group that gathered at David Caplan's San Francisco home represented fixtures of radical politics of the day: a coterie of international agitators bent on overturning American capitalism and replacing it with an idealistic workers' utopia by any means necessary. The campaign of their counterparts in Russia would succeed seven and a half years later in October 1917. But their larger cause in America was about to perish by their own folly as a plot began to take shape around the dinner table in Caplan's little house in the spring of 1910.

San Francisco was a natural setting for such a plot. With a population of 342,782 to L.A.'s 102,479, San Francisco could make its influence felt four hundred miles away. By the end of the century's first decade, however, all of that was beginning to change.

By 1910 Southern California had blossomed into an agricultural mecca, producing thirty thousand railcar-loads of citrus fruits annually and an abundance of almonds, figs, apricots, walnuts, peaches, and pears in its sunlit Mediterranean climate. Los Angeles itself had also tripled in size, bringing it into parity with San Francisco, whose population remained virtually stagnant. Largely by the design of General Otis and the MMA, wages remained remarkably low in L.A., but so too did the cost of living—far lower than in San Francisco, where jobs were becoming increasingly scarce. The building boom that had followed the great earthquake of 1906 had come to an end, and the northern city was slogging through a flat economy. Meanwhile, as thousands of automobiles began replacing the horse and buggy, the greater L.A. basin was sprouting oil wells, pumping fifty-eight million barrels annually to keep them running—hundreds of the wells located in the city proper. The budding motion picture industry, based on the East Coast, was just beginning to send crews to film scenes in Southern California, drawn by the abundant sunlight required—even for shooting "indoor" scenes—by the primitive filming technology of the day.

Union workers in the northern city had won higher wages and better working conditions for their memberships, but in the process had also raised production costs. A manufacturer of steel beams, say, could expect labor costs to be roughly 30 percent lower in Los Angeles than in San Francisco. Simple economics prompted manufacturers to shun San Francisco and gravitate to the south on a massive scale.

The open-shop principle had become the driving economic force behind this exodus, transforming an economic rivalry into a pitched struggle between two burgeoning American cities in which each felt mortally threatened by the other, impelling each side to marshal its resources and galvanize its supporters for the inevitable conflict ahead.

In the early summer of 1910, San Francisco Bay–area employers announced that they were not going to renew contracts with their unions unless San Francisco wages were brought in line with those paid in Los Angeles. What employers called "equalizing" could be accomplished either by San Francisco workers taking a massive pay cut, or by L.A. workers unionizing and demanding pay parity with their brethren to the north. Never was there any question as to which path the unions would take.

By June they created the General Strike Committee of Los Angeles, and their organizational efforts achieved success beyond any San Francisco unionist's wildest dreams. General Otis was outraged. All through the long hot summer of 1910 he watched the Los Angeles Central Labor Council grow exponentially.

"Not even the most sanguine organizer would have dared to dream a year ago that such a state of affairs could come to pass in Los Angeles," gushed Tveitmoe. Within a few short months, the San Francisco organizers had helped boost union membership in Los Angeles by 50 percent.

Local labor leaders railed against both the Republican and Democratic parties and invited the Socialist party to move its headquarters to the Labor Temple.

Otis and the MMA retaliated that summer with the enactment of the anti-picketing ordinance, which punished "loitering, picketing, carrying, or displaying banners" with fifty days in jail or a fine of $100, or both. The city council, which was all but handpicked by General Otis and the leadership of the MMA, promoted the ordinance, the handiwork of Earl Rogers, the city's most prominent attorney, as a deterrent to violence in the streets. Instead of deterring violence, however, the ordinance was threatening to shatter the city with civil unrest.

On August 5, 1910, striking ironworkers in Los Angeles voted unanimously at Tveitmoe's behest to defy the new law. Police in turn rounded up the pickets by the hundreds—on August 9 alone 173 pickets were hauled off from the site of the city's new Hall of Records, which was being erected by a nonunion construction company. Eventually 472 men were brought into court, and their trial date was set for February and March of 1911—a full eight months away, although the maximum sentence for the alleged offense was fifty days in jail. Those who could not post bail remained incarcerated pending trial, facing financial ruin. As a result, several judges relented, releasing men with large families on their own recognizance. Again, Otis was outraged.

Of the softhearted judges' actions, General Otis wrote threateningly: "The public servants who committed this improper act may have thought they were doing good politics. . . . This community is determined . . . to be done with the unlawful actions of members of labor union organizations and with the dangers that always accompany strikes where the strikers are permitted to picket. . . . He is a 'poor politician' who mistakes the temper of the people of Los Angeles on this [issue]."

In a single news article concerning the mass arrests, the *Times* referred to the unionists as "rowdies," "loafers," "blackguards," "hoodlums," "totemites," "roughnecks," "cowards," "firebrands," "agitators," and "jail flooders."

The crackdown ignited a political firestorm. Socialist attorney Job Harriman came to the rescue of many of the striking workers, defending many of them for free. Later that summer the Socialist Party put him up as their mayoral candidate, and his popularity mushroomed in direct proportion to the city's efforts to suppress the unions.

Meanwhile Tveitmoe and Johanssen rushed south to raise bail and money to pay the fines of the incarcerated unionists. When the *Times* got wind of their arrival, it published a scathing piece by reporter Churchill Harvey-Elder, datelined August 24, 1910, and headlined: "BRUTAL—BREAK HEADS IS THE ORDER—NOT ENOUGH BLOOD-SHED HERE FOR LABOR BOSSES." Below the lurid words, the news article said: "Tveitmoe and gang of labor union conspirators have arrived from San Francisco on a mischief bent.... 'Break more heads' is the order which the bull-dozing bosses of the unionites have sent forth."

The week before, Otis had written in an editorial of Johannsen: "It is through the libelous statements of such skunks as this foreigner that industrial troubles are started." On August 29 he editorialized: "To tyrannize, to subdue, and to completely enslave the working people is their aim and object. Once they succeed, their graft would make the United States mints look like dumping grounds of refuse."

On the same day, August 29, the Socialist Party of Los Angeles adopted a resolution at their county convention that stated: "We declare that in no city in the civilized world are there more honest men in jail, nor are there, population considered, more scoundrels in public office than there are in the city and county of Los Angeles."

Tveitmoe made his final trip to Los Angeles on September 13, 1910. He met with local union leaders and left on September 22. Five days later the General's newspaper editorially blasted what it called "the mad attempt of the San Francisco bosses to saddle this city with their rule."[6]

On September 30 an editorial page cartoon caricatured a "labor union grafter" with his hand in the pocket of a "deceived worker," who is grasping the unionist's wrist and saying, "No more." An editorial printed on the same page began, "Trade unions have been shown to be unnecessary in Los Angeles."

They would be the last words to appear on the editorial pages of the newspaper before the *Times* was destroyed.

Chapter 10

In November of 1909 Ortie McManigal received a telegram summoning him to the Bridge and Structural Iron Workers' union headquarters in the American Central Life building in downtown Indianapolis. It had been one of those bitingly cold days that Indianapolis regularly experiences in late November. He arrived wearing a bowler hat and a wool coat over his work clothes and was led by Mary Dye, the union's stenographer, through the outer offices to a large interior door. The door gave way to the union's inner conference room, where union president Frank Ryan and the thirty-four-year-old J. J. McNamara, the union's secretary-treasurer, stood at one end of a vast mahogany conference table. McManigal was offered a seat. Ryan explained that Ortie had been invited here to discuss a strategy for escalating the bombing campaign in the coming year. McManigal could not have felt more important.

Little in the way of new tactics was discussed at the meeting. But the strategy was clear: The dynamite campaign was going to be stepped up, and J. J. McNamara would be running the show.

McManigal was thoroughly impressed with J. J.'s charismatic management. The secretary-treasurer was wildly popular with the membership, having put his own life on the line as an ironworker early on, just as the men he now represented did day in and day out. He had also been recently credited with having delivered his men significantly higher wages, which, he readily acknowledged, was largely the upshot of McManigal's activities. Membership in the union was expanding rapidly, as were receipts from union dues, which now totaled nearly $5,000 per month. All of that accomplishment had given J. J. the ear of the national labor leadership; in fact, he was said to have become a close personal friend of none other than American Federation of Labor (AF of L) President Samuel Gompers.

J. J. was born in Cincinnati on December 23, 1876, and grew up in what neighbors described as a "poor but respectable" family. He would later relate that he got into the same sort of "petty mischief" that other kids did. His father had worked as a Cincinnati police officer, one of a legion of Irish cops, before the family was thrown on its ear. In 1894 Officer McNamara was charged with raping his twelve-year-old daughter, Alice. He was tried, convicted, and in April 1894 sentenced to life in prison.

While his father was incarcerated, J. J. at age seventeen became the de facto head of the household, ruling it with a heavy hand. In September of the same year that their father was hauled off to prison, Jimmy, six years younger than J. J., was sent off to the Cincinnati House of Refuge, where he remained for fourteen months. In his parole application he described how he had wound up there. "I played truant one day because I was too late that day for school. My older brother, Joseph [J. J.] said he would break my neck for me when he got hold of me, so my brother told me. They kept me about the yard all day. In the evening I ran away and stayed away from the house two or three nights. My little brother [Robert] would bring me food to the stable and I would sleep there. The stable was on our place. My brother Joseph whips me and treats me badly. My father is in Columbus." Authorities at the House of Refuge said that he "proved to be a model boy," and he was released in November 1895.

By then J. J. had dropped out of school to support his family, taking odd jobs. "It came natural for me to hustle. I worked hard because I liked to work," he wrote. He got his first job as a structural ironworker in 1898, working ten hours a day for $1.50 a day. There was no more dangerous work in America than that performed by the men hoisting the giant girders that formed the skeletal structures of America's great skyscrapers.

"I never planned my life far ahead," McNamara would later say. "The work of an ironworker probably precludes such planning for such as a man does not know when he leaves home in the morning that he will return at night. It probably tends towards fatalism."

At the same time, he began attending the Indianapolis College of Law by night. Bright and energetic, the Iron Workers Union hired him to represent men who had been injured on the job. But he found the work frustrating. If an injured man was a resident of one state and his employer was incorporated in another, the case would have to be tried in federal court, a complicated and expensive procedure in which the worker generally came out on the losing end even if the court ruled in his favor. McNamara, as facile with the pen as he was with the steel beam, also became the editor of the union's trade publication, *Bridgemen's Magazine,* and at age twenty-eight was elected secretary-treasurer of the union as part of a militant slate.

When it came to women, J. J.'s past had always had a seamy side that in some ways rivaled his brother's. He had once paid the rent at an Indianapolis boardinghouse for a woman named Katherine Kent, a "high-class" prostitute who entertained her other customers there. She was finally forced to vacate the boardinghouse in haste after one of her customers charged her with robbing him.

J. J. then began romancing another woman named Katherine, sometimes assigning her to union jobs. Detective William Burns would write later: "McNamara [put] her to good use . . . for she could get information at times without creating any suspicion, where a man would have no chance at all. . . . She made a number of trips about the country with McNamara. Finally, she went to a close friend, who afterward became our informant, and sought advice."

According to Burns, the conversation between the informant-friend and the second Katherine went like this:

Katherine: "I don't love this man or care for him enough to marry him. What shall I do?"

Friend: "Marry him. You will have a home, and this will prevent you from becoming a tramp."

Katherine took the advice, but she had no home with McNamara. He moved out of her life immediately after he married her. She also disappeared.

In the spring of 1909, he finally received a law degree from the Indiana School of Law and succeeded in getting his father pardoned from the Ohio penitentiary later that year. Upon his release the disgraced former police officer simply vanished. His family would never hear from him again.

J. J. appeared to have endured the family humiliation remarkably well.

"As for environment, I don't believe much in its effect," he would say. "I had no particular experiences to make me any different from my brothers."

Like his father, he was named John, but he never allowed anyone to call him that. He was either "Joe"—his middle name was Joseph—or J. J.

J. B.—or "Jim"—however, was another story. The shame of his father's odious act seemed to have left an indelible mark on his adolescent psyche, and now, as an adult, he was a rough-hewn contrast to his polished older brother. (He would also maintain a close bond with his violated sister, writing folksy letters in impeccable schoolboy penmanship to her regularly throughout his life. She, in turn, would treasure every one of them, never tossing away a single one.)

Indeed, to McManigal the two brothers must have seemed polar opposites. Nevertheless, it was said that J. J. loved his brother deeply, and McManigal too seemed to develop a fondness for the younger rapscallion as they worked side by side.

But fondness or not, McManigal was becoming increasingly concerned about the impetuousness of the hotheaded J. B., who shunned the restraints of vigilance and caution with such indifference that McManigal thought he might get them both killed.

But it was precisely J. B.'s insouciance that made him the ideal choice for the Los Angeles job.

Until now, every dynamite assignment had been directed at an open-shop construction job. Contractors were sent the implicit message—sign a deal with the union or face the greater costs of seeing your construction site a tangled shambles. But the Los Angeles job wasn't going to be a boiler room in a local foundry, a viaduct under construction, or a lonely construction derrick. This was going to be The Fortress, a building made of brick and granite in downtown Los Angeles, the cornerstone of Gen. Harrison Gray Otis's vast business empire—the building that housed the *Los Angeles Times*. And it was to include the murder of the city's two preeminent business leaders, Otis and MMA chief Felix Zeehandelaar.

The union barons of the West Coast and the East were about to join forces to pull off the most grandiose assault on capitalism in America ever. With this single assault they intended to rescue and preserve the cause of unionism in the state of California—indeed in all of the United States— by crushing the most stalwart proponents of the open shop, striking terror into the hearts of their cohorts, and forcing them to yield to the just demands of organized labor.

The initial plan as set out in the correspondence between Iron Workers West Coast chief Eugene Clancy and J. J. was to have Jack H. Barry, a union member from St. Louis, deliver the blow. Barry, however, developed misgivings about such an aggressive operation and eventually backed out. Herbert Hockin was then considered, as "Clancy believed that if a man of Hockin's type was sent out, he could accomplish their purpose," court documents would later relate. But Hockin had just been caught skimming McManigal's pay, and neither J. J. nor J. B. trusted him. So it was decided that J. B. would head to the West Coast theater of operations to give Los Angeles a "damned good cleaning up." J. B. wanted McManigal to go with him, but J. J. responded, "Nothing doing." McManigal, he must have thought, would likely have second thoughts, too.

Instead, McManigal would be dispatched to the Midwest, where he would step up his dynamite operations at open-shop work sites. J. B. would, in effect, be heading to the West Coast to open a second front.

Once the plans were firm and the round-trip train fares purchased, the West Coast labor leaders instantly became impatient. "Has Jim left for here yet?" Clancy wrote to J. J. in early August. "If not, send him out right away." He recognized that the summer of 1910 would be "the psychological moment" to strike, since union fervor in the city was swelling.

J. B. prepared to leave Indianapolis for California on the afternoon of August 15. He would be boarding the same train as McManigal, whose ticket would take him only to Omaha, where he was assigned to blow up a powerhouse. After the Omaha job, McManigal was due to return home to Chicago where he would be handed his next assignment, while J. B. continued on to San Francisco to meet with Clancy, Tveitmoe, and Johannsen.

Later that day J. B. and McManigal each carried two suitcases onboard the train, three of them holding several cans labeled "varnish" that were filled with nitroglycerin, the fourth containing a dozen infernal machines. While McNamara remained on the train, heading west, McManigal successfully carried out the Omaha job. He then returned to union headquarters in Indianapolis, only to be sent on his way again for another assignment in Milwaukee, then another in Duluth, followed by another in Superior, Wisconsin, and yet another in Kansas City, his suitcase literally dripping nitroglycerin everywhere he went. Then in late August a request came in for a bombing at the Lucas and Sons Foundry in Peoria, Illinois, and the Peoria rail yard where McClintock-Marshall had steel girders stored for a bridge project. "I want that damn shop laid flat on the ground," an agent for the Peoria union local demanded.

Before heading off to Peoria, however, McManigal returned to Indianapolis to refill his dwindling supply of nitroglycerin at the basement vault in union headquarters, as several dozen quarts had mysteriously disappeared at various caches across the country. J. J., however, had only four quarts of nitroglycerin stored there, so he sent McManigal on an assignment to pick up a supply from M. J. Morehart of the Independent Torpedo Company of Portland, Indiana.

McManigal arrived in Portland the following day and presented himself to Morehart as J. W. McGraw, an employee of a nonexistent Indianapolis rock quarry owned by the equally nonexistent "G. W. Clark." Together and with great care the two men successfully transferred one hundred quarts of nitroglycerin to a horse-drawn wagon McManigal had rented. Once the dangerous task was complete, Ortie paid Morehart in cash, signed the receipt with his alias, and then mentioned in passing that he had to deliver some of the "soup" to a job in Muncie. Ortie then bade farewell to Morehart and brought his hazardous load to a house on Ebright Street. McManigal spent the night in a Muncie hotel and then moved on to Indianapolis, where he delivered a few quarts to McNamara's downtown office as instructed.

"I'd just as soon have a can or two under my desk," J. J. remarked when Ortie arrived. "Nobody on earth will ever think of looking for the stuff here."

J. J. had another reason for keeping the nitroglycerin so close at hand. He had come to suspect that Hockin had something to do with the nitroglycerin that had recently gone missing. His suspicions were based on the obvious—that he was a thief, and that since his demotion he had been absolutely seething with resentment. However, J. J. told McManigal that he didn't want to confront Hockin about the missing nitro for fear of turning him against them further. So the bombers continued on their campaign with anxious misgivings about what Hockin might be up to.

McManigal arrived in Peoria at 6:00 p.m. September 3, 1910, with several quarts of nitroglycerin and four infernal machines in his suitcase, registering at the Metropolitan hotel as J. W. McGraw. That evening it began to rain. Once the weather passed, McManigal set out into the damp darkness, placing two ten-quart cans attached to two infernal machines in the Peoria railroad yard, and then moved on to the Lucas Brothers' Foundry. With two more infernal machines in his pocket and two cans of nitroglycerin in his hands, he scrambled over a board fence and entered the building. At 9:00 that night he set two devices to detonate at 10:30 p.m.

McManigal returned to his hotel at the Metropolitan and lay awake in bed waiting for the four explosions. The two blasts at the Lucas Brothers' Foundry occurred in quick succession, right at 10:30 p.m. A few minutes later, a third explosion sounded from the general direction of the railroad yard.

And then there was silence.

McManigal felt a chill come over him as he lay in bed waiting for the fourth explosion, the minutes quietly ticking away. But it never came. Had the alarm mechanism jammed? Had the wet weather shorted out a connection? (Current collectors of the Junior Tattoo clocks say that a known fault is that its alarm trip often fails to set off the alarm.)

McManigal realized he was utterly powerless. All he could do was leave town and abandon the conked-out infernal machine at the site. At midnight he caught a train for Chicago and the next day read the account of the three explosions at the breakfast table with his wife. The press account had them trembling: An infernal machine had been recovered by a night watchman at the Peoria, Illinois, railroad yard, it said, and he had turned it over to investigators.

Ortie and Emma continued to scan the newspapers daily for developments in the case, with each day's news deepening their concern. By September 6, the Chicago papers were reporting that the device was now in the possession of the well-known private detective William J. Burns, a short, stout, round-faced man who often affected a sword cane, a bowler, and a walrus mustache. Some called him a genius, others a charlatan. Since intriguing tales of his investigatory exploits regularly appeared in pulp magazines, he was familiar to Ortie and Emma, as he was to millions of Americans in 1910, as "the American Sherlock Holmes."

Chapter 11

In the 130 years that the weather has been tracked in Los Angeles, there was never a hotter April than April 1910. On April 22 temperatures soared to ninety nine degrees, then hit one hundred the next day. It hardly seemed like the right time for brewery workers in the city to go out on strike. But they did, and union members throughout the city supported them, boycotting "scab beer." Within months the beer bottlers were ready to capitulate.

Labor unions and Socialists had merged their political organizations and had nominated Socialist attorney Job Harriman as their mayoral candidate. Ten years earlier he had been Eugene Debs's vice-presidential running mate on the Social Democrat ticket. But he had spent the better part of the decade building a solid political base in Los Angeles, and some saw him as a strong contender for mayor against progressive Republican George Alexander, the incumbent, and former city auditor W. C. Mushet, the regular Republican candidate backed by the *Times*. Indeed, a few months later, in the October primary, Harriman would beat both Alexander and Mushet and seemed like a shoo-in come the runoff against Alexander in December.

The union cause had appeared to be unintentionally aided by the fierce crackdown by police and company guards on union pickets throughout the city and by the arrival of strikebreakers from all over the country at sites where union workers had walked off their jobs. Nowhere were the antagonisms so glaring and the consequences so devastating than at construction sites supervised by open-shop contractors.

Things came to a head in July 1910 at a construction site at Sixth and Spring Streets, where the Llewellyn Iron Works was erecting the Los Angeles Trust and Savings Building.

On July 16 Anton Johannsen arrived from San Francisco and gathered together a group of local organizers, who descended on the site and began shouting to the workers, urging them to leave their jobs and strike for better pay and safer working conditions. Word of the protest came to the attention of the two brothers who owned the ironworks, who quickly arrived at the scene with a team of police officers and demanded that the union organizers be arrested for violating the city's anti-picketing ordinance. In all, twenty-seven men were jailed that day.

The action backfired. Men at the building site, most of them Mexican Americans, began walking off the job or refusing to show up for work. The company responded by importing low-wage black workers from Texas to fill their places. On July 30 the first of these strikebreakers died in a construction accident at the site of the Los Angeles Gas Works that the Llewellyns were building. The coroner's verdict was that the man had suffered fatal injuries after being "caught by a falling derrick owing to an inadvertent error in orders and the literal execution of them by a fellow workman."

Throughout the following weeks, dozens of additional accidents ensued as massive iron and steel beams dropped from the hands of inexperienced workers. Others lost their balance and plummeted to the ground from the sky-high rafters.

Tensions between the union workers and the imported workers escalated. On September 2 one more worker brought in from Texas by the Llewellyns was killed when another construction derrick fell. (The man was later identified as a nephew of recently dethroned heavyweight champion Jim Jeffries.) Two others were injured. Out-of-work union men who were gathered nearby rushed to the scene. As the dead construction worker was being carried out, a woman in the crowd asked what had happened. When she was told, she remarked aloud, "That serves the scab right!" A black nonunion man helping with the corpse cursed her. That was all that was required to set off a riot.

It was aggravating enough that their jobs were being supplanted by these Texas outsiders, but a black man cursing a white woman in 1910 was a call to combat.

Union men, made conspicuous by their white badges, grappled with the nonunion workers. Police arrived, promptly picked off the unionists, and hauled them off to jail—among them, Los Angeles labor leader C. M. Feider, who had been scheduled to act as the grand marshal in a forthcoming labor parade.

In its report of the incident, the *Times* accused Feider of attacking the corpse! And indeed, Feider was duly charged with the crime and put on trial. The jury, however, was unable to reach a verdict, and Feider was released. In its report of the trial outcome, the *Times* insisted that the jury had split eleven to one for conviction, although other newspapers reported that the vote had been split fairly evenly. Of the one supposed holdout, the *Times* demanded: "He ought to be punished in some way."

On October 14 another one of the Llewellyn strikebreakers fell from the tenth floor of a new office building under construction, smashing a hole through the roof of a one-story building below him. As the man lay near death, the Llewellyn Company attorneys offered his family a $50 settlement.

Meanwhile, Harry Chandler and General Otis had other business on their minds. Indeed, during the period of the General's deployment to the Philippines, Chandler had moved not only to increase the *Times*'s land holdings close to home in the San Fernando Valley but also farther afield—in the Imperial Valley and Northern Mexico. While Otis was away, Chandler purchased an option to buy 862,000 acres in Mexico at 60 cents an acre. Three years later he formed another syndicate of investors and incorporated as the California-Mexico Land and Cattle Company (The C-M Co.) and began exercising the option. In a few years the land would produce more cotton than any area of the world. When Mexican President Porfirio Diaz was later overthrown, General Otis immediately launched a campaign for the annexation of Northern Mexico. When that campaign failed, he proposed that an independent North Mexican Republic be established as a buffer state.

In any case, by 1910 General Otis had grown deep roots into Mexican soil, and in late September, eight months before Diaz was ousted, he was appointed by President Taft to serve as a US delegate to Mexico's Centennial Anniversary. He was traveling in a luxury coach from the celebration when he received the telegram that would return him to full-time duty against his union foes.

Chapter 12

On August 19, 1910, a wiry young man with stringy hair, a scruffy beard, and an unkempt mustache walked through the massive wood-and-glass doors of the Argonaut Hotel in downtown San Francisco on Fourth Street between Market and Mission carrying two heavy suitcases. He approached the desk, set down his suitcases with a thud, and identified himself as J. B. Bryce. The clerk checked his reservation and asked him to sign in. In plain penmanship, the man signed the register and presented a cash deposit for the room. The clerk thereupon summoned a bellboy, Trevor McCachren, to attend to his luggage, but the man insisted on carrying the two heavy pieces himself. Only one of the two valises contained his clothes. The other contained the essential parts to create infernal machines.

A few minutes after the man checked in, a light on the hotel's Western Electric switchboard corresponding to his room lit up and the hotel operator answered. The hotel guest asked to be connected to MArket 1806, the telephone number of the San Francisco Building Trades Council. In relatively quick succession he placed two more calls to the same number. Presumably he had called Eugene Clancy, Olaf Tveitmoe, and Anton Johannsen. He had identified himself as "Jim" and arranged to meet with the three men the following day.

At the meeting at the Trades Council offices, Bryce (the erstwhile J. B. McNamara) described his infernal machines and told the San Francisco unionists how he intended to use them to terrorize Los Angeles and bring its tyrannous rulers to their knees. His listeners were impressed both by what he had to say and the glib, confident manner in which he said it.

"I'll need a couple of assistants," J. B. told them. Without hesitation the union leaders assigned David Caplan and Matthew Schmidt to him.

From the outset it was clear that they had made a wrongheaded choice. J. B.'s first meeting with Schmitty was like the encounter of flint and stone. On the one hand there was the burly Schmidt, with the bursting vocal cords and volcanic personality, raging against the capitalist system and drum-beating for Socialist causes. On the other hand there was the brooding J. B., with the surly smile and leering glint, seething with sociopathic paranoia, who at the time owed no group political allegiance.

J. B. made his dislike for Schmitty known to Tveitmoe the next day. He told him that he had a dynamite job to pull off in Oakland at the Pacific Coast Lumber Company that day and had planned to take Schmitty along with him to help out but had changed his mind.

"He talks too much," he said.

The next day the San Francisco newspapers headlined the story about the explosion in the neighboring city. Schmidt read it, found J. B., and asked him if he had been responsible. When J. B. replied that he had, Schmidt seemed overjoyed.

"Let's tell the old man," he said, referring to Tveitmoe, adding that he was sure they could "get some money from him and could go out and have a good time." When J. B. appeared reluctant, Schmidt paid a call on Tveitmoe himself and received $500. Together with J. B. he drove to a nearby cafe, loaded the car with prostitutes and liquor, and drove to a roadhouse. As if the day's explosion hadn't been loud enough, they now began to shivaree San Francisco like it had never been shivareed before. They spent $35 for taxi services alone. However, the original mutual contempt returned with a vengeance the following morning. Desperately hung over, they refused to speak to one another.

J. B.'s relationship with Caplan, a milder, less-volatile type than Schmidt, proved to be less bumpy. J. B. had planned to head to the Northwest, Caplan's home territory, to dynamite a few nonunion construction sites in Portland, Oregon, and Seattle before heading south to Los Angeles. Caplan offered the names of a few dynamite experts living in the Home Colony, outside Tacoma, one of whom was J. D. Waggoner, an electrician and teacher at a Seattle technical school. McNamara left for the Home Colony a few days later, first looking up Waggoner, who showed him how to detonate his infernal machine with the use of a fuse instead of an expensive and unreliable fulminating cap. The new method worked. On the night of August 31, J. B. employed it, blowing up the Lyon Building in Seattle, which was under construction by the open-shop Stone and Webster Company.

While J. B. was operating in Washington State, Clancy and Tveitmoe headed down to Los Angeles, prompting a *Los Angeles Times* report about how they had come under orders "to break more heads." Clancy became so livid that he decided that now was the time to strike a crushing blow at the city's power structure. He left the next day for Seattle to find J. B. McNamara.

On September 3, 1910, J. B. lay on his hotel-room bed in Seattle below a cloud of cigarette smoke, musing about the accomplishments of his one-man warfare. He was well aware that Seattle had become a hotbed of anarchists, communists, "Wobblies" (trade unionists who were members of the left-wing Industrial Workers of the World), and other radical groups who aspired to turn the city into the Western Front of class warfare. But what had they actually accomplished with all their inflammatory rhetoric? He, on the other hand, sufficiently armed and acting alone, could terrorize the capitalist class like no radical army in America had ever done and thereby better the lives of the proletariat.

His reverie was abruptly broken by a banging at the door.

"Who's there?" he called out.

From the hallway, Eugene Clancy identified himself. When J. B. opened the door, the San Francisco union boss barreled into the room, agitated and sputtering.

All of San Francisco, he said, was up in arms over the continued incarceration of dozens of Los Angeles ironworkers under the city's anti-picketing law. But their anger was like nothing compared with the fury of their brethren in Los Angeles itself, where even the men who had been released on their own recognizance were now being denied work—not only in the building trades but anywhere else that the Merchants and Manufacturers Association held sway.

General Otis, he said, had been trumpeting the alarm in his newspapers: "Hire the agitator at your peril! Let these hounds loose among your workers and they will contaminate all of them with their treachery." Variations of that theme were turning up in the *Times* on almost a daily basis. A climate had been created in which even men who had had nothing to do with the union protests but who were thought to have pro-union sympathies were being turned out of their jobs.

"Damn it," Clancy exhorted, "we must strike back!"

Until that moment, the union effort had been aimed at destroying property, sending a message to the "exploiting class" in a language that they easily grasped—money. Injuries had been few, and no one had been killed. Moreover, no one had been caught.

But the plan that J. B. McNamara laid out to Clancy, Tveitmoe, Johannsen, Schmidt, and Caplan back in San Francisco amounted to nothing short of an act of war. He would plant bombs not only at the *Los Angeles Times* but also at the homes of the two principal business leaders in the city: Gen. Harrison Gray Otis, the owner of the *Times,* and Felix Zeehandelaar, head of the Merchants and Manufacturers Association and Otis's powerful ally. The bombs would be set to go off at 1:00 a.m., when Otis and Zeehandelaar would certainly be home but when relatively few people would be at work at the *Times.*

If any member of the group was disturbed over the probable loss of life, their hesitance was overcome by McNamara's passion. In all great battles there is loss of life on both sides, he had repeatedly argued. Men must sometimes be sacrificed for the greater good of society. "As far as my act on the industrial field is concerned," he would later say in a letter to his mother, "I have never gave [sic] it a thought, and I never intend to. Why should I? Does a soldier worry about his act if it happens in the line of duty?" There was a religious fervency in the arguments of this Roman Catholic too. He was, he would later write, "daring to carry out the precepts of the Creator."

In McNamara's sociopathic mind, the strike against the *Times* and the killing of Otis and Zeehandelaar would encourage workers everywhere to rise up against their capitalist exploiters. "All through history peoples have fought peaceably and violently for the principles they thought were right," he would also write to his mother. "The day of reckoning is coming ... and I and others will draw compound interest for our tasks, for cannot we say, we done the best we could?"

It was an argument he had also undoubtedly made in the presence of his brother, and it was probably the reason why J. J. had sent him to California instead of Ortie McManigal.

But McNamara announced that he would not carry out the job if it meant working with Schmidt. He accused Schmidt of talking too much, telling too many people about his reckless ideas for waging war against capitalists, boasting of his ties to union leadership, caring nothing about workers except how he could be hoisted on their shoulders.

Not a person in the room came to the one-eyed man's defense.

Schmidt exploded. "Go to hell," he shouted. "Go to hell all of you!" He pounded the table and snorted threateningly, like a bull ready to charge, ready to take on one and all in the room.

"You bring in this outsider to do the work that men right here ought to be doing. Is it because none of you has the guts to do it? Well, I'll tell you, my friends, I'm going to do the job, even if I have to do it alone!"

The meeting erupted into a verbal ruckus that lasted well into the night. When tempers finally began to calm, it was agreed that Schmidt and Caplan should accompany J. B. to Los Angeles to "case" the job, and that a final decision on who would do what would be made upon their return.

They wasted no time. Two days later, after taking the train to Los Angeles, J. B. McNamara, accompanied by Schmidt and Caplan, walked into the lobby of the *Times* for the first time. The business counter in front of him had been constructed of wood from dozens of historical sites, including some of California's missions and a piece of the bed in which Abraham Lincoln died. He spotted a stack of postcards lying on the counter imprinted with the words "The Times for the News." J. B. snatched one from the top of the pile and used a pen and inkwell nearby to jot down a message on it to McManigal. "It will read 'News for The Times,'" he wrote.

On September 4, the group returned to San Francisco. J. B.'s relationship with Schmidt had somehow become smoother, and Schmidt even suggested that he check into Belle Lavin's boardinghouse, where he was staying, instead of the Argonaut Hotel. It was less expensive and would be more convenient for them to discuss their plans. J. B. agreed, but when they arrived, Mrs. Lavin told J. B. that she had no available rooms and directed him to another nearby boardinghouse, run by a friend, Mrs. D. H. Ingersoll.

J. B. set off on foot to Mrs. Ingersoll's boardinghouse and introduced himself to Lena as J. B. Bryce, a printer from Chicago.

"I usually stay at the Argonaut Hotel," he told her, "but I find it quite noisy." He asked her for a quiet room, which she showed him. He then paid her two weeks' rent, and she handed him the key. J. B. had just entered the room and set down his suitcase when the boardinghouse phone rang. Lena Ingersoll picked it up.

"Is Bryce there?" asked a voice she recognized as Matthew Schmidt's.

"Did you send him here, Schmitty?" she asked.

"That's right," Schmidt said. "I need to talk to him."

She placed the receiver on her desk, walked to J. B.'s room, and shouted that he had a telephone call. She then went about her business as J. B. engaged in what would be the first of many cryptic telephone conversations Mrs. Ingersoll would overhear.

That night at the Lavin house, Schmidt talked to another roomer, W. H. Brown, about his trip to Los Angeles. "They are having an awful time down there," he said, "beating up men. They won't give a union man a job in L.A.. But they are going to get theirs. Something is going to happen down there sure, and that, pretty soon."

Brown looked dubious. The unions, he pointed out, were under the thumb of General Otis—a man, he said, of "terrible power."

Schmidt replied: "There will something happen to him soon too!"

But if Schmidt talked too much, as J. B. McNamara had insisted, so also did J. B. A man seemingly incapable of love, J. B. gave none to Lena Ingersoll, but he was intimate with her—and often more than just physically. Lying next to her a few days after he took up residence in her boardinghouse, he awoke with a start.

He'd had a dream, he said. The *Los Angeles Times* plant had blown up just as the paper was going to press. In the dream he'd sensed that General Otis had been murdered.

The dream was lost on Lena. All she could do was try to calm her spooked bed partner, but the suspicions would linger.

A few days later J. B. left Lena's place altogether after having concluded that a boardinghouse with roomers coming and going, with mere plywood walls to dampen the voices of his coconspirators plotting a major act of terror, was not the place to be headquartered. On September 14 he returned to the Argonaut Hotel, leaving behind Lena and his paid-in-advance room.

～

On September 15 Bruce McCaul, chief invoice clerk for the Giant Powder Company near San Francisco, was sitting at his desk when the phone rang. On the other end: a man named Leonard. "This is the Bryson Construction Company of Sacramento," said the caller, who asked if Giant manufactured a 99 percent product. If so, Leonard would send a launch to collect a supply at the plant.

"Yes, we do indeed make a 99 percent gelatin," McCaul replied.

"I'll be in to see you tomorrow," Leonard remarked before clicking off.

The following day J. B. and Schmitty arrived at the offices of the Giant Powder Company in San Francisco, identifying themselves as Bryce and Leonard, employees of a "Mr. Clark" in Auburn. McCaul, the sales representative, became suspicious of the two men, especially of Leonard, "the man with the bad eye," and asked why they needed the 99 percent product.

"It's for blowing up tree stumps," Schmitty claimed.

"Usually 20 percent is all you need," McCaul said.

"They're pretty hard tree stumps. I've been using a stumping machine and have been breaking so many cables lately that we have decided to blow the stumps up."

McCaul shook his head. He wasn't selling this strange pair 99 percent dynamite. Schmitty insisted that he would settle for no less than 85 percent.

"That's what Mr. Clark wanted; that's what he will get."

The haggling didn't end until McCaul reluctantly agreed to sell them five hundred pounds of 80 percent dynamite. J. B. handed him $80 in cash and $2.10 in silver and told McCaul that he would return with a launch to pick up the order at Giant's wharf in a few days.

September 18, 1910. J. B. called the room clerk at the Argonaut Hotel to complain that his phone was not functioning properly and to advise that a friend would be joining him. Later that day, the clerk moved J. B. to another room and registered his friend, F. A. Perry.[7]

The following day, September 19, Schmitty walked to the *San Francisco Call* newspaper building and, identifying himself as a Mr. Perry, told clerk Marguerite Sheldon that he wanted to place an ad. He filled in the form that she handed him and scribbled the message:

WANTED—By party of men, 16–24 foot launch for 10 days to cruise around bay and tributaries: best of Refs.

The ad would appear the following day.

September 19, 1910. Schmitty, now using the alias Leonard again, phoned McCaul at the Giant Powder Company's San Francisco sales office. McCaul informed him that the company was preparing to make the dynamite sticks the following day. Leonard replied that a William Morris would pick up the order at the plant in Giant. "Morris" was now Caplan's nom de guerre.[8]

September 20, 1910. Caplan arrived at the Giant Powder Company's San Francisco office, where he told McCaul that he was William Morris, come to pick up the delivery documents for the dynamite his friends had ordered by phone. McCaul swiveled in his chair, reached for a printed form, dipped his pen into an inkwell, and began to write. Glancing up at Caplan, he asked:

"What would be the name of the launch?"

The question stunned Caplan, who was aware that at that very moment J. B. and Schmitty were trying to rent a launch but had not done so yet. Caplan, of course, had no idea what the name of it would be.

"I can't remember," he told McCaul.

"Look here, Mr. Morris. I must have the name of the launch."

Morris's memory still failed him.

McCaul called over B. H. Rennie, general sales manager of the company, and explained the situation to him. Rennie politely informed Caplan that the company would have to know the name of the launch before it could give him a delivery order.

"I'll be back later," Caplan remarked.

Things were also not going well for J. B. and Schmitty in Oakland. At the end of 12th Avenue on the waterfront, they had first called on Mrs. M. J. Peterson, who told them that her husband was away for the moment but informed them that his usual charge for the rental of his boat was $10 a day, "and he'll be happy to act as your guide."

J. B., however, insisted that they did not need a skipper—just the launch.

"Well, that's a different story," Mrs. Peterson responded. "No, my husband would not want to rent the launch without being on hand himself."

J. B. then offered to put up $500 as a good-faith guarantee of its safe return, but Mrs. Peterson still demurred.

J. B. angrily remarked: "We do not want the boat unless we can take it alone. We will go and see about the other one."

Mrs. Peterson watched them leave, gazing sadly at Schmitty and thinking to herself how terrible it must be for him to have to go through life with only one eye.

In fact, earlier in the day J. B. and Schmitty had set their eyes on the ideal launch for their purpose at a boathouse at the end of Webster Street in Oakland. It was called the *Pastime,* twenty-three feet overall, with a six-foot beam and a nine-horsepower engine. A tall cabin covered her almost completely from the bow to a point below the center of the craft ("abaft amidships"), the sides of the cabin being flush with the sides of the launch, so that there was no deck forward of the cockpit. It was, by any measure of comparison on San Francisco Bay, a strikingly peculiar-looking vessel. Nevertheless it was a near-perfect boat for hauling and concealing a large cargo.

The *Pastime* and several other boats anchored at the Webster Street dock were looked after by Captain John Stanley. When J. B. and Schmitty had first approached him that morning, Stanley informed them that the boat was not for rent.

"Now that would be a pity," J. B. responded. "And I understand why you would not want to entrust such a beautiful vessel to someone you did not know. But what if we was to put up a deposit of what she's worth to guarantee her safe return? Would that be of interest to you?"

Stanley told him it was not up to him, that he would have to speak to the boat's owners. He then phoned Douglas Burrowes, one of the two owners, who said that he would come down to the boathouse to meet them later.

He was waiting for them at the boathouse when J. B. and Schmitty ambled up from 12th Avenue after having been turned down by Mrs. Peterson. They told Burrowes the same story that they had told her. They were tourists from Chicago planning to cruise about the bay and the lower waters of the Sacramento River for a week or ten days. They were prepared to leave a security deposit.

Burrowes said he would charge them $30 for a week's rental or $40 for ten days. Now, about references and the security deposit . . .

"Would $250 be enough?" J. B. inquired.

Burrowes replied that he thought it might be, although the launch, he felt, was worth $900. Burrowes was far more interested in the money they intended to leave than in references. He told them that if his partner, E. Howard Baxter, would agree to the deal, he would turn the boat over to them.

"But you've got to talk to him yourselves. He'd want to meet the men he's doing business with." Burrowes phoned Baxter at his office in San Francisco and told him that the pair would call on him that afternoon.

By the time they crossed the bay again, it was already past 5:00 p.m. Baxter also was willing to rent the launch to them—but he insisted on a $500 security deposit rather than $250.

Schmitty merely pulled a roll of $10 and $20 bills from his shirt pocket and counted out an amount just less than $500 onto Baxter's desk.

He told Baxter: "Keep what you've got. I'll bring you the rest tomorrow, after the banks open."

Baxter wrote out a receipt for the deposit, Schmitty stuffed it into his shirt pocket, they shook hands with Baxter and left.

A while later they met Caplan, who filled them in on his experience at the powder company office.

"They wanted to know the name of the launch."

Maybe they wanted the name so that they could find out more about her, they wondered. They decided that they would change the name of the *Pastime* to the *Peerless*. They wouldn't be able to find out anything about her that way. She'd be pier-less, they chuckled.

The following morning Caplan returned to the Giant Powder Company office in San Francisco and gave McCaul and Rennie the name of the launch. McCaul thereupon phoned the factory in Giant and let them know that the launch *Peerless* would pick up the powder; he then wrote out the following delivery order:

"Please deliver to Mr. J. Bryson or bearer 500 lbs. of Gelatin.

"(S) McCaul"

Rennie handed the order to Caplan, and as he did so commented on his assumed name.

"Morris is a good American name. You look more like a Dago." Caplan's face flushed, and the Russian-born woodworker stormed out of the office without saying another word.

At 7:00 the next morning, Howard Baxter phoned Douglas Burrowes to tell him about his deal with "Bryce" and "Perry." A few hours later the two men arrived at Baxter's office with the rest of the deposit and Baxter wrote out a new receipt:

"September 20, 1910—Received of F. A. Perry and J. B. Bryce the sum of five hundred ($500) dollars as security on the launch *Pastime*, above sum to be returned to the above parties within forty-eight hours after return of said launch *Pastime* in condition as found at present date, less ordinary wear and tear. It is agreed that Mr. F. A. Perry and Mr. J. B. Bryce pay the sum of $30 for seven days' rental of the above launch and $40 for ten days. Owner is to furnish lubricating oil and above parties supplying the fuel.

(S) E. Howard Baxter, Douglas Burrowes (by E. H. B.)" He drew a rectangle under his name and asked the two renters to sign where indicated.

At about five o'clock that afternoon, J. B. and Schmitty found Burrowes at the Webster Street boat landing in Oakland and showed him the signed agreement. They immediately boarded the *Pastime,* and Schmitty quickly impressed Burrowes with his familiarity with the engine; he needed few instructions on how to run it. Burrowes was especially struck by the fact that Schmitty put on gloves when he started to handle the engine. J. B. wore no gloves, however. As the boat lurched through the water, he braced himself by holding on to the greasy wooden sides, leaving perfect handprints.

An enemy buccaneer would probably have attracted less notice than the *Pastime* during her voyage on the bay. She might just as well have flown a skull and crossbones, and her crew might as well have outfitted themselves in three-corner hats, peg legs, and eye patches (as a matter of fact, every voyager who spotted one-eyed Schmitty on the deck that week remembered him well).

In the late afternoon of Wednesday, September 21, the *Pastime* chugged into a channel in front of the Miramar Hotel in Sausalito. All three of the group onboard were wearing overalls and caps. Schmitty hailed the proprietors of the hotel, Mr. and Mrs. Paul J. Stuparich, and asked if they could get something to eat and made arrangements to stay the night.

The following morning J. B. and Schmitty arose early, breakfasted, and went out to the launch. They changed into overalls and busied themselves with the engine. When Schmitty asked Stuparich if he had any paint that he could spare, Stuparich found a nearly depleted can of dark green paint that he gave to the men.

A short while later they motored out toward San Francisco where they began shopping for two sets of aluminum letters to use to change the boat's name. And once again they attracted attention wherever they went. They first went to a hardware store, and when salesman Harry Bridgeman could not find letters of the proper size, they asked him to remove them from other signs he had on display in the store. The salesman refused.

They later found the letters they wanted at the Moise-Klinker Company. Salesman Harry M. Nutter couldn't help noticing that the men carried a thick wad of cash and that they didn't seem to care whether they spent 50 cents or $50 for the letters. (They spent $1.80—10 cents for two sets of nine letters each.) Schmitty's glass eye disturbed Nutter, and he avoided looking at him.

At about 6:00 p.m. the men decided to return to Sausalito. As they crossed the bay, they painted a board with the green paint and mounted the aluminum letters on that. For some reason—artistic? financial? slothful?—they decided to use the first letter in the word "Pastime" already painted onto the bow and mounted only the letters "eerless" on the green board, attaching it after the letter "P."

But the name change proved to be yet another forlorn exercise. When the boat returned to the Miramar, the proprietor immediately pointed out to his wife that the men had changed the launch's name. He later asked them why they had done so. They replied that they had just purchased it in Alameda and didn't want to keep the old name.

The Giant Powder Company was just a few minutes' cruise down the bay from the Miramar Hotel. Assistant Supervisor George Phillips met the trio when they arrived at the Giant wharf the next day.

Phillips had ten wooden crates holding more than five hundred pounds of 80 percent dynamite waiting for them, with "J. B. Bryson" stenciled on the sides of each case. Phillips, Schmitty, and Manuel Cortez, a Portuguese helper, loaded the heavy crates aboard. Phillips then handed a receipt to Schmitty, which he signed "J. B. Leonard."

Finally the *Peerless* cast off and motored away, the floorboards under the cargo hold beginning to buckle as the launch cut through the choppy waters, the tiny engine sputtering and occasionally cutting out as it propelled the overburdened vessel along at flank speed, overheating the engine and draining the fuel tank. The conspirators now had their deadly arsenal. Only 10 percent of it would be used for the planned operation in Los Angeles. The rest would be required to keep "capitalist tyrants" in the West terrorized for a long time to come.

The *Peerless* was certainly no speedboat. The bulky cabin of the *Peerless* may have effectively concealed the cargo, but it gave the boat a distinctive appearance that attracted notice everywhere it traveled. At least a half dozen boat owners and skippers would step forward later to positively identify the launch and describe Schmitty. Despite Schmitty's effort to power the boat beyond its designated full speed, it seemed to balk like a donkey resisting the spur, frequently coming to a halt as it returned across the choppy waters of the bay, the engine then grumbling and coughing whenever Schmitty attempted to rev it up again. Thwarted, the three-man crew decided simply to relax and watch the curtain of fog loom ever larger in front of them as the launch slowly putt-putted its way across the bay.

That afternoon they rented a bay horse and light spring wagon, loaded the ten cases of dynamite aboard, and clattered out to a house that Caplan had rented that morning at 1622 Nineteenth Avenue South. It was a fairly warm afternoon, and several neighbors were lounging on their front porches when the three men began unloading tarpaulin-covered crates into the house. When they were finished, Schmitty securely locked the front door and fastened the latches on the windows, tore down the FOR RENT sign in front of the house, hopped into the wagon with the others, and drove away with them. They again returned to the *Peerless* and headed for the Miramar Hotel in Sausalito.

The next afternoon Schmitty brought the *Peerless* into the Harrison Street wharf. Harry Piper, a seventeen-year-old jockey, was sitting on the wharf fishing. He looked up and saw "a big, heavy-set fellow, with a crossed eye" hurriedly walking toward him, perspiration dripping down his sunburned, peeling face.

Schmitty told Piper that he was going to fetch some gasoline and offered to pay him a half-dollar to look after the boat while he was gone.

Piper not only looked after it; he looked *into* it. He would later describe seeing "a big pile of bale rope and a lot of heavy twine" and rolls of burlap. Piper would also give this befuddled description of Schmitty's glass eye: "He was so cross-eyed that I couldn't tell where he was looking when he was talking to me. One of his eyes seemed to be very much crossed, and it made the other look crossed, too." Yes, Schmitty was not a man one soon forgot.

Every aspect connected with the rental of the boat originally christened the *Pastime* would turn out to be a fumbling miscalculation. To have negotiated with two owners on opposite sides of San Francisco Bay about the rental was a mistake. To have selected such a peculiar and identifiable boat was a mistake. To have tied her up in places where she would have attracted attention and comment was a mistake. Not to have inspected the batteries and engine more closely was a mistake.

And now the men would encounter all manner of complications merely returning the boat to its owners and getting their deposit money back. When they brought the *Pastime*, her original name now restored, back to the boat landing in Oakland where she had been berthed, Burrowes was nowhere to be found. They spent the morning and part of the afternoon lingering around the dock waiting for him. When he finally arrived, they asked him to inspect the boat for damage.

Does she appear to be in good condition? they asked. Burrowes replied that it did, except for a little paint missing from one side, where she had rubbed up against some object. Not to worry. He wouldn't ask them to pay for it.

They then asked for their deposit money back. But again they were informed that they would have to see Baxter in San Francisco. Schmitty reached him the next day. "We are back with the launch," he said. "It is in good condition and we would like to get our deposit because we are anxious to leave for Canada."

Baxter told Schmitty that he was ill, but said that if he would come to his home in Alameda that afternoon he would return the money. Schmitty arrived alone. Baxter told him the charge for renting the boat would be $30, plus $5 to touch up the paintwork where it had been rubbed, $2.50 for the fuel that had been in the boat when they picked it up, and $2 for the rental of a skiff belonging to Captain Stanley. The total came to $39.35. "Make it $40," said Schmitty with a wave of his hand. Baxter thanked him and said he would write out a refund check for $460.

A check! Where was the cash that had been deposited? Schmitty wanted to know. Well, said Baxter, he had deposited that in his personal account at the Crocker Bank in San Francisco. That would make things difficult, said Schmitty, not trying to mask his displeasure, as he and his friends were all strangers in town and would have difficulty cashing a check. Baxter remembered that his brother-in-law, Bert Scott, had an office in the Crocker building. He would simply make out the check to his brother-in-law, write a note to him asking him to cash it and to turn the money over to "Perry," and the problem would be solved. Clearly put out and nettled, Schmitty took leave of Baxter, arriving at the Crocker building a short while later and at long last receiving the deposit money back. That afternoon he and J. B. checked out of the Argonaut Hotel in San Francisco. They again refused to let bellhop E. E. McCracken take their suitcases. Another fierce argument between J. B. McNamara and Matthew Schmidt had put the two men on the outs with one another again, for it was decided that J. B. would go on to Los Angeles alone. J. B. then made his way to the station to board the Lark, the Santa Fe Railroad's nighttime coastal express, for Los Angeles.

On the afternoon of the following day, September 29, J. B. registered at the new Baltimore Hotel on East Fifth Street, near the Los Angeles Santa Fe train station. He signed the register J. B. Bryce from Chicago.

"I'm from Chicago too," the room clerk, C. A. "Kurt" Diekelman, remarked, and the two struck up a brief conversation before the visitor was assigned a room on the third floor. Although he struggled with two heavy suitcases, J. B. once again refused to allow the bellhop to help him.

At first light the next morning, he walked over to the Los Angeles Times Building, a few blocks away, and went straight in. The plant was in full swing, printing presses roaring and Linotype machines clattering with such a din that workers could communicate only by shouting. The sweet, pungent odor of newspaper ink was so heavy in the hot air that it could be tasted. J. B. took in the activity in the plant and chatted with several workers, including William Brown, a pressman. Giving his name as J. B. Bryce, a printer from Chicago, McNamara asked about the prospects for a job at the *Times*. The pressmen brushed him off, too busy to be bothered.

Returning to his hotel that afternoon, J. B. was ready to carry out the final steps of his mission. But he first dropped by the front desk to ask

Diekelman whether he would have to pay for a full day if he checked out in the afternoon around 3:00. Diekelman said the late checkout would be fine, that he would not be charged. The 3:00 p.m. checkout was critically important. Since his infernal machines could be timed to go off any time within twelve hours of setting them, J. B. needed those two hours between 1:00 p.m., the regular check-out time, and 3:00 p.m. to allow him to assemble each of his three devices and pack them up.

So in the silence of his hotel room, J. B. set to work, timing the first device, setting the clock, winding the spring, connecting the nine-foot coil of two-time fuse, and then carefully lowering it into a cardboard box that held sixteen sticks of dynamite. He then wrapped the box in white paper, as though it were a gift.

J. B. then timed the second device and lowered it into a small leather suitcase with a calico lining, which held another sixteen sticks of dynamite. Once this device was set, he placed the cardboard package and the leather suitcase into a larger suitcase that held a third device connected to another bundle of dynamite. His gifts were now ready to be delivered to the *Times* and to Otis and Zeehandelaar.

A few minutes before 3:00 p.m., Diekelman watched McNamara lug two heavy suitcases past his front desk. He asked if J. B. needed any help, and McNamara gruffly declined. He then shuffled out the door, down the sidewalk, and to the train station, where he checked the suitcase with his personal belongings in a storage locker and took with him the one holding the three infernal machines.

His first stop was the Zeehandelaar residence at 830 Garland Street. In the vague ambient light of dusk, he tightly wound the infernal machine's clock once again, set the alarm, and then placed its package by a rose bush next to the house under what turned out to be the Zeehandelaars' young daughter's bedroom. Then he was off, probably walking the ten blocks through the growing darkness to The Bivouac, General Otis's estate on Wilshire Boulevard, unaware that Otis was still in Mexico. Here he checked and wound the clock for the second device and left it in the leather suitcase in a flower bed under a bay window. Carrying the smaller suitcase, he made his way to the night's final stop at the *Los Angeles Times*.

J. B. knew exactly where he was going. Briskly moving along, he walked down the sidewalk on First Street, and then abruptly turned down Ink Alley, a covered corridor used principally as a storage area for barrels of printers' ink. Adjoining the alley was the great room that housed the *Times's* massive printing presses, while above it was the Linotype room. Standing among stacks of ink barrels, J. B. established that he was alone. Then, in the darkness, he found an empty barrel and lowered the suitcase into it, finally covering it with discarded editions of the *Times* lying nearby. He then placed a lid on top of the barrel and listened for the muted ticking of the clock as the building all around him throbbed with the activity of the one hundred or so workers and their machines. Satisfied with what he heard, he quietly emerged from the alley and walked toward one of the night entrances to the building.

As he approached the door he was stopped by the night watchman, who demanded to know where he was going. With a contrived air of authority, McNamara said he was heading to the compositing room, and the watchman let him pass. When he came to the door, he was again stopped, this time by a boy who also asked where he was going. When McNamara gave the same reply, the boy smiled, opened the door for him, and gave directions. Once inside, J. B. made his way directly downstairs to the belly of the beast, where he found the access to the gas cocks to the natural gas pipes. Using a set of pliers that he had brought along, he wrenched the cocks open, and then waited and listened to the hiss of the escaping gas until he could detect the unmistakable pungent odor. As he would later explain, he wanted the whole building "to go to hell."

From the basement he quickly headed upstairs, out the door, and walked directly to the Santa Fe depot a few blocks away on East First Street. He boarded Southern Pacific's all-sleeping-car Lark for its scheduled 9:00 p.m. departure for San Francisco, and quietly relaxed and smoked for the first hours of the four-hundred-mile, twelve-hour journey. Sometime before midnight he fell asleep. At 1:07 a.m. he was still asleep as the train sped northward through the night, already about 150 miles from downtown Los Angeles. It would be the last peaceful sleep of James Barnabas McNamara's young life.

Chapter 13

The special train that had brought Gen. Harrison Gray Otis and other dignitaries to Mexico for that country's Centennial Celebration and was now returning them home could not have been more ostentatious had it been designed for a European monarch. It consisted of elaborate Pullman cars that, as the *Times* reported, sported "drawing room sleepers," a "composite" car containing a club, buffet, bathroom, and barber shop, plus an elegant dining car and a baggage car.

It had been an eventful and memorable two weeks for the General, who had already become one of Mexico's wealthiest landowners and a power in his own right among the country's rulers.

Unlike other countries in the region, the United States had not dispatched troops to participate in the great army and navy parade in Veracruz to observe the centennial, but General Otis, a power unto himself, was present in the reviewing stands. He would do.

The general, now returning to his homeland in his luxurious train accommodations, his trip paid for by the government of Mexico, must have felt as if he had finally achieved the deference and eminence that he had long been intent on realizing. It had come late in life, but it had come. He only had to glance around him at his current surroundings to see how far he had come over the past fifteen years.

Back in Los Angeles on the night of September 30, Harry Chandler, now vice president and assistant general manager of the Times-Mirror Company, received a telephone call from his wife, Marian, demanding that he return home at once. He told her that he would be home in a few minutes and hung up. When he hadn't arrived by midnight, she came by his office in person. Employees passing by heard her rail, "Harry Chandler, if you don't drop everything this very minute and come home with me, I shall never believe you again!"

Chandler left a few minutes later, around 12:45 a.m.—a full hour earlier than his usual leaving time, after the *Times* had gone to press. Turning in early was probably for the best, he no doubt thought. Tomorrow promised to be an endless series of briefings and conferences as General Otis would be arriving from Mexico City.

Once Chandler had left the building, his secretary, J. Wesley Reaves, moved behind his boss's oak desk and began opening the night mail upon its vast polished surface. Directly beneath him was Ink Alley.

The temperature had barely slipped below seventy degrees at midnight as the first day of October 1910 began in Los Angeles. The city was experiencing a typical late-September/early-October heat wave, with daytime temperatures in the nineties, made especially uncomfortable by a reversal of airflow from the Pacific inland. A few hours earlier, a veil of heavy clouds coasted in from the ocean, dropping blobs of rain on the city streets, and many people sitting out on front porches or lying on the grasses of the city parks seeking escape from the thick heat trapped in their homes suddenly had to race for shelter. It was the sort of weather that would have signaled an approaching thunderstorm anywhere else. The wetness here, however, amounted only to a momentary sprinkle, and by midnight the clouds seemed lighter and the air cooler. Nevertheless, because of the balmy weather, more people were on the streets, in local bars, and awake in their homes than on an ordinary night in that burgeoning pueblo. Long before the invention of television, they were about to become mass witnesses to a historical event.

At J. T. Hinch's Saloon, abutting the Los Angeles Times Building at First and Broadway, Julian Johnson, the newspaper's drama critic, was holding forth on the current vaudeville fare at the Pantages Theatre. His audience was a number of *Times* reporters swigging one or more for the road home.[9]

At the Los Angeles Times Building next door, composers and Linotypers blended their racket to produce a cumulative roar as they worked away at their chattering machines, transposing a record of the day's events onto soft, hot lead, which, once cooled and slathered with ink, was eventually transmogrified into the printed word. It had proved to be a quiet news day on the national scene. In New York, John A. Dix had been nominated by the Democratic Party to be their gubernatorial candidate; artist Winslow Homer had died in Portland, Maine, at the age of seventy-four; the Chicago Cubs of the National League were set to face the Philadelphia Athletics of the American League in the World Series without the help of the middleman in the Cubs' famous Tinker-to-Evers-to-Chance double-play combination: Evers had broken his ankle.

Since the paper had now gone to press, the news and editorial department on the third floor had been left virtually empty. Churchill Harvey-Elder, who had been appointed night city editor and labor editor, remained at his desk. He had been at his supervisory post for only ten days and in the newspaper business for only five years. He was young (twenty-nine), handsome, and brilliant—some said a genius. Elder, who was of old California lineage from the Quaker suburb of Whittier—his grandfather, C. W. Harvey, was one of its founders—had seen much of the family fortune dissolve in recent years under an assault of taxes, water rights, and the heavy burden of exotic higher educations.

There, at the corner of First and Broadway, Elder had found an invaluable nexus of friendships and associations. Across the street from the *Times* stood the office of Earl Rogers, an old friend of his grandmother's and one of the most celebrated criminal attorneys in the country. In an era when drinking whisky was considered the principal entertainment among men, Rogers was often the most entertained man in his crowd.

Perhaps in an alcoholic's subconscious effort to preserve some semblance of symmetry and order, Rogers seemed to have taken a particular liking to the steady and dedicated Elder. Two days earlier, on the night of September 28, Elder had shown up at Rogers's office with sandwiches and beer. Adela, Rogers's sixteen-year-old daughter, would later recall Elder being "exuberant" as they chatted in the warm afterglow of his promotion. When Elder left, he was playfully "waving a hand that still had a bun in it."

Drunk or sober, Rogers was adored by the newsmen on the third floor of the Times Building, for it was "newsworthy to talk to Earl

Rogers." Previous city night editors had made it their business to form a friendly relationship with the attorney and drop by his office, where they were often rewarded with either a leak from the district attorney's office or a scoop on a prominent case he was handling. As "a young old friend" of the Rogers family, Elder regularly made his way to the office across the street, where the glass-shaded lamps burned around the clock. Within its lustrous paneled walls, he was given privileged access to the best inside information—the very currency of the Los Angeles newsman's trade—and it was only the width of First Street away. Typically Elder would find Rogers and his beautiful black-haired daughter casually leaning back in their chairs, a father and daughter discussing current local events and cases, the father sipping from an ever-present glass of bourbon, the adoring young woman, wise beyond her years, contentedly listening.

On the night of September 30, Harvey-Elder had dinner at a local restaurant with his cousin, Charles Elder, of the Los Angeles Investment Company. Charles would later recall their discussion concerning the smoldering dispute between the *Los Angeles Times* and the state's labor leaders. Elder detected the menacing spirit in the air of Los Angeles, mentioning to his cousin the pall of resentment all over the city that seemed to envelop the general and the *Times*. It wouldn't surprise him, he said, if The Fortress was blown up.

After dinner the cousins parted, and Elder returned to the Times Building to begin his nighttime shift on the third floor. A few hours later, country editor Charles Lovelace and deskman William Tribit found themselves in the editorial department with little to do other than keep Elder company. Perhaps it was his air of chivalry, manifest in the mysterious scars, perhaps the melding of his scholarly bearing and his down-at-heel nature. Whatever it was, people were drawn to this young man and his editorial desk. Sometime around 12:50 a.m. his grandmother dropped by for a surprise visit to see her grandson at his new nighttime editorial post. She left shortly before 1:00 a.m. "glowing with pleasure."

At the far end of the third floor, telegraph operator R. L. "Cy" Sawyer, a thirty-four-year-old hunchback with a wife and two children, was preparing to receive text via Morse code from a *New York Times* reporter in Minneola, New York. Sawyer was a talented telegraph operator, called in for special duty on this night because the *Times* was planning to issue an extra edition with the results of the 278-mile Vanderbilt Cup auto race.[10]

At 1:00 a.m., shortly after Elder's grandmother left the building, Sawyer tapped out his message to his *New York Times* counterpart, who received the message at 4:00 a.m. Eastern Standard Time: "Send us a good account of the race. At the crack of the [starting] pistol, begin sending the actual scenes on the track, describing in detail any accidents as they occur."

Word would be sent back to Sawyer but not received.

Approximately seven minutes later, the Junior Tattoo New Haven alarm clock began ringing inside the barrel in Ink Alley, and the alarm's wind-up handle began to turn. The brass post that had been soldered to it made contact with the tiny brass plate, completing the circuit that allowed the electrical charge to be sent to a Columbia dry-cell battery. Once the charge was received, the two-time fuse was ignited. The fuse burned for twenty seconds.

On the first floor of the Times Building, several workers emerged from the basement where they claimed they had smelled gas. The odor had been strong enough to sicken them.

At precisely 1:07 a.m. on October 1, 1910, the pale fizzing incandescence reached the sixteen sticks of dynamite stashed in the barrel in Ink Alley.

A. G. Schwalm was walking down the sidewalk in front of the Times Building when he was suddenly hurled into the street. G. F. Glick, walking in the opposite direction, was thrown against the Tajo Building with sufficient force to render him unconscious. Flying glass tore through Lustig's Saloon on the opposite corner. In midsentence, critic Julian Johnson was thrown from his stool at J. T. Hinch's Saloon. Earl Rogers was sitting behind his desk when the office window facing the Times Building blew inward.

The explosion was so powerful that people miles away witnessed it and for hours could see the flickering lightness in the eastern sky. Many ran into the streets, certain that the city was in the throes of an earthquake. But others seemed to know, almost intuitively, what was happening. Three miles away, Harry Andrews, managing editor of the *Times*, was walking up the steps of his residence near Westlake (now MacArthur) Park when he heard the explosion. With a sense of dread, he turned in the direction of the blast and cried out, "It's the *Times!*" He then scurried down the steps to his car, cranked the engine to a start, and drove toward the growing pillars of lurid red flames on the horizon. Harry Chandler, who was just climbing into bed at 1:07 a.m., made the same conclusion. Both men were certain it was the Times Building, and both were certain it had been bombed.

Within the building itself, Harvey Elder also knew in the horrifying instant of the blast what had happened. "My God, they have got us at last," he shouted at country editor Charles Lovelace. And now, the noise of the first ear-shattering explosion blended into the screams of the just-injured; those shouts were in turn drowned out at once by a series of smaller explosions as the gas mains ruptured, discharging a tremendous fireball of ignited gas. The lights went out and the giant newspaper machinery went silent as a colossal blast of flame fingered through shattered windows and doorways, turning men into fireballs and igniting dozens of smaller fires that singed hair and eyebrows. With the initial explosion, each of the building's six floors was lifted, heaving workers and their machines upward, much of which fell all the way to ground level as debris. Jagged slabs of plaster rained down, impaling people on the lower floors. Ink that had been stored in Ink Alley was vaporized, the tiny petroleum-based droplets forming a kind of inky black fog that, a moment later, ignited, sending all-engulfing flames throughout the rubble and ruin. Some of the ink geysered into the night sky, coating stunned workers in the engraving department on the sixth floor. A moment later, they were fighting for their lives as the intense heat ignited the ether and gun cotton that newspapers used to process photographs. The materials were stored everywhere. Now they were abetting the inferno.

Women on the second floor thought first of rushing to the cloak room to retrieve their wraps before leaving the building but were barred by the flames. On the sixth floor engraving room, men also dashed for their street clothes, somehow hoping to change out of their ink-stained aprons and work trousers, then realizing that there was no time to do so.

Solicitor Charles Career was one of the few fortunate employees working on the second floor who happened to be near the fire escape when the blast occurred. He watched a man and young woman fighting to get to the exit first. "The girl appeared to be badly injured and fainted to the floor," he would later relate, "and in the crush that followed, we left her on the floor partially hidden by the smoke. I tried to grab the girl, but a crowd joined us from behind, and I could not reach her. In going down the fire escape, a young man . . . who was covered with oil fainted across my back, and I turned and grabbed his arm, but the flesh came off with the cloth of his shirt in my hand, and it sickened me, and I let go of him."

The consuming flames lent only a hazy illumination to the smoking building. Some men discovered flashlights, but their lamps barely penetrated a few inches of the smoke. Those with handkerchiefs clamped them over their faces, but the air seemed hardly less suffocating. Workers roamed in the darkness with no sense of direction, stumbling over overturned chairs or chunks of plaster or iron beams, hoping they were heading toward fire escapes but often discovering themselves at windows high above the ground with a juggernaut of fire bearing down on them.

Panic turned the stairwells into death traps. Stereotyper William Latta was among a crowd of fugitives rushing down a flight of stairs to the ground floor. There was a shoving surge as a rush of flame threatened them, and Latta stumbled down twenty steps into a pile of sizzling debris. A few moments later, a young man stepped on Mary Copp's skirt as she fled down the stairs. She fainted. The young man and a printer, Charley Baker, picked her up and carried her out of the building and across the street to the corner drugstore.

Several of the men in the engraving department on the sixth floor made their way down to the third, where the Times Building connected to the roof of the Baumgardt Building, which also appeared threatened by the flames. Among this group was foreman George W. Long and workers Edward Ball, Harry Anderson, Charles Seebold, and Harvey Coleman. The men rushed to the end of the Baumgardt Building, but there was a short alleyway that barred further progress. The residents of a next-door rooming house had watched their escape, and one of them threw up a stepladder. It was just inches too short to reach across the gap. Swiftly improvising, two men held one end of the ladder, while resting the very tip of the far end on the ledge of the opposite roof. Upon this shaky bridge, the men crawled to safety. Foreman Long was last to make his way across. But as he conducted a head count, he discovered that one of his men, Huber Bruce, was still missing. Long decided to turn back, but just as he began to do so, Bruce was spotted climbing hand over hand down a cable connecting the buildings. A cheer arose as Bruce pulled himself onto the roof and joined them.

On the second floor nearly a dozen badly burned Linotypists found themselves penned into a corner by a wall of flames; behind them the floor fell away in an elevator shaft, down the center of which ran the hoisting rope. They had no choice but to leap for the rope and make their way down the shaft.

One of those Linotypists would later recall, "I could not see the rope in the elevator shaft and jumped for it blindly and missed, falling two stories to the basement. . . . There were a number of bodies lying at the bottom. [For eight men, the bottom of the elevator shaft was to be their tomb.] A heavy grating fell down the shaft and pinned me to a corner. . . . The flames came down and burned my ear and left arm. I beat my fists on the grating and smashed a hole through which I crawled and got into the job room. There I met Mr. Crabill [foreman of the composing room]. . . . He was pale as death and bloody. Then I lost him in the smoke and fell over a roll of paper. I thought it was all over. But I struggled up and met one of the stereotypers. . . . Together we groped to the mail chute and crawled up this to the street. I think we were the last men to leave the building alive."

As the two men emerged onto the street, the first horse-drawn fire wagon came clanging up. But it was a hose wagon; what was needed was a rescue vehicle, preferably a hook-and-ladder wagon with one of the fire company's new telescopic ladders.

"Nets—get nets, nets!" came a cry from the crowd, which now, barely ten minutes after the explosion, numbered more than a thousand. It watched horrified as men and women rushed to open windows and climbed out, holding on to the sills. "Don't jump," someone screamed. But to no avail. Flames were licking at the hands of the fugitives. They jumped.

The first police officers on the scene were two undercover detectives dressed in women's clothing and shoes returning to headquarters from Boyle Heights, where they had been attempting to lure a serial rapist into a trap. They had just stepped off a streetcar in front of the Times Building and were walking down First Street to the police station a block away when they were hurled against one another by the force of the explosion. "Then looking towards the west, we saw the first flames shooting from the floors of the Times Building ... and from the windows and the front door, came those poor souls crashing to the sidewalk with their clothing afire, and crashing to their death when they struck the sidewalk," one of them later wrote. "We dragged several dying employees back farther from that awful heat and got as many as we could away from the fire."

Times police reporter Paul G. Braud was three hundred feet away in the press room of the police station when the explosion occurred. As he raced to the burning building, he took in the incredible sight of a policeman running up the street with "a short ladder, pathetically inadequate. Someone called him a fool," he would write. Undeterred, the officer leaned it against the building, whereupon country editor Charles Lovelace miraculously jumped upon it from a smoking window on the third floor and, despite breaking a leg in the fall, was able to cling to its uppermost rungs.

Here was the kind of reckless initiative the emergency demanded, for Lovelace was then able to slide down the ladder and escape further injury. But it was the only life the tiny ladder would save. (The next day Lovelace would see his name on the list of the dead published in the *Times* and other newspapers.)

Nets had now arrived, but the heat from the inferno made it impossible for rescuers to approach the reddening walls with them. To the horror of the gathering crowd, workers on the uppermost stories began leaping to the ground, one after another, where they died upon impact; one man could be seen from the street framed in a window casing, then, after several agonizing minutes, he "threw up his hands and fell backward into the seething caldron behind and beneath him," Paul Braud would later report.

Among the thousands of onlookers and would-be rescuers who had gathered at the corner of First and Broadway was Earl Rogers, who ran out of his office across the street and immediately ran into the burning hulk to pull out an injured worker. After charging in for a second time, he came out alone with his face and hands burned and blistered, his eyebrows singed. He then roamed the vast perimeter of the ruin, searching for his young friend Elder. Elder's office, he knew, was on the third floor.

It was a dark sort of luck that Rogers would not directly witness what happened next. According to eyewitnesses, Elder suddenly appeared in a window frame on the third floor and crawled out, hanging by his fingers, looking below him at the pavement forty feet below. Flames began pouring out as the men and women below implored him to hang on awhile longer, declaring that help was on the way. Witnesses would later report that he was trying to communicate with the crowd, but that he was too high up to be heard, his voice muted by the wall itself. Several minutes passed, and no ladder or net materialized, and yet Elder still managed to hang on. The crowd beneath him grew and grew, cheering him, and it seemed as if he could hang there indefinitely. Then, without warning, Elder silently drifted through the darkness. There, at the feet of the crowd, he slammed onto the pavement, his body exploding internally, a leg breaking and splintering in a grotesque compound fracture. The brilliant young linguist with the two dueling scars and a promising career ahead of him was now a heap of crumpled flesh. Amazingly, he was not only alive but conscious. And in agonizing pain. Rescuers raced to him. He told them that others who were trapped inside the building were more in need of their help. "There is a lot of boys in there yet," he said.

In short order, Elder was carefully loaded onto a stretcher and rushed several blocks to Clara Barton Hospital, where an emergency receiving ward had been established. Elder's leg was reset. He was then so heavily dressed in bandages that the ubiquitous Braud, who had stopped by to report on the scene at the hospital, did not know who he was until his friend mumbled with dismay, "It's me, Elder."

Deskman William Tribit emerged from the inferno more or less unscathed and spotted his colleague, William Greenwood. Together they commandeered a Ford belonging to a spectator and raced away to pick up managing editor Harry Andrews.

Harry Chandler had already arrived at the scene by the time the three men returned. There was a hurried handclasp, a brief conversation between Chandler and Andrews, and the two senior executives quickly agreed on a course of action: Phone calls were to be made to the remaining *Times* employees. A telegram would have to be sent to General Otis. A printing force was to be rounded up. A secret auxiliary plant at San Fernando and College Streets, about a mile away, where printing presses with gasoline motors had been standing by awaiting just such an emergency was to be opened. Harry's nephew Ralph Chandler, the *Times*'s chief mechanic, was to be summoned to get the plant up and running. A representative of the *Herald*, an afternoon newspaper controlled by the *Times*, rushed up to offer editorial and engraving facilities.

Accountant H. E. Downing ran up to Chandler. He had left the company ledgers on his desk instead of putting them in the safe, he said. They were now in danger and so was everything in the safes, for that matter, if the temperature in the second-floor accounting room was allowed to continue to rise.

Chandler asked Fire Chief A. J. Eley, who had ordered all engine companies in the city to the scene, to turn some of his hoses on the area where the safes were kept. Later Downing would scramble across the rafters, holding on to blistering-hot pipes, and retrieve his now wet and scorched ledgers. It would take two days for the safes to cool down sufficiently so that they could be opened.

Chandler was then handed a list of names of the workers who were known to have escaped with their lives. His eyes welled as he scanned the list, which didn't include the name of his assistant, J. Wesley Reeves.

A massive section of the building's southeast wall collapsed, bringing down live electrical lines that whipped about, hissing across the sidewalk. Then, incredibly, men and women appeared and began climbing their way out of the wreckage, suddenly freed by the fallen wall. A badly injured fireman was spotted lying in the smoldering rubble and was dragged to safety.

Wild rumors had spread through the crowd· A hundred men and women had already died in the blaze, a hundred others were still inside. A woman's voice broke through the murmur of the crowd: "How many, oh for God's sake, how many are there in that place? My boy's there. He runs a Linotype. Hasn't anybody here seen my boy?" The scene would repeat itself with little variation throughout the night.

Within an hour of the explosion, the fire was brought under control. But the smell of death was in the air—a slaughterhouse stench. A steady caravan of horse-drawn ambulances had begun hauling away the injured. Glass was scattered everywhere, crunching under the feet of the crowd. Firemen entering the building reappeared carrying scorched tables and chairs and other charred items, stacking the ruined furniture in the street. Hollenbeck Kitchens owner John Mitchell arrived with steaming pails of coffee and hot rolls for the emergency workers.

Harry Chandler, Harry Andrews, Earl Rogers, Police Chief Alexander Galloway, and C. S. Holman, an agent of the Merchant's Fire Dispatch, gathered in the street to discuss possible causes of the explosion. Men in the basement were said to have smelled gas just before the explosion. Nonetheless, Holman had no doubts. The cause was dynamite.

"It could not have been the gas alone," he said. "A gas explosion would have blown the walls out sideways. This explosion lifted the floors up. . . . Such a condition indicates a dynamite explosion."

To the vocal majority in the crowd that morning, the suspects were a matter of equal certainty. Unionists had blown up the *Los Angeles Times*, the centerpiece of the city's business empire.

Harry Andrews turned to the crowd and shouted: "The scoundrels have blown up our building and have killed and crippled our men, but, by God, we'll carry on!"

Just before the sun rose over the San Gabriel Mountains, Earl Rogers walked back to his office with *Times* reporter Bert Cowan. According to Adela, her father was "black and tattered as something straight out of hell." Rogers found his daughter among the overturned furniture upon a floor awash in broken glass, the odor of printers' ink and scorched flesh everywhere. Adela saw at once that her father was in bad shape. When she took his trembling hand to comfort him, he winced.

His clothes torn to ribbons, his right hand raw, his lower lip bitten through, chin caked with dried blood, Rogers muttered through clenched teeth, "The murdering fiends," again and again. He then asked if anyone had heard from Elder. Cowan walked over to the blown-out window that opened onto the smoldering Times Building. He paused for a long moment and then said, "He jumped." Cowan then added that Elder had been taken to Clara Barton Hospital, terribly injured but alive.

Adela and the uninjured Cowan proceeded to lead the battered Earl Rogers out of his office and down five blocks to the hospital at Fifth and Grand. Thoroughly exhausted, perhaps even delusional with fatigue, Rogers began talking to himself as they walked. He spoke in the vaguely theatrical tones that celebrated lawyers affected in those days,

"The murdering fiends, the paranoiac assassins. They defeat their own ends, which are righteous.

"Senseless," he muttered. "I tell you, gentlemen, this is senseless. I am for the same cause, but we must use our brains."

"Gentlemen?" The only persons near Rogers were Adela and Cowan. After a long moment of confusion, Adela finally came to understand. Her delirious father was talking to an imaginary jury, speaking as though rehearsing his closing argument . . . for the prosecution. Forever the illustrious trial attorney, this was his manner of dealing with the trauma.

Clara Barton Hospital was a confusion of suffering and despair when they arrived. The dead, the dying, and the grievously injured were scattered about the emergency ward with more arriving by the minute, limping or being carried toward its parted doors. After wandering around the hospital for some time, the three found a female physician. "Our young friend Elder . . ." Rogers muttered.

The doctor, who recognized the celebrated attorney, interrupted. "He died an hour ago. And you may thank God for it." Noticing his badly burned hands and face, she gently added, "You need some attention your self, Earl."

The doctor led the beleaguered attorney away as his young daughter stood with Cowan, both of them trying to hold back tears, both trying to make sense of what had happened, neither able to imagine where all of this was about to lead.

"Somebody has to tell [Elder's sister] and grandmother," Adela eventually said.

"It don't have to be you," Cowan replied.

But it would be. Later that day, it would fall to the sixteen-year-old to shoulder that burden.

Chapter 14

At the Times Building the search for missing victims pressed on throughout the smoky glow of the early morning. The city's Board of Public Works gathered shortly after dawn and heard the tedious debate between investigators who worried over the possible destruction of evidence and those urging that the excavation for bodies begin immediately. The investigators also raised the possibility that unexploded bombs might still be planted at the site. They lost their argument. Public Works Commissioner Humphries explained: "There was a controversy over this, but we are going ahead. We will work the men in relays of one hundred each and continue until every body is recovered."

And so the grim excavation began.

At 9:00 a.m., in the area where Harry Chandler's office had stood, workers' picks dislodged the frame of a mangled typewriter. Digging deeper, they uncovered the body of Wesley Reaves, lying under the machine; the typewriter had been crushed into his chest. Chandler's splintered desk lay in jagged debris around him. Reaves's father had kept a constant vigil at the scene since his arrival at the building following Harry Chandler's phone call. A police officer who was among the men who had discovered the body was assigned to bring the news to the distraught man, who collapsed in grief.

Investigators meticulously combed the building. Near a printing press they found a gold tooth, placed it in a brown envelope, and jotted a description of the contents on the outside. Near the lethal elevator shaft they recovered a gold watch with the initials F. C. L., stopped at 1:18, in the small pocket of a piece of burned trousers. A picture of a woman was pasted in the cover. The watch was soon identified as belonging to thirty-six-year-old Linotype operator Fred Llewellyn. "Missing," said the note on the envelope. In all, nine watches were retrieved in the debris. Those in the area around the south end of the composing room were each stopped between 1:12 a.m. and 1:27 a.m. The others, found around the far end of the Linotype room, were stopped shortly after 2:00 a.m.

Outside the still-smoking building, thousands of onlookers looked on as the Public Works crews carried the remains of dead workers from the building in wicker caskets and loaded them onto horse-drawn hearses. Some of the caskets contained merely clumps of unidentifiable blackened flesh.

And then suddenly the crowd began to hear the cry of newsboys among them. "Extree, extree! Get your morning paper!" Incredibly the newspaper these boys were peddling in the smoldering city center of Los Angeles on this first day of October was the *Los Angeles Times*—a four-page wisp of itself, but still the *Times*.

Unbeknown to the public, Harry Chandler had negotiated a deal in 1904 to purchase 8,051 of the 10,000 outstanding shares of the *Herald*. (The newspaper had never editorially opposed a significant position taken by the *Times*.) Now, at 4:00 a.m., less than three hours after the explosion, Chandler had moved the *Times*'s editorial and preproduction staff—many of them among the walking wounded, heavily bandaged and blackened with soot and printers' ink—to the nominal rival and began putting together the early-morning edition of the paper.

Volunteers from off the street pitched in—the assistant postmaster, a theatrical printer, and an appellate judge who had been a reporter in his youth. In this ad hoc manner, against a backdrop of ongoing tragedy, workers assembled, and a process for producing that historic morning edition coalesced.

Chandler put in a call to the American Type Founders to order a new dress of display type. He then dispatched orders by telegraph for a battery of Linotypes, new presses, and stereotype machinery. Many of the editorial tasks could be handled at the *Herald*; production and printing would be handled at the *Times*'s auxiliary plant. He then rounded up his band of production staff and marched them down to the plant on Spring Street.

With inadvertent symbolism the masthead appeared damaged, the text riddled with the crudest typos that could only be regarded as evidence of the intense physical and psychological trauma under which the staff was working. Typically the masthead read "For Liberty and Law, Equal Rights, and Industrial Freedom." This morning, however, only part of the word "Industrial" made the folio, while "Freedom" had been altogether vanquished by the right margin.

That would be as far as the dynamiters would ever get to destroying the grandiloquent principles that drove the newspaper's antiunion owners. For behind the assortment of typefaces and the damaged masthead, the outrage of the paper's editorial staff was mustered in full display behind the headline "UNIONIST BOMBS WRECK THE TIMES; MANY SERIOUSLY INJURED." It was soon being shouted on the streets by the paper's grimy newsboys, heralding it with the obligatory cry, "Extree, extree, read all about it!"

Below the headline, the subhead read: "Terrific Explosion at 1 o'Clock This Morning Starts Fire Which Engulfs Score of Employes in Great Newspaper Plant—Many Victims—Great Property Loss." The story below had been hastily banged out by Paul Braud. Harry Andrews, the newspaper's managing editor, had written the defiant front-page editorial: "They can kill our men and can wreck our buildings, but by the God above, they cannot kill *The Times*."

The indictment, a clear rush to judgment by any journalistic standard, would not be lost on union leaders when they read it.

George Gunry, secretary-treasurer of the Metal Trades Workers local, issued a statement deploring the tragedy, but saying: "The unions declare that the statement in the *Times* that the explosion was caused by some persons or person connected with organized labor here or elsewhere is false."

Fred Wheeler, president of the Los Angeles Central Labor Council and Socialist candidate for lieutenant governor of California, declared: "Thousands of unthinking people said, 'The unions did it.' . . . Why wouldn't it be fair to presume that other enemies [of the *Times*] besides the unions were interested in the matter?"

Ralph L. Criswell, president of local 174 of the typographical union—an implacable opponent of the newspaper—offered union aid in getting out the *Times,* but asserted, "We do not believe that union labor men dynamited the *Times* plant or had any connection with its destruction."

And across the country the founding president of the American Federation of Labor, Samuel Gompers, released this statement: "The position of the *Los Angeles Times* as hostile to union labor is well known, but nothing has occurred recently to make the feeling of unionists more acute. I regret, as every person must, the loss of life and property, but I see no reason for thinking that unionists had anything to do with it."

In San Francisco, Olaf A. Tveitmoe, secretary-treasurer of the State Building Trades Council, offered a reward of $7,500 "for the arrest and conviction of the perpetrators of the outrage."

But of all the denials from labor leaders, none was stronger than that of J. J. McNamara, secretary-treasurer of the AF of L's International Association of Bridge and Structural Iron Workers Union. "Such an act is anarchy pure and simple. No sane organization would resort to anything of the kind under any circumstances. I do not believe that labor unions had anything to do with it."

By midmorning, all manner of sensational rumor was sweeping the city. Word of the explosion, which had first been carried from home to home by the morning milk deliverer or the iceman, was now being gruesomely embroidered. It was said that one hundred people had lost their lives in the disaster. It was also widely rumored that General Otis had dropped dead of a heart attack upon receiving the news on his homeward-bound train from Mexico.

Harry Andrews would dispose of the first rumor in a statement issued to the afternoon newspaper, the *Herald:* "I do not believe there were more than one hundred persons in the building [at the time of the explosion]. I was not there. Mr. Chandler was not there. . . . I feel sure most of our men escaped."

The second rumor was disposed of when a telegram to Harry Chandler arrived from General Otis, dispatched from a train stop at Imperial

Junction. Said the General to his son-in-law: "Your wire with its terrible news reached me this morning. Am amazed at the desperation of the criminal conspirators in destroying the Times Building and slaying its loyal defenders, whose loss I deeply deplore. But the *Times* itself will live on, bravely defending the vital and essential principle of industrial freedom under law, which must yet triumph in the entire nation. I will be home at 3:30. Meet me at the station."

"Meet me at the station!"—the General was back in command.

At 9:30 that morning, Mrs. Lois Zeehandelaar and her maid, Elizabeth Wilder, were watering the garden on the south side of the Garland Street home. As the two women worked their way through the flora, Miss Wilder noticed a white package lying behind a rose bush next to the house. She set down her watering can, picked up the heavy parcel, and gently shook it. She then put the package to her ear and thought she heard a muffled sound coming from inside. Maybe she was mistaken, but it sounded as though the package was ticking.

With a courage born of blissful ignorance, she brought the package to Mrs. Zeehandelaar and asked if it might have fallen from the bedroom window, as she had found the package directly beneath it. Mrs. Zeehandelaar was utterly puzzled and curious. She had no idea where it had come from.

As the two women stood in the garden conferring, the ticking package between them, Mrs. Zeehandelaar's neighbor, streetcar conductor J. W. Bringham, came walking by. One of the women asked Bringham if he knew anything about the package.

"All I know is that the *Times* has been bombed and that police expect that there might be other attacks," he said.

Hearing this, Ms. Wilder promptly set the package down and stepped away. She told him she had heard something ticking inside.

Flying in the face of common sense, Bringham got down on his hands and knees and put his ear to the box. He then dragged it out to the street and finally left the scene to telephone police.

At 10:00 a.m. Los Angeles Police Sergeant Dave Adams, along with Detectives Tom Rico and John Jarvis, arrived at the Zeehandelaar home. After clearing the immediate area, Rico approached the package and indicated that he too heard the ticking. A crowd gathered at a safe distance down the street as he drew a knife and gingerly cut open the white wrapping paper. Inside, nestled in cotton, was a mechanical device—a tiny alarm clock connected to a trail of wires, a fuse, a battery, and a bundle of sixteen sticks of dynamite. Rico quickly disconnected the wires, disarming it. He relaxed in silent triumph and began inspecting the dynamite on which was stenciled "Giant, California" and the date "September 20, 1910." Clearly something had gone wrong with the clock. Although the actual time was now a few minutes after 10:00 a.m., the three-inch dial indicated that it was a few minutes past 11:00. The alarm had been set to go off at 1:00, but the alarm spring had apparently been wound too tightly. Rico surmised that the mechanism had jammed, preventing it from detonating during the night while the Zeehandelaar family and their house staff slept.

◆

When W. H. Flockin, caretaker of General Otis's estate, heard through the grapevine of the Zeehandelaar bomb, he decided to make a thorough search of the General's premises. It would take him awhile, he figured, for The Bivouac, on Wilshire Boulevard and Park View, was vast and surrounded by dense gardens. But shortly into his search, he thought he saw an abandoned object under the bay window on the south side of the house behind a stand of bushes. Coming closer, his heart pounding, he saw that it was a leather suitcase. As he tentatively approached through the lush flora and columns of manicured topiary, he thought he heard a faint sound coming from the suitcase, a kind of patter. Once he had approached within a few feet, the sound became crisper; it seemed as though the suitcase were ticking.

At 1:45 p.m. Flockin called the Los Angeles Police Department. This time the chief himself arrived at the scene, accompanied by Sergeant Adams and Detectives Rico and Moore, whereupon Chief Galloway gave the absurdly reckless order to load the suitcase onto the police vehicle and transport it to headquarters. The three officers brought common sense to bear, urging the chief to allow them to open and defuse it on the spot. Galloway agreed.

Flush with his success of three and a half hours earlier, Rico again took charge, first carrying the suitcase to the curb, then unbuckling the leather straps that bound it. He then tried to force the lock open but failed, and so he began cutting through the leather cover and calico lining. Rico had just rolled back the covering to reveal the tiny Junior Tattoo New Haven alarm clock inside, one identical to the clock at the Zeehandelaar home, when it began ringing.

Rico's knife fell from his hand. He cried out, stood up, flung the suitcase onto the edge of the park across from the residence and began running for his life, his fellow officers sprinting behind him. They had covered just sixty feet when a blast with the familiar, strangely metallic note embedded in its shock wave—just like the one that shook the city thirteen hours earlier—rang out across the neighborhood. A huge crater was torn into the ground, windows across the neighborhood shattered, and debris rained down everywhere. The blast wave came against the officers' backs, hurling them to the ground—but none was seriously injured.

The city, however, was stunned as word spread in the immediate path of the impulse. Soon Los Angeles would find itself in the grip of panic, for no one could say how many such devices had been planted throughout the city.

The device found at the Zeehandelaar home was about to reveal a trove of clues. It also established that the *Times* explosion had indeed been a deliberate act of terror, not the result of a gas-main leak.

Not that the city elders were waiting for facts to be established. At 10:45 that morning (just as the strange white package at the Zeehandelaar home was discovered by the housemaid), the Los Angeles City Council came together in an emergency session and quickly appropriated $25,000 to be left at Mayor George Alexander's disposal to investigate the bombing. The mayor immediately announced that 10 percent of that amount would be used as a reward for anyone who came forth with information that would ultimately lead to the apprehension and conviction of the perpetrators. (Within days, the Merchants and Manufacturers Association appropriated an additional $50,000 in reward money for the capture of the "unionist fiends.")

The term "dragnet" had not yet entered police jargon in 1910, but that is essentially what police officials ordered in the hours following the bombing. In fact, within just one hour following the explosion, a half dozen suspects had already been rounded up.

Now, with the announcement of a bountiful reward, all manner of accusations, phony tips, and crank calls began flooding the police department's overtaxed switchboard.

A man described as "a known anarchist" was arrested in Westlake Park as he suspiciously happened to be tearing up a batch of letters. An anonymous tip from Portland, Oregon, sent police rushing up and down Vaughn Street in Los Angeles to arrest an allegedly discontented former employee of the *Times*. The street number, however, proved nonexistent. Newspaper editorials exhorted police to redouble their efforts. William Randolph Hearst's *Los Angeles Examiner*, pro-union and a longtime rival of the *Times*, demanded in a one-page editorial: "Let us have law and order at any costs. . . . Every suspicious character should be jailed."

Hearst's afternoon newspaper, the *Express*, claimed that a Western Union operator working at the *Times*, W. G. Furnam, had reported that the building had been filled with the odor of gas shortly before the explosion. Such testimony, the *Express* observed, from "an absolutely disinterested source," would have conclusively proved that the explosion was caused by gas and not by dynamite "if not for the war that has long been waged between the *Times* and union labor." On the other hand, the paper published accounts from witnesses who attested to having heard the unmistakable boom of a dynamite explosion. The Hearst papers also pitched in an additional $1,000 to the burgeoning reward fund.

The headline of the pro-labor *Los Angeles Record* made clear their point of view with the headline "LET US BE FAIR." The accompanying story went on to argue against any rush to judgment that it was indeed a dynamite explosion, and that unionists were behind it. "The *Times* owners are positive in their statements that the explosion was the work of union men. Perhaps it was, perhaps it was not. . . . Let us be fair and do everything we can to fix the real responsibility for the disaster."

The *Los Angeles Herald* accepted the theory that the bombing had been the work of unionists but expressed its conviction that it was not the act of any union member in Los Angeles. "During all the past history of this city, which has been at times marked by disagreements between employers and employed . . . no attack has been made upon property or human life, and we do not believe that the nature of the laborers of Los Angeles has changed at this late day," the *Herald* said in a front-page editorial. "We do believe, however, that the act was committed by some one of the thugs that labor troubles in the city of San Francisco have produced in such numbers."

In the immediate wake of the bombing, one thing was clear: Any investigation into the tragedy would be conducted in the glare of the political arena, in which every bit of evidence, every word of testimony, would be examined through partisan blinders.

And now thundering into the Southern Pacific train depot at 3:30 that afternoon came Gen. Harrison Gray Otis aboard his elaborate train carriage from Mexico. There to greet him were some two hundred members of the Merchants and Manufacturers Association, Harry Chandler, and Police Chief Galloway.

Galloway had brought two police officers along with him, assigning them as bodyguards to Chandler and the general. The general gruffly dismissed them, scowling, "I wouldn't give these murderers the satisfaction of seeing me walking around under the protection of a bodyguard." Besides, he suggested, he would be blessed with divine protection. "I believe there is still a God in Israel," he declared. Galloway, appalled by Otis's apparent recklessness, insisted, however, that the police officers continue to stick close to the *Times* executives. (*Times* editor Harry Carr would later recall: "The guard was the only man in town who never could find the general. One of the familiar sights of the *Times* office was this forlorn gunman wandering lonesomely around, trying to locate the man he was supposed to be guarding.")

From the train station the general was driven to the *Times*'s temporary editorial headquarters at the *Herald*, where the night staff was still on duty—bandaged, bleary-eyed, exhausted, and grieving, but boisterously scrambling to put out a Sunday edition. (Of the more than one hundred *Times* employees inside the building at the time of the explosion, not a single one escaped injury.) The general did not interrupt them with greetings or even condolences, but merely issued an order to his troops: "Get in all the news of the bombing, let the men go home early as possible, and be out on time."

He had now assumed operational command, invigorated and resolute, as if he had returned to the battlefield. In a way he had. He now left the building to visit the ruin that was once his newspaper.

By the time the general arrived at the Times Building, only a handful of the dead had been retrieved from the smoldering rubble. The wicker caskets were being loaded onto horse-drawn wagons and hauled off, the horses' hooves clattering over the pavement on their way to the temporary morgue at Clara Barton Hospital. The general, a 250-pound, six-foot-tall man, inspected the wreckage of his beloved Fortress wearing a heavy three-piece suit in the ninety-degree heat. His son-in-law and the fire chief escorted him as smoke rose up through the brick-and-granite rubble. With sentimental pride he pointed to the bronze eagle set atop the building that had somehow survived the blast.

Nearby, a local poet, Drayton Pitts, also observed the eagle and declaimed:

> High on the ruins of the battlement
> The Eagle stood, unscathed above the wreck
> Of dynamite and death . . .

For a man whose incendiary pen was legendary, Harrison Gray Otis's first editorial following the bombing began as a model of restraint: "In the early morning of October 1, the startling tidings of the terrible conspiracy against the *Times,* myself, and my loyal coworkers in the cause of industrial freedom reached me while en route home from the City of Mexico.

"I knew well enough beforehand the desperate nature of the conspiracy against my newspaper and the desperate character of some of the conspirators; yet I could not believe, until I was forced to believe, that they would go to the extremes to which they did go. . . ."

But by the time the general approached the end of his editorial, his fury had exploded in florid Victorian rhetoric and corrosive metaphor, as he directly addressed his perceived enemies: "O, you anarchic scum. You leeches upon honest labor, you midnight assassins, you whose hands are dripping with the innocent blood of your victims, you against whom the wails of poor widows and the cries of fatherless children are ascending to the Great White Throne, go, mingle with the crowd on the street corners, look upon the crumbled and blackened walls, look at the ruins wherein are buried the calcined remains of those whom you murdered. . . ."

While the general's editorial would be buried among miscellaneous items on the second page, on page one, a subhead summed it all up: "MUST BLAME UNIONS."

It was a conclusion that had also been hastily reached by newspapers and politicians, pro- and antiunion, throughout the state. *The San Francisco Chronicle* editorialized: "No one supposed that any labor organization would be guilty of such a crime, and yet it is impossible to doubt that the crime was committed in revenge for the attitudes of the *Los Angeles Times* toward organized labor.

"It is also true that the conduct of labor controversies is such as to produce the state of mind from which such crimes as this result."

Governor William Gillett echoed the sentiment: "Whether guilty or not," Gillett declared, "the labor unionists will have to be blamed for the crime until shown they are not guilty, as everything points to a desire to wipe out property and lives of those who have been fighting organized labor for years."

Gillett's opponent in the upcoming election, Otis-hating Hiram Johnson, declared: "I say to you, and I say it with the full measure of responsibility accruing to one who will be chief executive of the state, that if the awful crime was committed by a human being, no punishment is too great, no punishment is too malign to be meted out to the loathsome individual who committed that offense. . . . No man on the face of this earth can afford to condone or afford to forgive."

On Sunday morning, the day after the bombing, the ministers of the city also pointed accusing fingers at the unions from their pulpits. The Reverend Dr. J. Whitcomb Brougher told his flock, "If it is proven that union labor had anything to do with the awful destruction of property and life . . . then I shall be profoundly sorry for the cause of organized labor. It will have received a blow from which it can never recover in this city." The Reverend A. C. Smither of the First Christian Church sounded a similar note: "It is easy to believe that [the bombing] was done by the anarchists and assassins who have wrought much of the same in San Francisco and who have declared their purpose to unionize Los Angeles. They have committed one of the greatest crimes in modern civilization."

And throughout the country, fear arose that the bombing might have represented the first blast in a people's revolution, threatened until now by a fringe of implacable fanatics, who, if the *Times* attack was any indication, appeared to be mustering support for their call for a violent overthrow of capitalist society.

The Times Building still smoldered, its blackened granite front now resembling the ruins of a medieval castle. Like throngs of confused civilian survivors, the crowds continued to pack the streets outside. Many must have wondered, was this the scene of the first battlefield of a new civil war? If so, what had it accomplished? Why had so many men died? What had the deed triggered besides grief and mourning?

Chapter 15

Even while the work of retrieving the bodies of victims from the wreckage of the Times Building continued during daylight hours, plans were proceeding for the funerals of Churchill Harvey-Elder and Wesley Reaves at Rosedale Cemetery on Washington Boulevard.

At Elder's, the Reverend Dr. Robert J. Burdette declaimed from the mortuary pulpit: "He was young, and life was dear to him. . . . His feet were treading an upward path. Promotion in his chosen profession had come to him unsolicited. . . . Hope ran singing before him. . . . Then, the arrow, tipped with venom and winged with hate, sped by the hands of an assassin, hissed through the night, found the happy heart. . . . The pen fell from the ready hand, trailing a blur from the unfinished sentence. . . ."

In the meantime, the grisly recovery work continued at the Times Building. At 8:00 p.m. Sunday, recovery workers found a pelvis; at 9:15 p.m., a single unidentified rib. But the most gruesome scene still awaited recovery workers at 1:30 Monday morning. Discovered in the well of the freight elevator shaft at the northeast end of the building were seven or eight bodies (no one could say for sure), all of them men who had been at work in the composing room when the explosion occurred. The first body recovered was but a "headless, limbless, blackened trunk." By daybreak no one yet knew how high the number of confirmed deaths would rise. In the years before the development of forensic pathology, body counts were a complicated matter of putting together a gruesome puzzle, the pieces of which were human detritus, and waiting to hear from relatives and friends of those who were thought to be missing.

Wesley Reaves's funeral had also been scheduled to take place at Rosedale Cemetery. But as word came to General Otis that many of the remains found in the building could not be identified, he announced: "If the families of the men don't object, we will have them buried in one grave in my [family burial plot], and we will raise a monument to their memory, which will bear the names of all." The funeral was duly held at Hollywood Cemetery on October 9. A battalion of police officers kept a close eye on the mourners.

As Otis left his house to attend Reaves's funeral, he was approached by a police officer and told that he was being placed under arrest on charges of criminally libeling San Francisco union leaders for an article that had appeared in the *Times* claiming that they had come to Los Angeles to order local laborites to "break more heads." The article had been written by the late Churchill Harvey-Elder.

The arresting officer accompanied the further outraged General to the Reaves funeral and from there to Justice Court, where bail was arranged.

Conspicuous by his absence from the scene of the tragedy was the city's mayor, George B. Alexander. He had been holed up in his dimly lit office in City Hall receiving direct reports from the fire and police chiefs and from public and private investigators.

Beneath his snow-white goatee and furrowed brow, the mayor wore an expression of stolid determination. He resembled an Amish elder. For a future generation, he could have posed as Uncle Sam. Now in his early seventies, he had been courted to run for office in 1909 by the progressive Good Government Organization (the "Goo-Goos") and had won the city's first mayoral recall election handily. Over the ensuing year and a half, he had been able to establish himself as a centrist in a city that was being pulled by extremists.

Now, as he ensconced himself in City Hall studying the hand- and typewritten documents that the officials at the scene had brought to him, his was the one voice that remained oddly muted, even as critics outside his doors were loudly demanding that he display greater resolve in ensuring public safety. On the one hand, members of the Merchants and Manufacturers Association expressed anger that the mayor had refused to denounce the unions as the obvious culprits behind the bombing. On the other hand, he was being reviled by labor as a toady of business who had overseen the massive arrests of union members for violating the anti-picketing ordinance a few months earlier. The majority of Angelenos had not yet taken sides.

As the centrist mayor of a city divided against itself, Alexander saw it as his mission to gain the trust of the belligerents and to gain it quickly. Doing so meant fostering confidence that the investigation into the bombing would be carried out impartially—free of influence from the labor unions, and from General Otis and the MMA. The mayor could be sure that Otis and Chandler were going to bring to bear their considerable clout to take advantage of the tragedy by embarking on an escalated antiunion campaign that would likely call for the rounding up and jailing of every labor activist in the city and holding the lot for questioning until the perpetrators could be identified.

The labor unions, on the other hand, were by and large defending their name by attributing blame for the explosion to General Otis's faulty gas mains. Once news of the Zeehandelaar device began to circulate, a new theory emerged among the most radical in the ranks: the general had himself ordered the *Times* to be destroyed as part of a demented conspiracy that would allow him to blame the massive bloodshed on organized labor. In his typically shrill editorial voice, American Socialist Party leader Eugene Debs let loose in the party's weekly *Appeal to Reason* this unreasonable appeal: "I want to express my deliberate opinion that the *Times* and its crowd of union-haters are the instigators if not the actual perpetrators of that crime and the murder of twenty human beings. . . . Arouse ye hosts of labor and swear that the villainous plot shall not be consummated." In the cognitive realm of the conspiracy theorist, it all made credible sense. Hadn't Chandler unexpectedly left the building just minutes before the explosion? Wasn't General Otis originally scheduled to have been back from Mexico a day earlier? The answer to both questions was, of course, yes. And how did it just so happen that each of the bombs discovered at the Zeehandelaar and Otis estates turned out to be harmless duds?

Mayor Alexander recognized that any inquiry by the district attorney and police would be summarily spurned by a skeptical working class if it was not carried out with manifest impartiality. To that end, he dispatched a telegram to the most renowned detective in the nation, William J. Burns, who, as chance had it, happened to be on a train heading for Los Angeles for a conference of the American Bankers Association when the explosion occurred.

Chapter 16

Cigar smoke tinged with the stale scent of whiskey wafted intermittently like an Indian signal through the window transom above the door bearing the plaque reading THE OFFICE OF EARL ROGERS—the telltale indication that the city's illustrious trial lawyer was at work. Seated behind his imposing desk, piled high with legal notices, police records, and stenographic notes, Rogers was examining the nascent evidence in the bombing cases. The papers lay atop a green ink blotter marked with blurry circles formed by the condensation around his whiskey glass. The drink accentuated his gloom as he examined each official death report, and tears dripped from his eyes. As usual at this time of the early evening, Rogers was drunk.

That Mayor Alexander would call upon Rogers to direct the investigation of the dynamiting had been a foregone conclusion. Earl Rogers was the city's most renowned criminal attorney—and certainly its most spectacular. His revolutionary courtroom tactics had transformed criminal courtrooms into dramatic stages. He was the first attorney ever to attempt to re-create a crime in a courtroom using scale models, to use blackboard and chalk in court, to introduce ballistics tests as evidence. Rogers had personally conducted more than thirty autopsies and had been present for seventy others. But his genius was theater, as he developed revolutionary tactics that transformed criminal courtrooms into dramatic stages. Indeed, he spoke, as did many courtroom attorneys in those days, with the somewhat clipped, faintly British, accents of an actor. His performances in court were something to behold, and people lined up early at the courtroom doors to witness them. He quarreled with the prosecution, wept as his clients narrated their woeful tales.

He dressed flamboyantly, generally in long-tailed coats, black, brown, or gray. He wore spats, bright vests, and used lorgnettes as a prop—brandishing them in the air with a flourish to underscore a point, thrusting them at times under the nose of a judge or juror. He rarely sat in court, often stalking back and forth while the prosecutors questioned witnesses, nettling them.

He was idolized by his young assistant, Jerry Giesler, whose future career as the foremost attorney in Hollywood during its "golden age" would eclipse even Rogers's. Giesler would later say of him: "No man was ever more generously endowed with legal brains than Rogers. No man ever gave more of himself fighting for his clients."

He was also endowed with physical beauty. With his deep blue eyes, jet-black hair, and regal flair, his appearance was riveting. (He was nearly a dead ringer for the modern-day actor Leonardo DiCaprio.) Women swooned in his presence, sometimes on the witness stand.

He was once paid a fee of $10,000 to cross-examine a single witness at trial. But it was hardly a one-day job. Rogers knew that winning meant conducting a detailed study of the facts and testimony of any given case before stepping into the courtroom.

And he was alert. His hallmark was his ability to isolate the one critical overlooked fact, witness, or piece of evidence, and exploit it for all it was worth, a skill that complemented his vast knowledge of case law. From this deep well he drew novel theories of defense, which, over time, produced a remarkable series of acquittals. Of the seventy-seven significant murder cases he was involved in, he lost a total of three. But he did possess a conscience. Immediately after getting a client off for having murdered his wife, the man thanked Rogers profusely, to which the attorney replied, "Get away from me, you slimy pimp, you know you're guilty as hell."

By the first decade of the new century, Rogers's name had spread well beyond the region. His reputation would be carried down through posterity with what amounted to astounding legal hat tricks. The story of his most audacious courtroom ploy would be retold again and again by countless law professors for its intrinsic lawyerly lessons.

The extraordinary case originated in the town of Avalon on Catalina Island, where Al Boyd and Harry Johnson, two socially prominent young men, along with a professional gambler who went by the nickname "Louisville Sport," had gone into the card room of the swank Metropole Hotel. During the game, two gunshots sounded. Boyd and Johnson came out, leaving behind the body of Louisville Sport and the gun, which had been cleaned of all fingerprints. Both men were charged with the crime, and each accused the other of having fired the deadly shots. Shortly thereafter, Rogers learned that he had been retained by both Boyd and Johnson to represent them in separate trials.

During the first trial, Rogers argued that his client Boyd was innocent. He put forth considerable circumstantial evidence to support the claim that Johnson had fired the gun. He was then rewarded with a verdict of acquittal.

In the second trial, Rogers argued that Boyd had fired the deadly shots. This time, Rogers produced new exculpatory evidence that had been overlooked in the first trial. Thus Rogers won an acquittal for Johnson. Most significantly, Al Boyd could not be retried, as it would constitute double jeopardy for the same crime. Hence, both of his clients went free.

Rogers became so renowned for freeing accused murderers that he was once approached in his office by a wealthy Chinese merchant who wanted to know how much it would cost for Rogers to defend him against a murder charge. Rogers quoted a steep rate, and the man placed the amount in gold coins on his desk, bowed, and made his way toward the door. When Rogers asked him where he was going, the man replied, "I go to kill the man now."

Rogers's weakness was as legendary as his courtroom genius: He was an alcoholic (and in fact would die of alcoholism in 1922 at the age of fifty-two). He had instigated barroom brawls, had failed to appear in court on behalf of clients, had been seen in the company of "fast women," had been dropped from the Blue Book social register. Yet, drunk or sober, his legal talent was unassailable. If the dynamiters were to be brought to justice, Rogers's help would be wanted.

Some might have argued that Rogers had another fault. He could not fathom social causes, least of all the cause championed by radical Socialists. By 1910 capitalism was being challenged frequently, ardently, and often violently by a diverse international movement promoting a workers' revolution. America did not escape the ascendant movement.

He was the author of the statute on which the city rounded up the strikers and defended it this way: "You know that in these conflicts between the labor unions and their employers, men have been shot down, not by the dozen but by the score. The city of Los Angeles will have none of its people killed in rioting. It takes the riot question close up, right by the throat, and it says to its people, employees and employers, you may have your differences, you may have your strikes, you may fight between yourselves, but you must keep these strikes off the streets. That is all the city of Los Angeles says in the ordinance against picketing."

His labor-activist friends would later take him aside and plead, "Earl, don't you see that depriving working men of their right to take their grievances before the public, denying them their freedom of speech, will only frustrate them, turn their hatreds inward, fill their minds with violent dreams?" But in Rogers's mind, disputes among reasonable men ought to be settled reasonably between them.

In any case, Rogers was determined to focus his investigation of the Times Building bombing on the crime and not on the cause. On October 2, he jotted down a few notes, clipped together a few documents, and headed for an evening meeting of city officials and local businessmen to discuss his strategy for bringing the bombers to justice. The clear night air refreshed him as he made his way by foot to the meeting place, the offices of the Merchants and Manufacturers Association. Several of the VIPs had already arrived and were in animated discussion about the bombing. Rogers had just arrived and had begun mingling with the crowd of cigar-smoking moguls when General Otis burst into the room, waving a copy of his newspaper headlined, "BOMBS EXPLODED BY ENEMIES OF INDUSTRIAL FREEDOM."

As the general began to speak, Rogers brought him up short. Perhaps it was the effect of the witness statements that he had just pored over. Perhaps it was the effect of his treks to the bombed-out newspaper building. Perhaps it was the effect of his visits to the hospitals. Perhaps it was the effect of the whiskey. Whatever it was, uncharacteristic words emerged from Earl Rogers's lips and fell like a surprise assault on the formidable newspaper owner.

Pointing to the headline displayed behind the general's clutch, he said, "I won't fight under that banner, General," and then turning Otis's own motto against him, he added, "If you don't give industrial freedom to the workingman; if you let capital hog all the profits and refuse to share with them; if you don't do away with child labor, somebody else will clean your house for you, with dynamite! I want it understood that to me this is a murder case. I am after a murder indictment. Somebody dynamited innocent men and women, my friends." And referring to young Harvey-Elder, Rogers added: "They murdered a boy I loved, a boy I thought someday I might have as a son-in-law. I want to find the man who killed him." (Rogers was obviously unaware that Elder was already a married man. His wife, Leola, a former actress, had been working as a publicist for the Oakland Orpheum Theatre when the bombing occurred and was now heading for Los Angeles aboard the Southern Pacific Owl.)

Later the same evening Mayor Alexander informed Rogers that he would not be working alone; he wanted him to work side by side with Detective William Burns—a man with whom Rogers had collided three years earlier.

❧

At the end of the graft trials in San Francisco in 1907, when bribed and bribers—the mayor and members of the board of supervisors on the one hand and utility company executives on the other—were being sent off to San Quentin by the busload, Earl Rogers went north, successfully defended one of the accused bribe givers, and exposed the fact that sugar magnate Rudolph Spreckels, who was financing the graft trials, had no altruistic motive in doing so.

Spreckels and others, Rogers had revealed, had incorporated to build a trolley system in the city that would run on an underground electrical conduit (what became the city's famed "cable car" system). The supervisors were also considering an overhead electrical trolley system advocated by Patrick Calhoun of United Railroads. It would later turn out that United Railroads had passed nearly $200,000 in bribe money to members of the board of supervisors ("the boodle board") in return for their vote for its overhead system.

Spreckels had hired Burns to investigate rampant rumors that top city officials, despite their union connections, greedily sold their votes to officers of the telephone, street railway, gas, and electric companies. The climax of Burns's investigation came when he set up a sting operation in which he, along with two neutral witnesses, watched, through holes drilled in an office door, bribe money being passed to three supervisors, who later, given assurances of immunity, implicated all of their colleagues.

Burns happily took credit for breaking the boodle board and rescuing the city's virtue, even as attempts were made on the lives of the witnesses; a crusading newspaper publisher, Fremont Elder, was kidnapped; jurors were offered bribes; District Attorney Francis Heney was shot; and the man who pulled the trigger was himself found shot to death in his jail cell. But Earl Rogers had shown that Spreckels had his own reason for hiring Burns and exposing United Railroads as an instigator of San Francisco's corruption—to advance his own designs for a cable-car system in the city.

Rogers thus put a damper on Burns's victory celebration.

Chapter 17

On the morning of October 1, 1910, Matthew Schmidt was having a quiet breakfast with his paramour Belle Lavin in her room in San Francisco. Eventually he rose from the table and left to get the morning paper, as was his daily habit. He returned a few minutes later with the newspaper folded over and sat back down to finish his coffee. Then he opened it and took in the bold headlines: "LABOR UNIONS BLAMED BY CHIEF OF PUBLICATION." Below that was the subhead that brought home what he was reading: "EDITORS AND PRINTERS MEET AWFUL DEATH IN FLAMES AFTER BIG EXPLOSION."

He read each of the stories about the *Los Angeles Times* bombing aloud from beginning to end. Belle remarked at how horrible it all sounded, and then asked Schmitty why he was so intensely interested in the story. Schmitty said nothing. He merely folded up his paper and left the room. Later that evening he quietly moved out of Belle's boardinghouse, never to return.

⁓

At eleven o'clock that morning, J. B. McNamara telephoned Lena Ingersoll's San Francisco boardinghouse and, in a shaky voice, asked for a room. With an air of formality, Lena said she had no vacancies. J. B. pleaded, but Lena insisted that he find another place to stay. She'd heard the news from L.A. and no doubt surmised that the man on the other end of the line had something to do with it. Undeterred, J. B. showed up at her boardinghouse a few hours later, offering to take her out on the town. Through the bolted door, Lena shouted her refusal. J. B. groaned that he was tired. He had been on a train all night. He just needed to lie down—even on the davenport in the front room. Again she refused him. He would pay her a month's rent in advance, he pleaded. After a final refusal, J. B. finally left for the Argonaut Hotel.

Later that day he phoned Tveitmoe at the San Francisco Building Trades Council offices to arrange to collect the balance due him upon completion of the job in L.A.. For the second time that day he was unceremoniously rebuffed. Scores of people were dead or seriously injured, Tveitmoe scowled. Not only that, McNamara had bungled the bombing of the Otis and Zeehandelaar residences, and the authorities were now said to have the Zeehandelaar bomb in their possession. In short, J. B. had left an unmistakable trail that investigators could easily follow back to San Francisco. Tveitmoe then admonished J. B. never to contact him again and hung up.

McNamara was on his own. The man who imagined himself being welcomed back to San Francisco as a union-man's hero was now regarded as a pariah. His mind began to reel. He was angry, he later wrote, "because a majority was concerned about a few individuals and betrayed the issues interwoven into the principles, beliefs, and convictions of the broad masses . . . because a majority wanted to 'go along' the lines of least resistance, wanted to take 'the middle of the road.'" He may also have been troubled for another reason. In 1910 capital murder was punishable by hanging in the state of California.

He bought copies of each of the San Francisco newspapers, poring over the details of the bombing. The next day, Sunday, he bought the *Chronicle* extra edition, read the report about the investigation, then stuffed the newspaper, along with one of the Saturday editions, in a suitcase that still held two coils of one-hundred-foot fuse, an unopened box of blasting caps, a fuse cap with fuse attached, and a New Haven Junior Tattoo alarm clock. He closed the suitcase, fastened the two leather straps around it, and carried it to the dock, where he checked it at a ferry newsstand.

Through the course of his four-day stay in San Francisco, J. B. would turn to his old standbys, living almost exclusively on cigarettes and whiskey, and trolling the streets of San Francisco for loose women to soothe

the relentless psychic distress. Newspapers were now mentioning the unprecedented reward money being offered for information leading to the arrest of the perpetrators of the bombing. The following afternoon he picked up a local girl, hired a touring car and a chauffeur, and spent a good deal of what was left of his money at the area beach resorts. He flashed the huge roll of bills wherever he went, spending more than $100 on wine alone at various saloons. When the night was over, however, he refused to pay the chauffeur his fee of $25.

"All right," the driver said, "if you don't [pay] I'll call that policeman at the corner and he will settle with you."

"No jail for me, kid," J. B. replied. He then pulled out his ever-diminishing wad and paid the driver, adding a 10-cent tip.

As details of the atrocity and the subsequent investigation spread, J. B. realized just how obvious a trail he had left. He knew that he had to get out of town. Before leaving he took four infernal machines down to the wharfs between San Francisco and Oakland and dumped them into the bay.

On October 5 he boarded a train for Indianapolis. As he headed eastward, J. B. found himself gripped by a nightmarish panic, with his fellow passengers dwelling on the topic of the *Los Angeles Times* bombing. At every stop newspapers plastered with reports about new clues and information concerning the state of the investigation were brought aboard. The outraged passengers couldn't get enough and snapped them up. J. B. McNamara sat helpless, listening to snatches of their conversations condemning "the cowardly fiends," "the murderous maniacs." Moreover, there was the ever-present threat that one of his fellow passengers might somehow connect him to the newspaper descriptions of J. B. Bryce. He was trapped on a locomotive, speeding through a vast wilderness with no means of escape should that happen.

Finally the sheer helplessness of life as a captive train passenger became too much. "Coming back on the train [to Indianapolis]," J. B. would later relate, "everybody was reading about the *L.A. Times* disaster and I thought everybody was looking at me." When the train pulled into the Salt Lake City station, he got off.

Immediately after detraining, he contacted John E. Munsey, a business agent for the Iron Workers Union and occasional union bomber himself. That evening Munsey sent a wire to J. J. McNamara, who had become worried that J. B. had been arrested, as he hadn't heard from him for several days now, nor had he arrived in Indianapolis as planned. Munsey's message was cryptic and concise: "Patient out of danger." The prognosis was wrong.

Munsey was shocked by his old friend's emaciated appearance, the hunted look in his bulging eyes, his palsied movements, all of which were exaggerated by his strict tobacco-and-whiskey diet. Rolling a cigarette with his shaking brown-and-yellow-stained fingers, McNamara said he needed a place to hide out for a while. After conferring once again with J. J. McNamara by telephone, he had J. B. move on to the home of the McNamaras' sister, Alice Nabb, in Ballagh, Nebraska, where J. J. said he would meet them in a few days' time. Here J. B. would be in the care of his mother, Mary McNamara, who happened to be staying with the Nabb family at the time. But it was the prospect of his older brother's company that eased J. B.'s mind the most.

Like all who saw him, Alice and her mother were horrified by J. B.'s wasted appearance. He was now almost unrecognizable, due in part to the ragged beard he had been growing in an effort to disguise himself. Feeling hunted and haunted, he refused food. He also began angrily demanding that J. J. come as he'd promised. Alarmed at her brother's drunken temper, Alice called J. J. in Indianapolis, who in turn called an old family friend, Frank Eckhoff, for help. J. J. explained that he couldn't come to his brother's aid, as he believed he himself was now being watched by detectives, and asked Eckhoff to go in his stead. Eckhoff, an old neighbor of the McNamaras, and now a "handyman" for the Executive Committee in Indianapolis, agreed.

"I guess you read about it," J. J. told Eckhoff on the phone. "I'm afraid we are in bad."

He then wired Eckhoff some cash along with instructions for his brother. J. B. was to go to Sioux City, Iowa, change his name, and find work.

Little did Eckhoff know what he was in for. When he arrived at the Nabb house, J. B. was furious. He'd expected J. J. Eckhoff explained that he was just doing what his brother had requested, and then gave J. B. his instructions and money. J. B. was hardly calmed; he was tired and scared, and didn't want to keep moving.

"Let's take a walk," he remarked, and as they trod down a path toward the stable, J. B. muttered, "I guess you know all about it, don't you?"

Eckhoff nodded. J. B. then turned to face his old friend. "I want you to go out hunting with me and kill me," he said. "You can say it was accidental, and it will be getting me out of this trouble. I know they are going to get me."

Eckhoff, taken aback, refused. Nevertheless, he was moved by the man's apparent remorse and distress. But, in an instant, it became evident that conscience had less to do with J. B.'s anguish than fear and alcohol did.

All right, J. B. spat out, if Eckhoff wouldn't do what he had asked, there was something else he could do for him. He wanted Eckhoff to go to Indianapolis and kill the stenographer at union headquarters. Her name was Mary Dye, and she simply knew too much; she had written too many letters concerning dynamitings, and J. B. didn't trust her. He maniacally laid out a plan for Eckhoff to follow her onto the train she took to work every morning and plant an infernal machine under her seat. Eckhoff could then depart the train at a nearby station and be miles away when the explosion occurred.

Appalled, Eckhoff again refused. He wasn't averse to carrying out a few odd jobs for the union, but the idea of possibly wiping out a train full of people was not something he would be a part of, he told J. B. It was at this point in their conversation that Eckhoff privately began to question whether the deaths of the people in the Times Building that night was accidental, as he had been told. Anyone who got in J. B.'s way, it seemed, was a potential accident. The two men began arguing loudly over Eckhoff's refusal to murder the stenographer. The argument became so loud that it disturbed J. B.'s mother, who had been asleep inside the house and now called out the window to ask what the fuss was all about.

"It's nothing, Mother," J. B. called back. "Just some union business."

Chapter 18

As a young man, William J. Burns had aspired to become an actor but instead eventually became what the *New York Times* would call "the only detective of genius whom the country has produced." His original ambition fit his talents, possessing as he did a remarkably retentive memory for his lines. William J. Burns also possessed a flair for the dramatic that would serve him well as a detective, effortlessly drawing publicity. Indeed, he himself often wrote about his exploits in the kind of pulp magazines that piled up on the tables of barber shops all over the country. By the turn of the century, he was an international celebrity. "[H]e lives in the glare of publicity," the *London Spectator* wrote. "When he walks abroad, he is followed by a small army of reporters to see what he does."

Burns had come into detective work without having received any formal training, but he had broken an unprecedented number of cases, from counterfeiting to land fraud to murder. He went on to serve as the chief of the Secret Service, a new agency of the federal government, founded in the aftermath of the assassination of President McKinley at the hands of anarchist/Socialist Leon Czolgosz in 1901. Six years later he became the lead investigator in the celebrated graft trials in San Francisco, sending corrupt public officials to San Quentin en masse.

In March 1910 he founded the Chicago-based William J. Burns National Detective Agency, and the following June pulled off an astonishing coup. By underbidding the Pinkerton Agency, Burns landed his competitor's most prestigious account, that of the American Bankers Association.

Burns, along with Walter Drew, a full-time legal counsel for the National Erectors Association (NEA), had been hired by the McClintock-Marshall construction conglomerate to look into what was suspected to have been a union bombing in Illinois. At daybreak on September 4, 1910, a watchman at the Peoria railroad yard had noticed something peculiar tucked among a stack of steel girders. It turned out to be an infernal machine that had failed to go off. Later that day Burns received a telephone call at his Chicago office, and that night he was on a commuter train traveling through a warm rain to the nearby city to look at the device.

"It had been made as prettily as a toy," William J. Burns wrote of the recovered device, "and it was evident that the man who had made it was expert with his tools and took joy in his work. The soldering was 'professional.' The wiring was neat. . . . You could imagine the man who made it holding it on the palm of his hand, and putting his head on one side, and being proud of it."

Each component was all but impossible to trace, being ordinary stock items found in nearly every corner hardware store in the country. The Junior Tattoo alarm clocks were one of the most commonly available in America.

Only the can of nitroglycerin offered any useful clues. Although it bore no trademark, a cryptic legend was embossed on it: X PENNSYL OLD METHOD IX OPEN HEARTH X CUMMY MCFARLAND AND CO. In the course of his investigation, Burns learned that it was standard practice for manufacturers of nitroglycerin to order specially made cans that held the explosive "soup." With this in mind, he released a description of the can with the peculiar legend to the press, and within days was contacted by M. J. Morehart, an agent for the Independent Torpedo Company of Portland, Indiana, who confirmed that the nitroglycerin had come from his factory. Checking his company ledgers to find the purchaser, the agent's finger had lit upon the name of J. W. McGraw. Morehart remembered him well and recounted how he sold the nitroglycerin to McGraw and helped him load it aboard a horse-drawn express wagon. McGraw had paid him $130, said he was heading for Muncie, and that was the last he had ever seen of him.

Burns moved his investigation on to nearby Muncie, where he thumbed through the registers of the local hotels, eventually coming across the entry: "J. W. McGraw, Indianapolis." He traced a sample of McGraw's handwriting and moved on again, this time to the livery stable where McGraw had hired the express wagon and a farm where he had helped himself to sawdust for the packing crates. Burns noted that the sawdust was of "a peculiar cut and color" and matched that found with the unexploded Peoria device as well as sawdust found around the area where the three other infernal machines had detonated. He even came across several people who had met McGraw during his stay and could give detailed and corroborating physical descriptions of him, all of which matched the description given by Morehart. McGraw was consistently described as having a full face, "even features," a mustache, and "warm, dark eyes." He was also rather short and always wore a cap.

From Muncie, Burns moved on to Indianapolis, where McGraw's ostensible boss, G. W. Clark, was said to operate a stone quarry. But Burns found no such quarry, and no G. W. Clark. The trail quickly went cold, and Burns left the investigation in the capable hands of his son, Raymond.

But for the time being, it appeared that J. W. McGraw, whose real name, Burns would one day learn, was Ortie McManigal, had made a clean getaway.

The porter on the train to Los Angeles woke Burns with the news from Los Angeles, then handed him the urgent wire from Mayor Alexander. The peripatetic detective, whose life in recent months seemed to be spent almost exclusively on train carriages, struggled to wake himself. After reading the message, he then went to work, scribbling out a barrage of telegrams that he dispatched at the Western Union office at the next station, redirecting his operatives across the country to what promised to be a lucrative new assignment.

Upon arriving in Los Angeles, the famous sleuth was met by an LAPD detective who drove him directly to the ruins of the Times Building, briefing him en route about the state of the investigation. Little in the way of useful information could be gathered from the smoldering hulk, Burns quickly realized. What he wanted to see was what everyone knew to be by far the most valuable piece of evidence the police had in their possession—the device recovered from the Zeehandelaar residence. None of Mayor Alexander's detectives had ever seen anything like it.

But William J. Burns had.

It was "identical in every detail to the unexploded bomb in Peoria," Burns would later write, "except for the use of sixteen sticks of 80 percent dynamite instead of nitroglycerin."

Tying the crimes together across half a continent was the peculiar little Junior Tattoo alarm clock and, it would seem, the same craftsman's invisible hand.

Still, Burns hesitated at taking the assignment to track down the dynamiters. He told Mayor Alexander that under no circumstance would he work with Earl Rogers.

Burns bitterly resented Rogers's courtroom success in the waning days of the boodle board fight, and his paintbrush-size mustache did not mask his displeasure when Mayor Alexander insisted that he wanted Rogers to investigate the bombing too. He would write later:

"I promptly told him . . . I would certainly not cooperate with Rodgers [sic], that he was a lawyer and not a detective and what they needed at that time was the service of the latter."

But the mayor was undeterred. He knew that General Otis hated Burns. Everyone in Southern California knew it. The feud had begun during the graft trials in San Francisco, when Burns had investigated one of Otis's allies for corruption. The dispute between the detective and the publisher had been well chronicled in the press. The mayor was frank with the detective: If he was not careful in his choice of the lead investigator, it could appear as though City Hall were in league with Otis in a conspiracy designed to crush labor in Southern California.

"It looks like we've got a madman running around with enough dynamite to blow up all Los Angeles," the anxious mayor explained. "We don't need a labor war as well."

He had the same reason for bringing Rogers onboard as a special prosecutor in the case. Rogers would be working under the auspices of District Attorney John Fredericks, whose credentials as an antilabor prosecutor were far too well established for any pretense of impartiality. And although an attorney for the rich and famous, Rogers possessed the common touch. At least twenty Angelenos had been murdered, and

Alexander was in no mood to be turned down because of a personality conflict. The mayor appealed to Burns's vanity, telling him that he was looking to hire his "reputation as well as skill." Then he moved on to what he knew to be Burns's weakness: money. He offered him lots of it with incredible terms.

"I am delegating you to run [the dynamiters] to earth," the mayor shouted, "no matter what the cost—and no matter who they are!" Burns could name his own fee. He would receive a bonus of $100,000, an incredible sum in 1910, should he catch the bombers. There was also the enormous reward money, the most that had ever been offered in North America, an escalating sum that promised to dwarf all other fees and bonuses. Moreover, the mayor assured Burns that Rogers would only assess Burns's evidence and not interfere with the investigation itself.

Still, the swarthy detective demurred, but with less ardor. With more artful nudging by the mayor, Burns finally agreed to at least meet with Rogers.

The next day Rogers appeared at the mayor's office sartorially dressed, sober, his blistered hands still bandaged. Burns was all business, but affable. Rogers mustered all his persuasive gifts as an attorney, which were considerable, and in short order the two men began to talk about "burying the hatchet." Burns, however, would not mention how the evidence the LAPD had obtained was likely connected to the bombings in the Midwest.

This secrecy would not change when he left the meeting. Burns trusted no one but his own men; never would he trust Earl Rogers. He told the mayor, "I accept the responsibility of this investigation on the condition that I will be obliged to report to no one—not even you—until the job has been brought to a successful conclusion." Alexander promptly agreed to the terms.

Indeed, every lead Burns developed would be kept to himself, his eyes focused on the luminous pot of gold at the end of his investigation.

<hr />

The unexploded Zeehandelaar bomb provided the embryo of the investigation. The dynamite sticks had been labeled "Giant, California"—a fact that was reported the next day in newspapers throughout the country. By

Sunday evening reporters had interviewed the manager of the dynamite plant in Giant, who gave them a description of the purchasers, neither of whom matched Burns's mysterious "round-faced" nitroglycerin expert from the Midwest who had called himself J. W. McGraw. Still, it was a foregone conclusion that Burns and Rogers would begin their hunt for the dynamiters by visiting the Giant plant.

They wasted no time. Shortly after the hatchet burial they boarded the Southern Pacific Lark for San Francisco in plush sleeper cars with a contingent of LAPD officers accompanying them. They neither shared rail carriages nor one another's company. Later Burns would publicly refuse to have his photograph taken with the attorney.

News of the men's visit to San Francisco preceded them, and they were met by a crush of newspaper reporters at the station and plied with questions about the reward money, which was now said to be approaching $200,000. As they made their way to the hotel, the posh St. Francis, they were besieged by men claiming to have confidential information about the bombing. Once ensconced in their hotel headquarters, the telephone in Rogers's room began ringing with one crank caller after another, each ready to provide clues—for a price. Exasperated, Rogers held an impromptu news conference in the hotel lobby.

"I regard it as exceedingly unfortunate," he began in his confident, theatrical voice, "that such huge rewards have been offered for the apprehension and conviction of the dynamiters. While it is well enough that it be generally known that Los Angeles is prepared to spend any amount of money in good faith, I don't care for this putting of prices on heads. Every county constable, every rural deputy, every private detective, so-called, in the United States will be solving this mystery."

And they were. Newspapers across the country were running stories about local law officials who had clapped dynamite suspects in jail. Some authorities sent Rogers wires setting out details about the suspects that they had picked up. One of them inquired about his own liability if he arrested two men he suspected of being the dynamiters if it developed that they were not the men wanted. Several persons wrote claiming to have clues but told Rogers that they did not want to turn them over to their local officers for fear they would not receive the reward money if the clues proved accurate.

Rogers told the news conference: "The man who ordinarily would be quite willing to talk to you will shortly become averse to giving you facts because he thinks he holds the key to the whole situation."

And Rogers had another fretful worry about the reward fund, which had now risen to nearly half a million dollars: "Suppose four men say to each other: 'Here is an immense sum which we can get—a fortune for each of us.' And forthwith they commence to frame up 'evidence' against an innocent man. This thing has been done often. Every man who deals with criminals knows that many innocent men have been convicted upon perjured testimony bought by a great reward."

~

The next day Earl Rogers crossed the bay to visit the little town with the grandiose name where the dynamite used in the bombing had been manufactured. Although a rickety tram line using a system of wooden trestles had been laid between San Francisco and the Glen Cove area near Giant, Rogers elected to take the more-reliable boat route. The spicy, somewhat acrid odor of dynamite hit his senses as he stepped ashore. Making his way from the dock over a narrow dirt road, he saw a green, pastoral landscape dotted here and there by gable-roofed cottages, outbuildings, tank houses, and barns. Locals in the area called it "Little Switzerland." Indeed, the Giant Powder Works seemed designed to fit right in: Taking in the scene, Rogers saw four small, dusty-gray wooden buildings on one side of the road with a sign, barely noticeable, on one reading DEAN'S CONDENSED SAFETY NITRO-GLYCERINE, a somewhat larger building on the opposite side housing the boilers, and up the road, a shack described as the "Powder Magazine," all enclosed by rough wooden fences tacked with more signs reading BEWARE OF FIRE. (A local newspaper reporter, writing a feature about the company, remarked that the warnings may cause "the nervous to think that there are safer places than around that locality.")

Over the next three weeks, Rogers would return to this bucolic out-country a half dozen times, gathering evidence, pumping witnesses, then returning to San Francisco and Los Angeles to fit his puzzle together. By the end of that time, his sorted files would produce a tangled chronicle of what had transpired in Giant and elsewhere in the Bay Area during the months prior to October 1, 1910.

Chapter 19

Back in Indianapolis, Ortie McManigal arose early each morning to buy the paper as soon as it hit the streets. The stories about the aftermath of the *Times* bombing had banished other salient news items off the front page of the *Indianapolis Star*. There was one about the rising casualty toll, another about the enormous reward, another about America's most famous detective being called in to investigate, another about the accusations mounting against the unions. One item said that police investigators were close to making arrests.

McManigal realized that authorities might soon be moving in on him. He decided to visit the office of J. J. McNamara, where he found the secretary-treasurer of the Iron Workers Union reading the same paper he had already devoured.

"Seen the morning paper?" McNamara asked McManigal as he came into his office.

"It's about as bad as it can get," McManigal replied. Unaware that J. B. had acted alone, he fairly shouted at McNamara, "Those fellows killed a lot of people."

McNamara appeared downright nonchalant about it all, McManigal thought, as he pointed out that J. B. had accomplished just what he had set out to do. Those who died were "scabs," McNamara said. "This will make them sit up and take notice." Indeed, he now wanted to step up the bombings. He told McManigal of his plan to have explosions occur in Omaha and Columbus, Indiana, on the same night.

"I want them to go off about the same time, so they will wonder how the fellow was in Omaha and Columbus the same night. What I am going to do is to get about six or eight good fellows and I am going to station them all around the country, and I am going to have explosions all come off at one time, one right after the other. I will make them sit up and take notice."

That night McManigal was sent off to Massachusetts. Despite realizing that he could be picked up at any moment as an associate of a mass murderer, he hardly hesitated at detonating eight quarts of nitroglycerin under a derrick car in Worcester, at midnight, just five days after the Los Angeles explosion. McManigal then moved on to Boston and New York, achieving the same successful results, finally returning to Indianapolis on October 15. A few days later he was off again to scope out a bridge under construction by the American Bridge Company in the fittingly named town of Highbridge, Kentucky. But when McManigal wired back to Indianapolis that it looked like an easy target, McNamara ordered him to hold off and to head back to Chicago.

Chapter 20

Bruce McCaul, chief invoice clerk for the Giant Powder Company, who usually worked in the company's San Francisco offices, and George Phillips, the company's assistant supervisor, were waiting in the Giant office when Earl Rogers arrived.

They had an extraordinary account to relate about the men who had wanted to buy 99 percent dynamite from them but who had settled on 80 percent. They told him of Perry, the unkempt "beefy red-faced man" with a "bad eye." Then there was Bryce, the man who had met McCaul in his San Francisco office, a "dark-haired little fellow," who remained relatively silent compared to his talkative companion. Phillips told Rogers that after the men picked up their dynamite order, he felt overwhelmed with pity for the "man with the bad eye."

The following day LAPD detective Samuel Browne reported to Rogers that he'd located the *Pastime/Peerless* at an Oakland boathouse. George Phillips confirmed that it was "identical to the one used by the men who purchased the powder." After hearing Phillips's identification, Rogers told a *Times* reporter that there was no doubt in his mind "about that being the boat used by the men we are after."

Onboard, detectives found two pairs of blue overalls, which were sent off to Los Angeles to be tested for trace evidence of nitroglycerin, and a torn piece of a boat's nameplates "bearing some other name."

Like composing the layout of a newspaper, Earl Rogers had begun piecing together clips of testimony and photographs of evidence to form a fairly complex chronicle of the activities of the suspects. To Rogers's elegant lodgings at the St. Francis Hotel came a procession of witnesses and would-be witnesses, all with absorbing—sometimes even spellbinding—tales.

At first the investigators tried diligently to keep their stories out of the papers. But newspaper reporters soon began staking out the St. Francis and buttonholed witnesses as they came away after visiting Rogers. Word soon spread that the newspapers were willing to pay for stories about the dynamiters. Baxter and Burrowes, the two owners of the *Pastime*, were each commissioned to tell about their meeting with the men in front-page articles that appeared in the *San Francisco Chronicle* under their bylines. Frank H. DePue, director of the State Bureau of Identification, announced that he had been able to secure some excellent fingerprints from the cabin of the *Pastime*. He had also put the gloves and overalls that had been found on the launch through a chemical process and discovered faint traces of nitroglycerin on them.

Indeed, only five days after the bombing, the *Chronicle* was commenting: "The remarkable thing about the case is the amount of direct evidence which has been gathered before the arrest of any of the principals in the crime has been announced."

Telephone calls placed from the Argonaut Hotel by "Bryce" and "Perry" were checked. On October 7, the *Los Angeles Times* reported that "Perry," the man with the glass eye, had been seen on several recent occasions at the Hoffman Cafe in San Francisco with a friend named "Morris" who, with his wire-rimmed spectacles, it was said, looked the part of an intellectual. Morris's identification was made by Sam Bernard, the cafe's proprietor, and was backed up by the cafe's bartender, Charles Williams; incredibly, Morris had also given Bernard's name as a reference upon renting the *Pastime*. Bernard and Williams identified the man with the glass eye as Matthew Schmidt, whose last known residence was a boardinghouse at No. 2410 Mission Street. Patrons of the cafe were questioned. One of them, explaining Schmitty's odd appearance to a reporter, said that it reminded him of the joke about the man who bumped into another man and said, "Why don't you look where you're going?" to which the other replied, "Why don't you go where you're looking?"

What made Bernard and Williams's story so explosive was their assertion that Schmidt had regularly frequented the cafe with Olaf Tveitmoe,

the San Francisco labor boss. This one connection, as slender and pre-
liminary as it was, demonstrated just how high the stakes in this case had
become for the labor movement. In a few days' time, Schmidt would be
identified as an anarchist with a penchant for anticapitalist rants advocating the violent overthrow of the US government. If Tveitmoe was found
to have any meaningful connection to the bombers, then the entire labor
movement would find itself in mortal danger, and labor leaders everywhere knew it. So too did General Otis and Harry Chandler.

Reporters tailed Tveitmoe and Johannsen relentlessly. The two men
refused to meet with Rogers or Burns, grumbling to the press that they
were being set up and predicting that Rogers would make every effort to
have a special grand jury indict them.

Five days later came yet another breakthrough for Rogers and
Burns. D. H. Ingersoll contacted San Francisco police detectives and
claimed that a man calling himself J. B. Bryce had been a boarder at
the boardinghouse run by his wife Lena. Bryce, he said, had a friend
who lived in a boardinghouse nearby, "a squint-eyed man" calling himself Schmidt. When city police detectives dropped by to interview the
married couple, it became clear that their marriage was a briar patch of
domestic contempt. Lena, they would later relate to *Los Angeles Times*
reporters, had "broken her home and endangered her eight-year-old
boy's future." At first she refused to speak to Rogers, agreeing to do so
only after being granted immunity from prosecution. Bryce, she told
him, had been her boarder from September 4 through September 14.
He then moved on to the Argonaut Hotel, whereupon she lost track
of him. While he boarded with her, however, she had heard "through
a keyhole" and the "thin plywood walls" Bryce and Schmidt "plotting
against someone and [using] the word 'dynamite.'" She said that she felt
certain that she could identify Bryce.

After being questioned by the attorney, Mrs. Ingersoll promised him
that she would not to speak to reporters, but she was quickly enticed by
the *Los Angeles Times* into publicly revealing the details of her relationship
with J. B. and Schmitty. She painted her husband as a "drunken rowdy,"

although upon publication, the *Times* depicted him as "a decent industrious man who has been too lenient with her faults." Even the boarders in Mrs. Lavin's and Mrs. Ingersoll's rooming houses were being quoted about the romantic dramas they had witnessed.

Then on October 16, just fifteen days after the bombing, James C. O'Brien, who owned the cottage on Nineteenth Avenue South that Caplan had rented, decided to visit his new tenants. Neighbors had told him that they had not seen anyone coming or going from the cottage since that night when a group of men had arrived with a strange cargo of boxes. No curtains had been hung over the windows. No lights had been lit in the evening.

O'Brien knocked on the door of the cottage, waited, then knocked again. When no one answered, the cigar-chomping landlord let himself in with a skeleton key. He glanced around the front room—no furniture, no suitcases, no sign that anyone was living there. Just a stack of boxes, covered with a canvas tarpaulin. Each of the boxes had been covered with burlap and tied securely with rope.

"I did not know what was under the canvas, but I was afraid something was wrong," O'Brien would later relate. "When I lifted the canvas and uncovered one of the boxes, I saw some funny-looking sticks. I thought they were about the funniest looking candles I had ever seen and picked one up and tried to break it on the side of the box.

"I dropped some of the ashes from my cigar into the box too. I kept on investigating, and when I finally saw the marking on the side of the boxes which read 'nitroglycerin 80 percent,' I got so excited, I dropped my cigar. I threw up both hands and yelled, 'Goodnight! Dynamite!' and then I ran out of that house as fast as I could go."

The five hundred pounds of dynamite could have blown up the entire neighborhood. Only a few days earlier, a fire at the nearby Catholic orphanage had showered sparks all over the street, some of them flitting down onto the roof of the dynamite house. The roof of the house next door had in fact erupted into fire in several places, and a nearby outhouse had gone up in flames. A slight change in the winds and the *Times* bombing would have been like nothing compared to the devastation that might have befallen Nineteenth Avenue.

For Rogers and Burns, the O'Brien discovery turned out to be a big break.

The dynamite recovered at the Zeehandelaar home was immediately sent up from Los Angeles. Within hours of its arrival investigators had determined that the newly discovered sticks were indeed part of the same batch, making a three-way chemical match with the special high-grade dynamite purchased by Bryce, Perry, and Morris at the Giant Powder Works. Detectives also found a pair of striped overalls and a jumper in the cottage, exactly like ones left behind on the *Pastime*.

The immediate impact of the discovery lay in the fact that the bombers had lost a significant lethal arsenal. But there was a secondary impact. O'Brien was able to provide Rogers and Burns with the name and address of his former tenant, David Caplan, a bookish young man, he said, who wore wire-rimmed spectacles and also happened to match the general description of the man who had most consistently used the alias "Morris."

Rogers accompanied police to the apartment at 1641 A Fulton Street that Caplan had rented from O'Brien, where they found a piece of cardboard about "one-quarter the size of a comic postcard" with the initials O. A. T. on one side (Olaf A. Tveitmoe?) and the cryptic words, "I'll do it" printed out on the other. They also found a bit of a card with the words "Russian Progressive Society, S.F." They gathered up clippings from Russian newspapers about labor topics in the apartment as well as copies of Caplan's correspondence, including letters to a man named Bryce. While police scoured the place, Caplan's wife and daughter looked on glumly, saying hardly a word. They insisted that they had no idea where Caplan had gone.

It was in the rooming house in Corte Madera, where Schmitty had lived while he was working on Anton Johannsen's house that investigators found the first evidence directly linking the dynamite buyers to the *Times*. They discovered, stuffed into a cushion on the lower end of a couch, a rumpled pink cloth, normally used for polishing eyeglasses and lenses (and glass eyes?). On it were the tracings of a building marked "T" with an alleyway clearly indicated. It was obviously the Times Building. Also drawn on the cloth was a crude outline of San Francisco Bay, with key points along the route that the *Peerless* took clearly marked.

For the Los Angeles investigators, the discovery was, well, explosive.

Chapter 21

Three weeks after the bombing, Ortie McManigal, accompanied by his wife Emma, took the train to Indianapolis, where he expected to receive new assignments. The morning after they arrived, Emma picked up the phone and listened as a man at the other end told her: "Tell Mac his friend Mr. Clark wants to see him at 11:00 a.m. at the Briggs Hotel." McManigal's wife duly delivered the message. "Clark," he knew, was J. J. McNamara.

Later that morning McManigal met McNamara in the lobby of the hotel. The two men glanced around them, then walked outside.

As they strolled down the street, McNamara suddenly swore, then remarked: "Things are red hot. There's a hell of a smear around there."

McManigal figured that McNamara might have learned that his brother had been arrested and asked, "Is he clear? Is he out of the way?"

"He is away, but he is not clear yet." J. B., he said, needed to be removed to some remote place where he could be protected. J. J. asked McManigal about his upcoming plans. McManigal said that he was about to go on a hunting trip with some friends. J. J. knew them—Louis Zeiss, George Sharp, and William and Charlie Lawrence.

McNamara told McManigal: "You are going to pick up an additional member for your hunting party."

On November 5 Ortie McManigal kissed his wife and children goodbye and headed for the Chicago train station, carrying a valise and three shotguns in cases. He took a short, fifty-two-mile trip to Kenosha, Wisconsin, where he dropped off the guns at George Sharp's home. He then returned to the train station with Sharp, and at 3:55 p.m. they welcomed J. B. McNamara, who now called himself Frank Sullivan.

McManigal, like the others, was taken aback by his appearance. "I was greatly surprised at the change that had taken place in him," he would write later. "He was haggard. His eyes roamed in every direction as though he was expecting arrest at any moment. He appeared greatly excited and said he wanted to get somewhere where he could be certain not to see anyone he knew. He said he had been hiding since the destruction of the Times Building, and if he could get off into some woods where nobody went he would feel better."

But there was first the not-so-small matter of obtaining hunting permits. By law, it would be necessary for each of the men to give the license agent his complete description. At first J. B. balked. "It's too risky," he told the others, urging them to skip the procedure and just head out to the woods. But McManigal replied that the risk of being arrested for hunting without a license would be even more dangerous. The following day the group gathered at the license bureau and obtained the proper documents. "Sullivan" said that he was an office worker on holiday to regain his health. McManigal would remark later: "He did look yellow and peaked."

The hunting party now made the 250-mile train trip to Conover, Wisconsin, where they bought winter hunting gear, rented a cabin, and trekked to their camp near Pioneer Lake.

McManigal mailed a note to J. J. McNamara: "Met the old carpenter. He is looking fine."

Chapter 22

"This is the most important discovery made since it was found that the dynamite that was used to blow up the *Los Angeles Times* was purchased at Giant," Earl Rogers told reporters following the discovery at the O'Brien house. "We have been looking for this dynamite, and it clears up a lot of things. Enough was taken away to blow up the Times Building."

He described how investigators had found in a hallway a pair of striped overalls and a jumper, exactly like ones that had been left behind in the *Pastime*.

Tracing the purchase of the tarpaulin, Rogers disclosed, they found that it had been ordered by a "William Capp" and had been delivered to David Caplan's apartment.

Later, Harry Piper, the jockey who had been paid a half-dollar to look after the *Peerless,* identified the burlap and bale rope as the same sort he had seen in the cabin of the launch when he looked inside. Police concluded that the burlap had been used to disguise the boxes, or in any case to cover up the labeling.

Police had staked out Lena Ingersoll's boardinghouse. At the time, she was still refusing to talk to them. But, they surmised, maybe one of the dynamiters might return there. They kept an around-the-clock watch on the house. And then at 2:30 in the morning of Friday, October 14, they spotted a man trying to force the door of the boardinghouse. They quickly pounced on the man—who identified himself as D. H. Ingersoll.

"My wife's in there with the dynamiters. She's protecting them!" he shouted. The lights went on in the boardinghouse, and Lena Ingersoll emerged, glaring at the cops and the disheveled man they had just nabbed.

"They know they're in there. I told them," D. H. Ingersoll shouted to her.

"There's no one here but me and the boarders, and I won't have them disturbed because of this lunatic," Mrs. Ingersoll shouted back.

Sgt. Lionel Shaw released the hapless man and asked Mrs. Ingersoll to come to the station the next day. In her written statement to police, Mrs. Ingersoll called her husband's accusations "nothing but the ravings of a man crazed by drink and jealousy. He claims to be in love with me, and it was when I refused him admittance last night that he threatened to make trouble for me by telling the detectives and a newspaper a made-up story of my dealings with the supposed dynamiters."

Mrs. Ingersoll's reluctance to cooperate did not last long. As each damning bit of evidence pointed to her involvement with the suspects, as each lodger in her house testified about what they heard through the thin walls there, Earl Rogers returned to the boardinghouse to confront her with what he had learned. Finally, he put it to her that unless she cooperated she would be placing herself in danger of being indicted as a coconspirator. Three days after she gave San Francisco police her statement about her husband's attempted break-in, she returned to the police station again and gave them a detailed account of her relationship with the suspects.

When a bundle of laundry arrived for "Bryce" the following day, she turned it over to the police. They examined the laundry marks and immediately sent out a circular to every police bureau in the country, saying: "We wish to notify all Chiefs of Police in the United States to select a careful man to interview all laundries and to watch all laundries in their jurisdiction, to instruct the laundry workers to watch carefully all laundry which passes through their hands and to be on the lookout for the marks 'XX2' and 'A2410.' If this laundry shows, have the laundry notify your department and arrest the owner of such at once. Keep this from the press."

The press published the notice on the same day it was distributed.

Investigators were quick to notice that one of the laundry marks, "A2410," was the same number as Belle Lavin's boardinghouse address on Mission Street. They had already made three visits to the place to question her. But she taunted them with conflicting stories about her involvement with the dynamiters. Finally, on Tuesday, October 18, after three hours of grueling and frustrating questioning by Chief Seymour, Earl Rogers was sent for. He arrived at police headquarters at 2:00 p.m., his Beau Brummel appearance causing heads to turn as he dashingly strode into the interrogation room. He wore a dark tailored suit, with silk shirt and jeweled cuff links. Across his vest, a gold chain dipped into a small watch pocket. He was the natty dresser down to his custom-made shoes and spats.

"Mr. Rogers, this woman is lying," Seymour said. "I will turn her over to you."

Rogers gently took the woman's hand and led her out of the interrogation room and into a private office. His soft, resonant voice, well practiced for this sort of dramatic tableau, fairly stroked the young woman. He told her why he had taken the case, how he had raced to the Times Building shortly after hearing the explosion to witness a nightmarish scene. Still holding her hand, the handsome attorney attempted to impart the emotions he felt on that night to the woman sitting before him.

"If you had seen what I saw after the dynamiting of the Los Angeles Times Building, I believe you would take a different view of this affair," he told her. "I saw crowds fight to get through police lines to assist in dragging forth the mangled victims of that terrible crime. I saw fourteen bodies of men who were the sole support of wives, children, mothers, brothers, and sisters in a single coffin, an unrecognizable mass. I saw things that would bring tears to the eyes of a fiend. If you had seen those things, I believe you would tell what you know of the fiends who are responsible for that horrible crime."

He let the words sink in as he looked directly at the woman, his eyes moist and pleading.

Belle Lavin was not moved.

It wasn't all a contrived act for Rogers, not a case of assuming a dramatic pose that could soften up his audience of one. What he had witnessed in Los Angeles had come to haunt him, and he had mustered every device in his considerable bag of talents to persuade witnesses to testify. Many were terrified that if the dynamiters found out, they too would become targets. But Rogers had reasoned with them, coaxed them, assuaged their fears with the not-too-assuring argument that telling him what they knew was the right thing to do.

But Belle Lavin was another case entirely. Rogers told her that he had given her every chance to tell what she knew.

"Because you haven't, madam, understood your position, I am going to take you to jail."

For the first time Belle Lavin seemed to lose her composure. Her hands gripped the handles of her chair, and she leaned forward.

"Where? Where?" she asked.

"To the county jail of Los Angeles, madam," replied Rogers.

"How are you going to do it?"

If his behavior had seemed somewhat melodramatic up to now, it now went over the top. He drew back his coat, displaying the badge of a deputy sheriff of the County of Los Angeles. "By virtue of the authority I have as a deputy sheriff and this warrant charging you with murder."

He handed her a warrant charging "Jane Doe" with murder committed on the morning of October 1 in Los Angeles. It was one of several warrants that had duly been issued by a justice of the peace in Los Angeles upon the telegraphic request of Rogers; a San Francisco Superior Court judge had authorized the service of the warrant on Mrs. Lavin.

Rogers conducted her to a waiting police car, which drove her to her home, where she was allowed to fetch clothes and other necessities for her sojourn in the Los Angeles County Jail.

At the train station in San Francisco that night, Mrs. Lavin was accosted by a horde of journalists and photographers "until she was almost in hysterics," the *Los Angeles Times* reported. She then boarded the Lark with Rogers and sped through the night for the scene of her alleged lover's alleged crime. Upon arrival she was hauled off to the county jail, where she was booked, immediately released, and then given a "neat, prettily furnished apartment with softened lights," where she was finally allowed to rest.

On Sunday afternoon, October 23, Earl Rogers and Belle Lavin went for an automobile outing. They headed for the ruins of the Times

Building, driving around the block several times, Rogers telling her about the friends he had lost in the explosion, describing to her in ghastly detail how they had died or had been maimed. As he watched her take in the scene—the blackened walls, the piles of rubble, the dust-covered cleanup crews, the downcast passersby—he sensed that the enormity of the crime had at last been brought home to her. At the end of their journey, he told reporters that he thought Mrs. Lavin would now become more cooperative.

Earl Rogers had now rounded up a herd of witnesses and collected a hefty load of evidence in San Francisco. His files on the case were now bulging with notes and documents. He had everything he needed to go to trial—except the dynamiters. And they had made a clean escape. "The world is not big enough to conceal them," Rogers declared during one interview. But it was doing a good job of it then.

～～

From the beginning of the investigation, William Burns had kept his distance from Rogers—out of jealousy, mistrust, and a sensible suspicion that if Rogers nabbed the dynamiters, the reward money would go to him. He was just as uncommunicative and remote with Los Angeles authorities, even with the man who had hired him, Mayor Alexander. Two weeks after he was recruited, Burns, who had last been seen questioning witnesses in San Francisco, seemingly vanished. No one—not the press, not the mayor, not the city council, not General Otis, not Earl Rogers—had any idea where he was, let alone what he was up to.

Rogers, meanwhile, was being lavished with praise. In San Francisco "they still loved Earl Rogers," daughter Adela would later write. "He was their boy." The reverence in which he seemed to be held by the press and local politicians must have poured more fuel on Burns's suspicions and jealousy. Burns's own secretiveness seemed to play into the hands of his critics, who now wanted to know what the detective was doing with the large sums of cash being disbursed to him out of the city's treasury.

Burns sent not a single report to Mayor Alexander or District Attorney Fredericks. He realized that any details about the progress of his investigation might wind up in public circulation, providing valuable leads that any Johnny-come-lately investigator in the mayor's or district attorney's offices might follow to capture the dynamiters and claim the reward money.

It would have been an act of professional suicide for any private investigator other than the World Famous Sleuth to simply disappear from the scene of a major investigation shortly after having received public money from a district attorney's office. But Burns understood that, his national reputation being as esteemed as it was, Mayor Alexander trusted him implicitly.

By the end of October, the grand jury had been summoned to investigate the investigator. Earl Rogers was appointed an assistant district attorney and charged with tracking down Burns. The mayor was then instructed to stop sending money to Burns.

Soon after Burns learned that the San Francisco suspects, David Caplan and the man known as Bryce, had lived for a time at the Home Colony in Washington State, he presumably concluded that the notorious anarchist commune might have been the breeding ground for the bombing. He certainly must have felt that, at the very least, he would be able to track down information about where the two men might be hiding. He immediately assigned two of his agents to the colony, where they easily infiltrated its core, passing themselves off as fellow radicals. Then, without informing his men, Burns himself suddenly pulled up stakes in San Francisco, headed for the train station, and boarded a northbound train for Tacoma.

The hunter found no prey in the Home Colony. He did track down J. D. Waggoner, the teacher and electrician who had given Bryce advice on how to set off dynamite without a blasting cap. The teacher recalled that Bryce had shown him a can containing two sticks of dynamite. The can had been labeled "Portland." When the teacher remarked that he wasn't aware that dynamite was manufactured in Portland, Bryce had replied: "Not Portland, Oregon—Portland, Indiana."

That seemingly trivial remark would turn out to be the most propitious lead that Burns would come up with during his feigned hunting trip into the North Country. He immediately recalled that the first unexploded infernal machine that he had seen in Peoria a month before the *Times* explosion contained nitroglycerin that had been manufactured by the Independent Torpedo Company of Portland, Indiana. He subsequently learned that it had been purchased by a man named J. W. McGraw.

What perplexed Burns somewhat was that none of the men who had plotted the bombing in San Francisco answered the description of McGraw. He figured that there could only be one explanation: a ring of dynamiters, each of them knowledgeable of and adept at constructing the same sort of infernal machine.

Still, Burns's trail had turned cold in Washington, and it might have frozen over if Herbert S. Hockin hadn't entered the picture. Hockin decided to present himself to the iron contractors and provide them with inside information about union plots—for a price. Meanwhile, he continued working in his reduced position at the union.

On November 2, 1910, Lindsay L. Jewell, construction superintendent for the McClintock-Marshall Company, arranged a secret meeting between Hockin and Raymond Burns, son of the detective.

Hockin would provide the younger Burns with the crucial information that would break the case. McGraw, the Peoria dynamiter, he said, was actually Ortie McManigal of Chicago, and J. B. Bryce was actually James B. McNamara of Indianapolis, the younger brother of John J. McNamara, the secretary-treasurer of the Iron Workers Union.

William J. Burns showed no sign of being elated when he received the news from his son. It was as if some unwelcome accomplice had shown up at a poker game and had begun to signal the contents of the other players' hands to him. He had little patience with disgruntled employees who ratted on their associates. He found dealing with them singularly distasteful—the reason, perhaps, that he asked his son to question Hockin first.

His antipathy toward Hockin was intensely apparent when he resumed the questioning that Raymond had begun. He told Hockin that he was already aware that he and J. J. McNamara had been trying to sell union "protection" to the iron contractors in and around Peoria. He pounded the desk sharply. Hockin jumped, reacting as if Burns's fist had struck him.

Burns roared: "You are coming late in the day when we are about to grab you and J. J. McNamara."

At that moment, Hockin might as well have been walking on a steel girder a hundred feet in the air—carefully negotiating his every move, keenly mindful that any misstep could prove to be his undoing.

He told Burns that he had decided to speak out because he did not like the idea of wholesale destruction and murder. He said that he merely wanted to help Burns.

What is he up to—this smarmy double-crosser? Burns must have thought. Money? He decided to test him. He offered to hire Hockin as a "special investigator" to keep tabs on the activities of the Iron Workers' leaders.

"No need to pay me," Hockin replied. His words astonished Burns, but only for a split second, for Hockin quickly added: "I just want to be reimbursed for expenses." At the moment, Burns had no knowledge of Hockin's talent for expense-account padding.

By the end of their meeting, Burns had also agreed to protect Hockin if he should ever be jailed by the authorities; he would pay him $2,500 a year for two years upon his release.

Three days later Burns would receive his first communication from his new special agent. "McManigal left here [Chicago] today," Hockin wrote him. "He said he was going on a hunting trip. I know he is to meet J. B. within a day or two. . . . Caplan is in the Dakotas some where and is heading for New York." J. B., he said, was now calling himself Frank Sullivan.

The Los Angeles Times Building located at the northeast corner of First and Spring Streets prior to 1891, when an enormous iron eagle would perch on its turret.

Ortie McManigal's wife, Emma, and their two children, Evelyn and Walter. Of all the principals in the dynamite conspiracy, he was the only family man, and the case might have turned out far differently had he not been.

Ortie McManigal, posing with an infernal machine and describing how it functioned.
HUNTINGTON LIBRARY, ART COLLECTIONS AND BOTANICAL GARDENS

J. J. McNamara posing with Bible and rosary beads as a youth. COURTESY ARCHIVES
AND RARE BOOKS LIBRARY, UNIVERSITY OF CINCINNATI

J. B. McNamara at about the time his brother J. J. recruited him to join the
bombing conspiracy. COURTESY ARCHIVES AND RARE BOOKS LIBRARY, UNIVERSITY OF
CINCINNATI

Portrait of J. J. McNamara as secretary-treasurer of the Iron Workers Union. The half-smile never seemed to leave his face. COURTESY ARCHIVES AND RARE BOOKS LIBRARY, UNIVERSITY OF CINCINNATI

Dear Alice:

Two copies of Marie, in her wedding dress, are on their way. I am very sorry for the delay. After Mother passed away I didn't give it any thought; am glad you had Margaret call my attention to it. You should find original enclosed. Too bad it is out of focus. You can notice it in the eyes.— I had some copies of Mother taken from a snap shot. You will recognize them. I didn't know what to do with them so I sent them along. You can give them to members of the family if you wish.— Received letter from

J. J. McNamara upon graduation from the University of Indiana School of Law. Although J. B. McNamara refused interviews, he wrote hundreds of chatty letters to his sister Alice, who treasured every one and eventually donated them to the University of Cincinnati. COURTESY ARCHIVES AND RARE BOOKS LIBRARY, UNIVERSITY OF CINCINNATI

The executive board of the Iron Workers Union (1907–08) as they appeared in its official organ, the *Bridgemen's Magazine.*

The young Harry Chandler. Journalism held little interest for him. Wealth and power did. He would build the *Los Angeles Times* into the city's most dominant institution.

Harrison Gray Otis ran the *Times* as if it were a military operation, and he would often show up for work in full uniform. He called the Times Building The Fortress. His home on Wilshire Boulevard was The Bivouac. A second residence in the Hollywood Hills was called The Outpost.

A crowd of 40,000 gathered for the opening of the Los Angeles Aqueduct on November 13, 1913. Engiineer William Mulholland delivered an inaugural address of five words: "There it is. Take it!" PHOTOGRAPH BY: *LOS ANGELES TIMES*

A photographer caught this scene of the inferno at about 1:40 a.m., a half-hour after the blast occurred. COURTESY HUNTINGTON LIBRARY, ART COLLECTIONS AND BOTANICAL GARDENS

In the daylight hours of October 1, 1910, tens of thousands of citizens gathered at the corner of First and Spring Streets to watch the continuing search-and-rescue/recovery activities.

The charred ruins of the front counter of the Times Building that had been fashioned from wood from Union and Confederate ships, from California missions, from Lincoln's death bed, and "from the mast of the USS *Hartford* to which Admiral Farragut was lashed." COURTESY HUNTINGTON LIBRARY, ART COLLECTIONS AND BOTANICAL GARDENS

Looking like a gutted structure on a field of battle—which, in effect, it was —the front entrance to the Los Angeles Times Building had defied the holocaust that had leveled the rest of the structure. COURTESY HUNTINGTON LIBRARY, ART COLLECTIONS AND BOTANICAL GARDENS

The Times LOS ANGELES

For Liberty and Law, Equal Rights and Industrial Freedom

PER ANNUM, $9.00 | SATURDAY MORNING, OCTOBER 1, 1910. | 5 CENTS

UNIONIST BOMBS WRECK THE TIMES; MANY SERIOUSLY INJURED

Terrific Explosion at 1 o'Clock This Morning Starts Fire Which Engulfs Score of Employes in Great Newspaper Plant---Many Victims ---Great Property Loss.

Many lives were jeopardized and half a million dollars' worth of property was sacrificed on the altar of hatred of the labor unions at 1 o'clock this morning, when the plant of the Los Angeles Times was blown up and burned, following numerous threats by the laborites.

Not quite as many of the employes were on duty as would have been the case earlier in the night, when all departments were working in full blast, but even so, the murderous cowards knew that fully 100 people were in the building at the time.

With the suddenness of an earthquake, an explosion, of which the dry, snappy sound left no room to doubt of its origin in dynamite, tore down the whole first floor wall of the building on Broadway, just back of the entrance to the business offices. In as many seconds, four or five other explosions of lesser volume were heard.

In the time it took to run at full speed from the police station to the corner of First and Broadway, a distance of less than half a block, the entire building was in flames on three floors. Almost in the same instant flames and smoke filled the east stairway on First street, driving down in a frenzied panic those employes of the composing room who had been so fortunate as to reach the landing in time.

Elbowing past the last of these fugitives, men fought their way up to the first floor with flash lights and handkerchiefs over their faces. There efforts were unavailing, the blistering hot smoke and the lurid light of the flames almost upon them and licking down at them fiercely, drove the would-be rescuers back, hurriedly.

Although they could hear clearly the cries of distress, the groans and screams of the men and women who, mangled and crippled by flying debris from the explosion, lay imprisoned by the flames, about to be cremated alive.

Along the windows of the editorial and city rooms, on the south side of the building, through a choking volume of black smoke, could be seen men and women crowding each other about the windows of the third floor. The cries for ladders went up, frantic.

A fire wagon drove up at full speed. Groans greeted it when it was seen that it was but a hose wagon instead of the hook and ladder truck.

"Nets; get nets, nets!" was the yell.

A policeman came running up from headquarters, carrying a short ladder, pathetically inadequate. Some one called him a fool. But the ladder saved the live of Lovelace, the country editor, who jumped upon it and escaped with broken leg and some minor burns.

Other fire apparatus thundered up. The nets were jerked out in less time than it takes to tell, but by that time the fire had surged through the building with such rapidity that it was impossible to approach the reddening walls with them, and those unfortunates who had not jumped with Lovelace were doomed.

In less than four minutes from the time the explosion was heard the entire building was ablaze.

The Work of Demons

It reeked little to the man who placed the bombs which wrecked a splendid newspaper plant that 100 men were at work on the various floors, busily engaged in getting out the great newspaper. That the instant that the bombs were exploded their lives were in peril; that as a result of the hellish work lives were probably lost and other lives precious to wives, children and relatives were in deadly peril.

The bombs were planted by experienced hands. They did the work for which they were intended, at least temporarily, to cripple a great newspaper.

At 1 o'clock the Times plant was humming in every department. Forms were being closed up, stereotyped and sent down to the press room. An hour later the great presses would run at lightning speed to print the many thousands of papers which carriers were waiting to serve to their customers.

A second hell broke loose. A deafening detonation, a sickening uplift of men's hearts and lungs, then vivid tongues of flames, dense, stifling smoke which obscured the electric lights on every floor.

One instant busy occupation, lights, the whirr of machinery, the next, black midnight, smoke that overpowers, flames that shot their wicked tongues from basement to roof.

Trapped on all floors, the men of the Times, picked men they were, preserved their coolness in the midst of this appalling scene.

But it would seem that there was no escape. The murderers had planned with hellish cunning. The broad stairways were filled with deadly smoke almost as soon as the echo of the dynamite bomb had died away. The building was on fire on every side. But there

INJURED

E. B. ASPINALL, linotype operator. Cut over left eye; nose cut; right wrist strained.

S. W. CRABILL, foreman composing room. Burned and cut with flying glass.

WILL LATTA, sterotyper. Burned arms and back.

U. S. G. PENTZ, linotype operator. Jumped from window; wrist broken.

G. RICHARD, cut.

M. WESTON, cut on shoulders.

RANDOLPH ROSS, lynotype operator. Jumped from second story window; abrasion left knee; ankle sprained.

CHARLES VON VELSEN, fireman. Cut on left hand.

MRS. J. B. ULRICH, fell down elevator.

CHARLES E. LOVELACE, editorial staff. Jumped from third floor window; injuries perhaps fatal.

AUGUST KOTSCH, compositor. Slightly burned.

J. F. LINK, glass cuts on head.

CHURCHILL HARVEY-ELDER, burned over body and head; broken right leg; will probably die.

RICHARD GOFF, slight burns and cuts.

MISSING

J. C. GALLIHER, 40, linotype operator, married and five children.

W. G. TUNSTALL, 45, linotype operator, married.

FRED LLEWELLYN, 36, operator, married.

JOHN HOWARD, 45, printer, married and one child.

GRANT MOORE, 42, machinist, married and three children.

ED. WASSON, 35, printer, married.

ELMER FRINK, 25, operator, married.

EUGENE CARESS, 35, operator, married and one child.

DON E. JOHNSON, 36, operator, married.

ERNEST JORDAN, 32, operator, married and one child.

FRANK UNDERWOOD, 48, printer, married and one child.

J. WESLEY REAVER, stenographer.

R. L. SAWYER, 34, telegraph operator, married and two children.

HARRY L. CRANE, 38, assistant telegraph editor, married and one child.

CHARLES GULLIVER, 35, compositor, married.

A PLAIN STATEMENT

By the Managing Editor of The Times

The Times building was destroyed this morning by the enemies of industrial freedom by dynamite bombs and fire.

Numerous threats to do this dastardly deed had been received.

The Times itself cannot be destroyed. It will be issued every day and will fight its battles to the end.

The elements that conspired to perpetrate this horror must not be permitted to pursue their awful campaign of intimidation and terror. Never will the Times cease its warfare against them.

Gen. Otis, the principal owner of the Times, is on his way home from Mexico and will arrive here this afternoon.

The Times has a complete auxiliary plant from which this issue was printed on its own presses.

The management is under great obligations to The Herald for hearty assistance and to the Examiner for friendly offers.

The Times will soon be itself again. All business will be conducted at the Times Branch Office, 531 South Spring street.

A further statement cannot be made at this hour in the presence of frightful death and destruction.

Harry Chandler, assistant general manager of the Times, happened to be on the street when the explosion occurred and immediately took command of the situation.

They can kill our men and can wreck our buildings, but by the God above they cannot kill The Times.

HARRY E. ANDREWS,
Managing Editor of The Times.

CHIEF'S STATEMENT

OUT OF THE JAWS OF DEATH

All Business for THE TIMES Will be Transacted at Their Branch Office 531 SOUTH SPRING ST.

N. Y. DEMOCRATS SELECT DIX FOR STANDARD BEARER

State Chairman Finally Agrees to Run for Governor of the Empire State

FULL TICKET IS NOMINATED

When Independence League Is Mentioned It Is Greeted with a Storm of Hisses

WINSLOW HOMER, NOTED ARTIST, DIES, AGED 74

The *Times* uses the editorial offices of the *Herald* and an auxiliary printing plant to report on its own destruction on the morning of October 1, 1910. COURTESY HUNTINGTON LIBRARY, ART COLLECTIONS AND BOTANICAL GARDENS

Arriving back in Los Angeles from a formal trip to Mexico, General Otis was immediately driven to the wrecked Times Building, where he immediately took command.

FUNERAL AND MEMORIAL SERVICE
FOR VICTIMS OF TIMES DISASTER
SUNDAY OCTOBER 9, 1910 AT 2 P. M.

ADMIT BEARER TO RESERVED SECTION

AT AUDITORIUM AND SPECIAL CARS

TO HOLLYWOOD CEMETERY

AND RETURN

The mass burial at Hollywood Cemetery on October 9, 1910. Many of the victims could not be identified. The large floral piece is a reproduction of the Times Building.

The Pacific Mutual
Life Insurance Company
(of Los Angeles)

immediately pays $6000 under
an Accident Policy, upon the
simple statement of the
"Times" foreman that the
policyholder was in the building at the time of the fire.

This policy doubled from $3,000 to $6,000 because death occurred in a burning building and the annual premium was only $15.00

In the program for a charity show to benefit the bombing victims and their families, a life insurance company took out an ad displaying a replica of a check that it had written to the widow of a *Times* worker for $6,000, a double indemnity payout, it noted, "because death occurred in a burning building."

The program for a benefit to raise funds for the *Times* victims and their families. The five-hour vaudeville show concluded with acts by Piquo, the Acrobatic Clown, followed by Helen Bertram, "Prima Donna Soprano."

A Junior Tattoo New Haven alarm clock of the type used in the bombers' infernal machines.

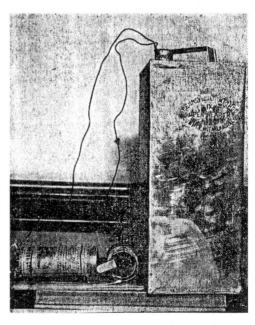

The unexploded infernal machine attached to a can of nitroglycerin discovered at the Lucas Iron Works in Peoria in September 1910. It was the first clue in the trail that led to the dynamiters.

Chapter 23

From the moment that Ortie McManigal walked out the door of his Chicago home carrying his suitcase and hunting weapons, he had been shadowed by W. J. Ots, an operative for William Burns's detective agency. Ots bought a ticket on the train that took McManigal to Kenosha; he was standing nearby when McManigal and Sharp returned to the station to meet J. B. McNamara's train and heard McManigal introduce McNamara to Sharp as "Frank Sullivan, an old friend of mine." When the trio bought their train tickets to Conover, Wisconsin, Ots did the same, stopping to make a phone call to a colleague after he did so. Now, at Conover, some 250 miles deep into the northern woods near the border of the upper peninsula of Michigan, Ots was joined by three other Burns detectives who bought hunting gear and rented a cabin in the woods. J. B. McNamara remained as nervous as a hunted stag. The trip into the wilderness country had not calmed him as he had hoped. In the morning, after provisioning, he and Ortie headed out by foot to the hunting camp three miles from town on Pioneer Lake where Ortie had rented a cabin. There J. B. delivered a detailed account of his expeditions to San Francisco and Los Angeles.

"We gave them a real good cleaning out," he boasted. His listener simply stared at him. And McNamara's mood suddenly descended again. "I am sorry so many were killed," he moaned. "I wish now that I hadn't done it, and if it was to do over again, I wouldn't do it either. . . . If they ever catch me, they'll take me back to Los Angeles and hang me without a trial."

But then, after a few moments of silence: "I hoped to get General Otis."

There was no predicting the mood swings of J. B. McNamara during that hunting trip. On November 9 McManigal awoke to find McNamara gone. He picked up his rifle and set out to look for deer. He was climbing onto a tree stump when he heard the crack of a pistol and a bullet whizz by his ear. He leaped down, glanced across a gully, and spotted J. B., wearing a red hunting cap, as was required by Wisconsin law, and aiming a rifle in his direction. J. B. was laughing raucously.

"I was just shooting at a rabbit," he yelled.

McManigal's eyes took in the area around him and landed on the spot where the bullet had hit soft loam. There were no traces of rabbit tracks.

"I think you were taking a shot at me," he yelled back. "If you do, you had better do a good job of it. This is a fine place up here to get rid of a man—just shoot him and the coyotes will eat up his body."

J. B. was now convulsed with laughter. "Oh, no, I was just shooting at a rabbit."

The two men and their hunting companions soon became friendly with a group of four hunters at a nearby campsite dressed in gabardine rather than hunting attire. The other men—one identified himself as a mining engineer; the others, stone cutters—had brought a prodigious supply of food and whiskey with them and formed a particularly tight friendship with J. B. One of the men had also brought along a Kodak Brownie camera and snapped a photo of J. B. posing with the group. They often invited him to join them for dinner at the Conover home of Tessie Steinmetz, who took table boarders.

One evening at dinner, the mining engineer claimed that he had once witnessed a big girder fall twenty feet and not even get a kink in it.

The next day, after J. B. returned to his campsite, he went for a walk in the woods with McManigal and told him about the engineer's remark.

"He can't get by me with any stories like that, and I told him so."

McManigal, who was suspicious of the men from the day they all arrived together, exploded. "You damn fool," he shouted at J. B., "I suppose you've been drunk and telling them all you know. How do you know but that they are detectives?"

J. B. refused to believe that his new friends could be detectives, but after receiving the dressing-down McManigal had delivered, it did seem to him now that the campers were always trying to get him to pose for pictures with them. On one occasion one of them attempted to take a snapshot of J. B. posing with a girlfriend he had picked up. It was a dreary day, and J. B. advised the man to set the Brownie for a time exposure. When the detective snapped the shutter, J. B. moved his head slightly so that his face would be blurred.

On another occasion, J. B. himself secretly adjusted the Brownie to "time." But when he inspected it again later, he noticed that the camper had reset the lever back to "snapshot." He moved it back again.

On yet another occasion, while reprovisioning in Conover with J. B., the Burns men were approached by a local girl McNamara had dated, who asked if one of the detectives would take a picture of her with Sullivan. While J. B. demurred, feigning shyness, the girl insisted that a picture of her two-year-old daughter be taken with her boyfriend holding the child in his arms. In a single abrupt motion, the girl handed the toddler over and stood at J. B.'s side in an impromptu family-like pose. Not quite believing his sudden luck, the detective took a few steps back and steadied his camera. The hapless J. B. found himself trapped with his girlfriend's child squirming in his lap as the detective quickly counted down: "On three. One, two . . ." And on "three," J. B. once again moved his head.

Later in the afternoon the detective slipped off to the telegraph office in the Conover General Store and wired Burns that he would be sending the roll of negatives along in the morning mail. An elated Burns received and developed the film. Although the picture of J. B. was indeed badly blurred, Burns thought, it was clear enough for the San Francisco witnesses. Judging from their descriptions, he felt certain that he was looking at the man who had called himself J. B. Bryce and had gone on to bomb the *Times*.

On still another occasion, J. B. was invited by the Burns men to their cabin for breakfast. He arrived bleary-eyed, his hands trembling. During the meal he told his friends that he had been drinking too much with them and that he needed to dry out. He was hoping to put a fishing party together and hike to Scott Lake, six miles south of Conover, where he knew he could not get any liquor.

"I'm drinking too much because I'm worrying too much," he confided to his friends.

"What was the good of worrying?" one of them asked.

"That's all I have done for a month is worry," J. B. replied, "and I am going to cut it out. It does not get anyone anything. What is done cannot be undone."

Ots wired back to William Burns that J. B. "seems worried and told me he has lost about ten pounds in the last month but passed it off by saying he guessed he wasn't drinking enough out here."

J. B. was in fact a drunken emotional wreck.

The trip to the lake never materialized. On the contrary, J. B. began spending more time at the Steinmetz home in Conover, getting loaded on booze. One day he told McManigal that he was going into town because he was expecting a letter from his brother. He did not return to the camp for three days.

On November 26 one of the campers who had befriended J. B. arrived at the Steinmetz house for a meal and, as he approached, saw the two Steinmetz children, Marguerite, sixteen, and Alice, fourteen, racing out of the house, screaming. People in the general store and the post office, hearing the commotion, ran outside to see what was causing it. The two girls ran to the camper and told him that everyone in the house was fighting and that "Sullivan" (J. B. McNamara) had drawn his revolver.

The camper would later write: "I ran into the house, entering through the sitting-room, as I knew they were in the kitchen. I remained in the dining room and looked through the window into the kitchen and saw Mrs. Steinmetz receive a blow in the jaw from Sullivan as she was holding her husband. Sullivan also punched him in the jaw and ear, cutting both places. Sullivan was very drunk. He then rolled over on the floor for a nap. At 4:30 the section foreman pulled out the hand car to take Sullivan back to his camp. He got him to the station, but he fell forward on his face, making his nose bleed. He went back to the Steinmetz house. He was taken upstairs and put to bed."

The following morning, the camper again called at the Steinmetz home and found J. B. off on a new bender with two boarders. He invited them all to his cabin.

By afternoon the commotion in the cabin attracted the attention of Ortie McManigal, who wandered over to see what the noise was all about. The cabin door was open, and when McManigal looked in, he saw J. B., well boozed, shouting unintelligibly as his friends filled his glass. (Said McManigal later: "When I saw J. B. in the company of the detectives [he had little doubt who they were], I thought the game was up.")

McManigal vented his outrage at McNamara the next day. He had been assigned by J. J. to look after him, and instead J. B. had put himself in greater danger, he told him. Who were these men who were always liquoring him up but drinking little themselves? Why were they still camping out in the woods in late November when everyone else had long left? Why hadn't they bagged a single deer?

J. B. responded to none of this. He told McManigal that at the post office he had "heard good news and I had to celebrate" and then walked over to the Steinmetz home and "I drank every drop they had in the house."

It is not difficult to surmise what sort of "good news" J. B. McNamara had received at the post office. Life, his brother had probably written, had returned to normal in Indianapolis. News reports from Los Angeles were indicating that the trail of the dynamiters had gone cold. William J. Burns had apparently disappeared off the face of the earth after pocketing a veritable fortune from the city, reports had said. So confident were J. J. and Tveitmoe in San Francisco in these recent developments that they were now calling for a resumption of the bombing campaign in Los Angeles.

J. B. and McManigal tied one on around the campfire that night, relieved by the news from Indianapolis. Then, in the small hours of morning, J. B., Ortie, and their three friends quietly arose, packed their clothes and hunting weapons, and sauntered away from the smoldering campfire, vanishing into the cold mist of the northern woodlands.

Burns's men awoke at dawn to a quiet hunting camp. They casually walked over to the neighboring cabin but saw that the bombers were gone—and so were most of their things. Alarmed, they hurriedly walked the three miles back to town, where they asked the townspeople about the Sullivan party's whereabouts. No one had seen them. The day passed, and there was still no sign of their neighbors.

Once the realization had fully sunk in, the two detectives strode into the telegraph office in the Conover General Store and reported to their stunned boss in Chicago the exasperating news.

Ortie McManigal and J. B. McNamara were back in circulation.

Chapter 24

Had authorities in Los Angeles been aware that William Burns had Ortie McManigal and J. B. McNamara in his clutches and let them slip away, they would have been outraged—perhaps justifiably so. After all, they might have argued, Burns now had in his possession an entire catalogue of material evidence, an army of witnesses, volumes of fingerprints and handwriting samples. All that was needed were the bombers themselves, whom his men could have arrested at any moment had they been given the order. Even McManigal and McNamara, who had been vaguely suspicious of their hunting companions, had reasoned that if they were really out to nab them, they would have acted long ago.

So why indeed hadn't Burns ordered his men to handcuff the two dynamiters and haul them back to Los Angeles to face charges?

"I wasn't ready to strike yet," Burns would later claim, "not by a long shot. There were certain phases about this case, certain peculiar situations which comprised its background, that convinced me that arrests at that particular time would be most inopportune."

The implication was clear: Arresting a couple of henchmen would have alerted the higher-ups who had employed them, and Burns had reason to believe they held positions in the highest levels of the union movement. Premature arrests would only have served to alert them, allowing them to clear out their records, dispose of remaining evidence, and make the case that the two men his detectives had been tracking were merely rogues whose activities were not just officially sanctioned but deplored.

Burns would write: "I was satisfied that J. J. McNamara, sooner or later, would personally participate in these dynamitings, and I had in mind all the while that it would take evidence of the very strongest and most conclusive character to convict him, because of the fact that he was a lawyer and he occupied an important position—that of secretary and treasurer of the International Union."

On November 25, 1910, Burns suddenly returned to Los Angeles after more than a month's disappearance without so much as a single letter or report or telephone call to Mayor Alexander. He audaciously showed up at the mayor's home incognito and hat in hand, requesting the $5,000 of promised funds for investigative services that he claimed to have rendered. He offered the mayor no written report, only a few blurry photographs of a man in the Wisconsin woods who Burns claimed was the suspect who had blown up the Times Building.

The *Times* duly reported the meeting, noting that the mayor "admitted yesterday that he had seen the detective Tuesday morning, and that he had paid him a large sum for his services and expenses up to date."

Earl Rogers erupted. "What were the taxpayers getting for their money?" he asked Alexander. "What evidence was the Burns investigation producing?"

The mayor couldn't cite any specific pieces of evidence—other than the photographs. Rogers promptly fired off a message to Burns, asking him to make copies of the photos and send them to him. When he received them, he mixed one of the photos with about a dozen of other men and showed them to Lena Ingersoll. She had no problem selecting the correct photo.

"That's the man," she told Rogers. "His name is James Bryce."

Burns himself showed the same photos to Kurt Diekelman, the desk clerk at the Baltimore Hotel on East Fifth Street near the Southern Pacific train station. Diekelman vividly remembered the man who had arrived the day prior to the bombing, struggling with two heavy suitcases but refusing to allow the bellboy to help him. He had checked out just hours before the explosion.

Diekelman positively identified the man in the photos too.

Nevertheless, photos of a man in the woods linking him to a bombing suspect using an alias seemed like a scanty return for the thousands of dollars that the city had dispensed to Burns. The city council forthwith demanded that the Burns Agency provide daily reports on the investigation from that moment on. Moreover, it said, it would provide no additional funds to the World Famous Sleuth, thereby seeming to insist on a bargain that made absolutely no sense—daily reports in exchange for nothing.

When Burns got word of the action, he appeared dumbfounded. He declined the new conditions but was still free to pursue the reward as he pleased—which ostensibly meant that he would have to continue the investigation at his own expense. The upside of that option was that he could continue to keep the evidence he had gathered confidential.

Burns's relentless insistence on secrecy was based on straightforward financial considerations.

Rogers was essentially working on the case for a salary from the city; Burns, primarily for reward money. Salaries were reliable; reward money, notoriously otherwise—often withdrawn when claims for them were made, and almost always challenged. (While Burns could continue to bill the McClintock-Marshall Company for his services—and did—it was only liable for his investigations that could be shown to be directly related to the Peoria bombings.) He thereupon began financing the investigation using his own resources—first underwriting it out of his own pocket, then borrowing additional funds from friends in order to complete the investigation. It would cost him the equivalent of more than a half million dollars in today's currency before his work was over. But Burns was confident of the outcome.

"I knew that our operatives were watching the right rat holes," he would say years later, "and I intended to keep them there as long as I could raise the money to pay their wages."

After pulling up stakes at their Wisconsin campgrounds, Ortie McManigal and J. B. McNamara headed back to Chicago. McManigal was able to reunite with his wife and children, while J. B. tried to unwind. But Chicago was also the home base of the Burns Detective Agency, and one day while J. B. was walking near McManigal's home, he spotted one of the hunters. The man greeted him warmly, acting as if it were all a coincidence. Perhaps it was; perhaps it was not. J. B. figured that somehow he had been tracked down. Still, days went by and neither McNamara nor McManigal came across any of the hunters again.

On December 6 the two men reported to J. J. McNamara in Indianapolis and gave him an account of their hunting trip. J. B. told him how he had run into one of the strange-acting hunters on the street in Chicago.

J. J. appeared elated at the news. The half-smile that he wore perpetually widened into a grin. If the World Famous Sleuth had any hard evidence against his brother and McManigal, he figured, they would have been in his custody by now. That they had been allowed to come and go as they pleased indicated to him that Burns had nothing.

Nevertheless—just in case—he now had a plan that would cast all suspicion away from his brother. Since J. B. was likely the suspect in the Los Angeles bombing, he wanted him now to hide in plain sight—allowing the detectives to follow him, while McManigal would go to Los Angeles and set off a new series of explosions. Tveitmoe, it seems, was requesting a "Christmas present" in the form of bombings at Baker Iron Works, Llewellyn Iron Works, and the *Los Angeles Times*'s auxiliary plant.

Shutting down the *Times* was still the principal aim of the San Francisco gang. As McManigal would later recall, J. J. McNamara displayed no misgivings about the original employee fatalities. He ordered McManigal: "Put a good mess of it under the *Times*'s auxiliary plant, and add a few more to the list of dead. They've been questioning Tveitmoe and Johannsen out there [in San Francisco], and we'll throw them off the track."

J. B. seemed relieved, if not downright thrilled, by his older brother's tough-mindedness—in particular, because he now realized he had J. J.'s unequivocal blessing and support. Both brothers possessed only rudimentary acquaintance with radical socialism, but both shared similar beliefs about what it would take for workers to make real progress in a society dominated by wealthy capitalists. Like himself, J. B. must have thought, J. J. understood the larger issue—that in the battle for the working man, the only thing that could lead to victory was the use of unsparing force. And if some workers needed to be sacrificed for the common good—well, that was an inexorable part of any great struggle.

Ortie McManigal was motivated by no such social conscience. He had taken care throughout his dynamiting career to avoid injuring workers, and he had nearly always been successful. He knew that many of them were, as he had been, family men just scraping by to support the wives and children they loved. It was one thing for him to destroy buildings and bridges on orders from his union; it was quite another to destroy lives.

He was wary even of traveling to Los Angeles barely nine weeks after the *Times* bombing. Certainly, he thought, police there would have been ordered to be especially vigilant. Private security measures would have been redoubled. The city would still be on tenterhooks.

"That's a hell of a trip," McManigal remarked, clearly ruffled. J. J. ignored him.

On December 9 McManigal boarded a train for his longest trip yet, his suitcase holding twelve quarts of nitroglycerin. He arrived at the Santa Fe station four days later and headed directly to a nearby gravel pit on the Los Angeles River that he had spotted as the train pulled into town, where he buried his explosives. He spent the next few days playing the part of the tourist, relaxing in the sunny, dry December weather, which illuminated his mood.

Only at night did McManigal's attention return to business, engaging in a very different kind of sightseeing. He set out first to locate the Llewellyn Iron Works. J. B. McNamara had already cased the building but had given him only the most general directions to find it. He had told him to walk north to where the east-to-west streets bore names instead of numbers. He walked past First Street and finally found it at the corner of Redondo and Main Streets. At night the grounds where the service tracks entered the property hardly seemed to be patrolled at all. It was a different story at the Baker Iron Works. It took him days to find the plant; then, to his dismay, he discovered that it was heavily guarded around the clock. It would be impossible for him to access any area of the property where explosives could wreak extensive damage. That left the *Los Angeles Times*'s auxiliary plant. "They were setting up a new press there at the time. I had a long talk with the watchman. I looked the place over and decided it was too well guarded to do anything there."

He waited until Christmas Eve before returning to the Llewellyn plant. He figured that on that night the few guards who ordinarily would have been stationed at the plant might have been given the night off. At about 7:30 p.m., under cover of nightfall and the overcast skies, McManigal carried a suitcase containing three infernal machines and two quarts of nitroglycerin onto the grounds of the Llewellyn Iron Works. As he crept through the darkness laden with the delicate materiel, he slipped on the icy ground and "slid for some distance," causing one of the fulminating caps to explode spontaneously, injuring his hand. "That put me out of humor," he would say later. Still, the remainder of his supply had not gone off in the fall, and McManigal thought to himself, "Certainly I was not born to be blown up."

He decided at that moment to use all twelve quarts of the nitroglycerin on the Llewellyn job and drop the other two assignments altogether.

"I left my grip [suitcase] in the right place," he would say later—a critical area near the center of the building. "There was enough nitroglycerin there to plane the place." He then set the alarm clock to go off at two o'clock on Christmas morning. Tveitmoe's Christmas present thus delivered, McManigal returned to his room at the Rosslyn Hotel, where he was registered under the name of J. M. McKee, packed his belongings, paid his bill, and was aboard the Southern Pacific Valley train by 9:00 p.m., on his way to San Francisco.

The following morning the Junior Tattoo alarm clock rang on schedule, triggering a massive explosion that tore a hole in the Llewellyn Iron Works and injured a night watchman when a fragment of plummeting debris severed the tendons of his right hand. Otherwise McManigal's bomb had done what it was intended to do. No one had died, and in annihilating itself, the device was eliminated as a source of evidence. However, it had failed to level the plant. McManigal, the explosives expert, would later explain, "There was no force to prevent it from expanding. That is the reason it only damaged the plant."

Nevertheless, the city of Los Angeles was gripped by fear and panic again. Many people remained at home on Christmas Day rather than attend church or visit friends—afraid that the terrorists might strike again.

While the Llewellyn plant still smoldered, the *Times* fulminated. "Smitten by a bomb of terrible power, placed at a vulnerable point by hands long trained to such coward's work," it editorialized, "the Llewellyn Iron Works had bidden a brave defiance to the enemies that stab in the dark and run." In other words, the building remained standing. "Another chapter in the history of an attempted reign of industrial terror has been written," it continued. "Skulkers in dark places once more have tried to strike fear into the hearts of independent employers through a blow at their own stronghold. Once again they have failed."

That law-enforcement authorities and the city's government appeared impotent in the face of continued terrorism was a fact that further enraged the *Times:* "The city council appropriated a large sum of money to ferret out the dynamiters and has spent thousands of dollars (mostly paid to William J. Burns)—and to what avail? Fellow citizens, what are you going to do about it? . . . The *Times* will suggest that certain undesirables should be driven out of the city and kept out."

As fate would have it, there was no need to drive Ortie McManigal out of the city. He was spending Christmas Day seeing the sights of San Francisco.

In the late afternoon of December 26, Ortie McManigal dropped by the Union Labor Temple in San Francisco to pay a call on Olaf Tveitmoe— "the big chief," as he called him—and Eugene Clancy. Tveitmoe, he was told, was not expected, but he did find Clancy, whom he had never met. McManigal was in such high spirits on this day that he decided to play a practical joke on the union leader. Pretending to be a police detective, he told Clancy, "I've come to get the Los Angeles dynamiters." Clancy paled. McManigal roared with laughter, introduced himself, and told Clancy, "Tell the old man [Tveitmoe] his Christmas present has been delivered."

McManigal was back in Chicago in time to ring in the New Year with his wife and children.

Two weeks later he received a call from J. J. McNamara, who wanted Ortie down in Indianapolis as soon as he could get there.

McManigal had no way of knowing that he was heading in a direct route to trouble—not from the law but from his boss. J. J. McNamara met him at the train station in Indianapolis in a fit of fury. He told McManigal that he had gone to great expense to send him on a round-trip to Los Angeles and San Francisco. He had also paid him a large fee for his assignment. He had paid for the nitroglycerin as well as the hardware for the infernal machines. And what had McManigal delivered in exchange? A hole blown in the side of one building. And that appeared to be such a botched job that some local newspapers were openly theorizing that it could not have possibly been carried out by the same men who had blown up the *Times*.

He also demanded to know "why in hell" he had made no attempt on the *Times*'s auxiliary plant. "You should have gotten a bunch of that soup in the *Times* and given them a shaking up."

"My God, it did not look good to me," McManigal replied. "It looked like suicide."

J. J.'s assault took McManigal aback, especially since he had nearly blown himself up in the operation. The Llewellyn brothers had been delivered a pointed message, and unionist morale on the West Coast was once again on the up-tick after the murderously feckless disaster J. J.'s brother had pulled off three months earlier. But the tirade was revelatory to McManigal, for it underlined the reckless extremes to which J. J. was willing to go less than three months after the *Los Angeles Times* disaster. Indeed, it gave him an altogether different perspective of the man who conducted the bombing operations. Until now, J. J. McNamara had seemed like a cool, confident operator to McManigal. There was that half-smile. There was that roguish charm even as he carefully calculated his every word for the desired effect. The bombings were nothing more than a strategic response to heedless corporate wrongdoing, he would say. But now, for the first time, McManigal saw on McNamara's angry face the wild eyes of a certifiable fanatic.

As he and McNamara walked away from the train station, McManigal made it clear that he wasn't about to tolerate McNamara's temper, saying, "You were lucky to have had an explosion there at all." At this point, J. J. checked himself, repeating only that the union had spent too much money for too little damage. He then changed the drift of the conversation and asked about the state of the *Times* investigation, whether things had cooled down in Los Angeles.

Far from it, McManigal grimly reported, the investigation was in the process of becoming fully nationalized. In fact, just a few days earlier in a Chicago saloon he had seen a wanted poster for the three dynamiters (Caplan, Schmidt, and "Bryce").

J. J. McNamara was not a man to dwell on unhappy news. Instead he presented a new tactical policy for future bombings. Henceforth, dynamite alone would be used; nitroglycerin was out. Furthermore, the dynamite would be stolen, thus eliminating the generation of sales records. All identifying markings on the sticks were to be cut off. J. J. also proposed a bold new plan of action that included a new modus operandi—the mail bomb, which would be addressed to the homes and offices of various non-union industrialists around the country.

McManigal saw the wisdom of using stolen dynamite. Delivering bombs by mail, however, was madness. Packages were delivered by train, which could easily detonate the dynamite en route, killing trainloads of innocent people. And who knew if a child might open up a package. A long-standing campaign of this sort would inevitably produce more outraged Americans than newly tamed industrialists. In the end, McNamara agreed with him.

So dynamite was needed, and dynamite would be got, chiefly by pilfering it from stone quarries, as their grade tended to be some of the most powerful manufactured. The first target in McManigal's hunt would be Nat France's stone quarry outside Bloomville, Ohio, since he knew it well. In a laborious process over the course of several days in January 1911, McManigal made off with more than a half ton of dynamite, creeping into the quarry by night, removing the dynamite, and transporting it to a hiding place behind his father's house ten miles away in Tiffin.

When he was finished, McManigal tossed a few of the sticks into his suitcase and headed back to Indianapolis. He lugged his samples into the union headquarters and walked up the stairs to the office of J. J. McNamara, who now welcomed him with open arms. When he told J. J. that he had made off with 1,200 pounds, the union executive seemed impressed.

The next day McNamara and McManigal returned to Ohio, retrieved the 1,200 pounds of dynamite, loaded it onto a horse-drawn wagon, and transported it back to Indiana. They then drove to a farmhouse near Indianapolis owned by T. P. Jones, who had advertised in the newspaper that he had a barn for rent. Jones stood silently at the door while the two well-dressed strangers whispered to one another as they carefully inspected the place. Finally McManigal and McNamara explained to Jones that they had several cases of union records that they needed to store, and that his barn would provide the perfect place for them. A deal was struck in Jones's farmhouse, Jones handed McNamara a key to the barn door, and the two men headed back to their vehicle. As they walked away, McManigal suddenly turned to the farmer and asked, "Do any children play around the barn?"

"No," the farmer replied. "No children."

"Fine," said McManigal cheerily as he and J. J. departed.

A few days later, an enormous piano box containing the half ton of union "records" was delivered to the barn.

Thus opened a new chapter in the nationwide dynamite campaign. Operations resumed with McManigal busily planting infernal machines in Midwest cities between January and March. In mid-March, McManigal happened across J. B. in Indianapolis, looking as happy and healthy as he'd been before the *Los Angeles Times* bombing.

"I've got the mess in this suitcase for the French Lick job," he said cheerfully. Indeed, a few days later, on March 20, 1911, the new addition to the French Lick Springs Hotel being built by an open-shop construction company eighty-nine miles south of Indianapolis exploded in the night. J. B. McNamara was his old self with a vengeance.

So business as usual had resumed for the two dynamiters. Yet, despite J. J. McNamara's dismissive assertions that the authorities would surely have arrested them if they had been able to pin anything on them, both men inexplicably sensed from time to time that they were being shadowed. As ambiguous as the feeling was, it was also undeniable. J. J. scoffed at what he regarded as their paranoia, insisting—with very little evidence—that the investigation was utterly stymied.

But the two men decided to put their suspicions to the test. They would suddenly turn a corner, then hide and wait to see if anyone also came around. They would walk long distances on streets that they ordinarily did not frequent, glancing behind them. They would jump on a streetcar, ride a short distance, then get off and travel in another direction in another car, watching to see if anyone else made the same trip. Their tests proved to be useless.

But of course they were being followed. Burns would say later that the first maneuver he taught a new operative was tailing. "It's what good palming is to sleight of hand. It's the thing the operative has to learn before he can move on a case at all. He has to learn to follow a man on the street, in railroad trains, on streetcars, in hotels, picking him up and dropping him and picking him up again, without ever really losing sight of him and without ever being seen or suspected himself. We kept track of McManigal and Jim McNamara in that way for months."

In April McManigal returned to Indianapolis after having cased a job in Detroit. Upon entering the union offices in the American Central Life Insurance Building, he spotted J. J. in the lobby. Then, glancing behind him, he noticed another man, someone who seemed maddeningly familiar but whose face he could not place, someone who had perhaps been on the train from Detroit. Cautiously he approached the union's secretary-treasurer and remarked, "J. J. McNamara, you can say what you please, but there's a man behind me right now." McManigal glanced over in the direction of the elevator where he had seen the suspicious character a moment before, but there was no one there now. J. J. followed his gaze, then turned to McManigal and remarked, his half-smile playing over his face, "Guilty conscience."

In spite of his skepticism, J. J. decided to remove the remaining dynamite that he kept stored in the union offices and transfer it to a storage room in the basement of the building. It was a strangely anxious and wearying task, secretly ferrying explosives down the elevator, as only a few sticks could be moved at a time. But it was necessary. Should detectives suddenly storm through the door waving warrants, searching in file cabinets and closets, they would find not a trace of evidence.

Now, as he sat in his office suite overlooking the booming city of Indianapolis, the task completed, J. J. McNamara must have thought that he was home free.

Chapter 25

The new round of bombings of 1911 was making news across the country. But news was all it made. The campaign wasn't resonating in the American public's mind nor in the industrial community's—particularly in Los Angeles, where union organizational activity was being thwarted with renewed zeal by General Otis, the MMA, and the city council. Industry had simply begun to discount this commonplace, low-grade terrorism as one of the costs of doing business. The city's return to a placid normalcy infuriated J. J. McNamara. What was needed, he now concluded, was to deliver a crippling blow that would bring industrialist America to its knees,

Emboldened by the fact that his union had now been able to pull off nearly two hundred bombings successfully, McNamara summoned his brother and Ortie McManigal to a meeting on April 7, 1911, and described his most ambitious—and lunatic—scheme yet.

It was a plan to destroy the entire city of Los Angeles.

He would send both J. B. and McManigal there and have them plant a number of infernal machines along the new aqueduct under construction and principal water mains. They would be set to go off simultaneously. A few minutes later, a number of fires would be ignited in key locations all over town, set off by timing devices. Without water to put them out, said J. J., "the whole scab city would be wiped off the map."

A second scheme was more grandiose still—and, to McManigal, even more harebrained.

In the spring of 1911, the Panama Canal was in its latter stages of construction, the main contractor of which was the McClintock-Marshall Company. J. J.'s plan was to dispatch McManigal to Panama and, while there, steal a magazine of construction dynamite and dump it into one of the canal locks.

McManigal protested that there would probably be too many guards on duty.

J. J. had that figured out, too: McManigal would enlist in the US Army and request to be detailed to Panama.

That wouldn't work either, protested McManigal; an enlisted man had nothing to say about where he was detailed. J. J. was not dissuaded. Irritably he said, "Well, go down anyway and put it in by the wagon load."

McManigal was not confident that he could even pull off another bombing close to home. He told J. J. that he and his wife had recently been hunting for a new home in Chicago and that they both felt certain that they were being followed closely from house to house.

J. J. remarked that he had a scheme to get rid of Burns himself: McManigal would rent a room next to Burns's Chicago office, place a bomb in his desk, run an electric wire from the bomb between the two rooms, and when Burns sat down at his desk, all McManigal would have to do would be to plug the wire into a socket. And then he wouldn't have to dodge any more detectives.

McManigal would have none of it and quietly left.

Three days later on April 10, J. J. McNamara telephoned McManigal to tell him that the union's executive council was about to hold its quarterly meeting. He wanted both McManigal and J. B. to go to Detroit together and pull off five assigned jobs to impress the council with what he had been doing. He told McManigal: "You've got to get out and pull off something to make the boys feel good when they get here."

That was the kind of work McManigal was comfortable doing. And he knew Detroit well. It was, in fact, where his dynamiting career had begun four years earlier.

On that same day, McManigal's wife sat down with her favorite fortune-teller in Chicago. The clairvoyant described to the woman an unsettling vision of her husband being followed by police. In her vision McManigal drew a pistol and shot himself. Mrs. McManigal was terrified. Could such a thing be prevented? Should she tell her husband what the fortune-teller had foreseen? No, she concluded, he would not like it if he knew she was spending money on fortune-tellers. She would tell him that she had had a dream in which she herself saw the same scene. Mrs. McManigal told the fortune-teller about her plan, paid her, and left.

A few minutes later Malcolm McLaren, an adroit veteran operative of the Burns agency, paid a visit to the fortune-teller, took the seat Emma McManigal had just vacated, and offered to pay for information about Mrs. McManigal. The woman told the detective about the "vision" she had described. And how, the detective asked, did she come up with such a story? Well, the woman admitted, she knew that the husband lived a mysterious life, and so she had "taken a chance on the story of the police and McManigal." The Burns operative paid the fortune-teller for the consultation and left.

━◦━

"I decided that we had all the evidence we needed and couldn't get any more without an expenditure that I couldn't afford to make," Burns would later tell a reporter. Indeed, he was already close to going broke.

The duplicitous Hockin, who was now on Burns's payroll as his principal informant, now revealed to him the plans for a massive bombing operation in Detroit, including the destruction of a new train station that had been built by nonunion labor. On April 11 Burns's son, Raymond, and two Chicago police officers, Guy Biddinger and William Reed, began trailing McManigal and J. B. from the moment they left their homes in Chicago and Cincinnati, respectively, until they arrived in Toledo, where they greeted each other at the train station. The detectives took positions nearby, keeping an eye on them as McManigal pulled out a map, unfolded it, sat down on a bench, and began discussing it with J. B., who leaned over and made some marks on the map with a pencil. After about ten minutes, McManigal folded the map again, and the two men and their tails trooped out of the station and up the street to the Meyerhoff Hotel, where J. B. and McManigal signed the register.

The two officers remained in the Meyerhoff lobby with McManigal and McNamara while Raymond returned to the train station and telephoned his father back in Chicago with the message, "Number one met number two."

"That was the signal to begin," the elder Burns would later relate.

Raymond Burns and the two detectives registered at a hotel directly across the street and from their room on the third floor kept their eyes on the entrance to the Meyerhoff throughout the day. That evening McNamara and McManigal went out to a vaudeville theater together, returning to the Meyerhoff at 11:10 p.m.

At 8:45 a.m. the detectives spotted the two suspects through the glass doors of their hotel sitting in the lobby on rocking chairs, engaged in animated conversation.

About an hour later the pair checked out of the hotel and walked out into the street, carrying their suitcases. At 10:30 they boarded their train, with the Burns men and Chicago police following right behind.

The train was crowded with travelers, who included women and children—and the detectives, eying the bulky suitcases carried by the men, decided to delay an arrest. Their prey, they thought, just might decide to escape, or put up a fight.

As the train pulled into Detroit, McManigal and J. B., seated in opposite chairs, pressed their heads against the train window, pointing out various bridges and buildings in the distance to one another and discussing them.

The train arrived at the Detroit terminal at 12:25 p.m., and as the two men disembarked, they hesitated on the station platform for a while, scrutinizing the other people getting off. They then picked up their heavy bags and exited, their two shadows right behind. Down the street from the station, they entered the Oxford Hotel and identified themselves at the desk as G. Foster and F. Caldwell of Cleveland. The desk clerk informed them that their room was not available at the moment, that they would have to return later. The men responded angrily, but the clerk was insistent—he had no rooms available. He could, however, accommodate them by checking their bags. After receiving claim checks, they elbowed their way through a large theatrical troupe that was crowding the lobby, J. B. leading the way. As he reached the front door, Raymond Burns pressed against McManigal, and at the same moment clamped handcuffs on his wrist.

J. B. turned and shouted, "Well, what the hell's the matter?" At which point the two detectives. shoved revolvers against him and cuffed him too. "What's this for?" he demanded.

One of the detectives informed him that they were being arrested on a charge of safe-cracking committed in Chicago the previous Saturday. McManigal admitted that he had been in Chicago that Saturday but insisted that he had been shopping with his wife and children on State Street all day.

"So you think I kicked in a jug on Saturday night, do you? Say, bo, you may think you're a wise one, but I'll kill this with an alibi."

J. B. protested that he had been in Cincinnati. They were taken to Detroit police headquarters, where they were duly booked as yeggmen (itinerant burglars).

As it happened, the Burns Agency had in fact been investigating a series of high-profile safe-cracking jobs committed against their new account in Chicago, the American Bankers Association. Making the trumped-up (albeit plausible) charge allowed Burns to conceal the monumental news that he had just arrested two of the men he believed to have been behind the *Los Angeles Times* disaster, thus greatly reducing the chances that J. J. McNamara would begin destroying evidence back in Indianapolis once the arrests were reported.

After the pair were driven off, the Burns detectives returned to the Oxford, where they collected the checked suitcases. Inside they found among the men's personal effects: two revolvers; a rifle fitted with a Maxim silencer; and twelve infernal machines "such as have been used in the bomb outrages," the *New York Times* reported on April 23, 1911, noting that they "had fuses and caps attached and were ready for use." In addition, there were blasting caps, wires, tools, and a battery tester. Meanwhile, at the train station J. B. had spotted a pair of Detroit police officers and began shouting out to them that he and his friend had been kidnapped. His intent, apparently, was to avoid being whisked out of town without being able to get word to his brother of his predicament. But the ploy failed to work.

The Burns men, the Chicago police officers, McNamara, and McManigal drove to a nearby police station, joined by the Detroit officers.

The ploy almost worked. The Chicago officers identified themselves and described the men as fugitives. Did they have an extradition warrant? the Detroit police wanted to know. Somehow they had neglected to obtain one, it turned out. Well, then, McNamara and McManigal would have to remain behind bars in Detroit pending an extradition order—unless, of course, they signed a waiver.

McManigal, confident that he'd beat the Chicago safe-cracking charge and realizing he had all his money in Chicago, readily signed an extradition waiver. J. B. was suspicious and balked, but in the end he signed too, and they returned to the train station, where they took seats in a plush drawing-room car.

Burns watched his captives carefully as they twisted nervously in their seats. "They were both frightened," Burns would later write. "They didn't know what they were really wanted for, and they didn't know how to find out." Burns was pleased with how smoothly the capture had been executed, and he knew his father would be too.

On the train Burns said little himself, just listened as the men talked. Lawmen in those days were not required to inform suspects of their right to remain silent, and J. B. McNamara probably would not have exercised that right anyway. McManigal said practically nothing.

At one point McNamara blurted out, "You fellows don't want me for no [safe] blowing. Why, I never cracked a safe in my life. You want me for a Los Angeles job."

Burns stared blankly at him. But McManigal, who was stretched out on the upper berth above McNamara, reached below and grabbed him by the hair.

"Say, fellow, do you know what you are talking about?" he demanded.

"I know what I'm talking about, you pinhead," he replied.

McManigal let loose of McNamara's hair and dropped back into his berth, remarking as he did so, "All right, if you do, go ahead."

J. B., agitated and single-mindedly aiming to put an end to his detention, began talking about the *Times* bombing, then telling Burns, "We can prove that it was caused by gas. . . . Well, they will never convict me if they take me back to that scabby [expletive deleted] town in California."

Burns continued staring ahead, his silence infuriating McNamara.

J. B. then changed his tack. Invoking the clichéd language of bribers, he told the detectives that he knew they were not fools and knew good money when they saw it.

"All you fellows have your price. Now what is it?"

Burns remained expressionless. But Biddinger told him that it would take a great deal since there were a large number of men who had been involved in the arrests.

McNamara then offered $2,000 to let them go. Burns continued to say nothing. Biddinger scoffed at the amount.

J. B. then began upping the bribe offer. When he reached $20,000, Burns broke his silence to reply that the offer was still not high enough and that it would "have to go too many ways." J. B. tried $30,000.

"How will you raise any such money?" Burns asked.

"Never mind how I'll raise it," J. B. replied. "All you've got to do is to let me get to a telegraph office for ten minutes. If you take me to Chicago it will be too late." He asked for thirty-six hours to reach "the man upstairs" and come up with the bribe money.

With a wave of the hand, Burns turned him down. At which point McNamara blurted out a statement that the Burns men would later report to the press, thereby handing the antiunion industrialists one of their most sensational morsels of propaganda yet in the case.

"You're making the mistake of your life," he said. "Remember, I've got a lot of backing, and if you fellows don't come across, we'll get you, and you, and you," and he pointed threateningly at each of his captors. And now, to compound his strategic blunder, he remarked. "I have got the American Federation of Labor behind me with hundreds of thousands of dollars." Raymond Burns jotted down the remark in his notebook. For decades to come, it would haunt the American labor movement.

In any case, the Burns men had no intention of taking a bribe—no matter how much J. B. offered.

Later during the trip, Ortie McManigal—testing—remarked to one of the detectives, "You don't know anything about me."

Detective Malcolm McLaren replied, "Why I even know where you bought the shoes you've got on."

McManigal laughed nervously. "OK, where did I buy them?"

"At No. 117 State Street, Chicago. They are Walkover shoes, and you bought them on the evening of April 8." A pause, while this little tidbit took effect, and then: "I can even tell you what your wife dreamed the night before you left home."

McManigal stared, challengingly.

"She dreamed that the police were after you, and that you had drawn your pistol, and that you had shot yourself."

The following day, Ortie McManigal confessed.

Chapter 26

Upon their arrival in Chicago, McNamara and McManigal were placed in separate rooms in the three-story home of Sgt. William Reed, one of the Chicago detectives who had participated in the arrests in Detroit. They were taken to the house instead of jail—and kept there incommunicado—so that, in the words of William Burns himself, "we would not have to waste time in fighting habeas corpus proceedings and other obstacles."

At the same time, he sent a telegram to his Los Angeles office, not mentioning the actual names of the pair his men had arrested. "We have under arrest and hidden away here Bryce and John Doe, who did Llewellyn job. Have police department proceed immediately to Sacramento, get requisition [he presumably meant "extradition"] papers on Illinois, and come here quick as possible. We won't let arrest be known here until officers arrive with papers or they would spend hundred thousand dollars on habeas corpus proceedings, and all sorts of trouble; they offered us $30,000 to release them."

When the elder Burns arrived at Reed's Chicago home, he decided to interview J. B. first, since he had been the more talkative one on the train. "I am not an officer of any kind—merely a private detective," he said as he sat down before the *Times* bomber. "I suppose you know who I am."

Much to the World Famous Sleuth's chagrin, J. B. claimed he did not. Burns then introduced himself, whereupon J. B. truculently admitted that he knew all about the famous sleuth, but he wouldn't be getting any confession. He exuded defiance. Burns didn't press the issue.

After all, he had a mountain of evidence against McNamara already. Burns was aware that too many times suspects had successfully claimed in court that they had been tricked into confessing or had been tortured into doing so. He was not about to give McNamara the opportunity to make a similar claim. J. B. sat in silence as Burns turned and left the room.

Burns then called on McManigal, who was in a room down the hall, and "told him that I had seen him say goodbye to his wife and children. I described how he had kissed them, and informed him that there was a good chance that he never would see them again as a free man, and that it was his duty to save them."

He then told McManigal, "Perhaps you feel that because you did not accompany J. B. McNamara to Los Angeles on the occasion of his blowing up the *Times* that you are in no way responsible for his act. On the other hand, when I explain the law of conspiracy, you will find you were equally responsible." Burns explained that if he was in any way connected with a general murder conspiracy, then, under the eyes of the law, he was as guilty of murder as the man who planted the bomb. And he could be executed for that crime.

Burns could almost hear the gears in McManigal's mind grinding in the silence. "Now, I can't promise you anything—no immunity whatever," he concluded. "But you've got to decide what you'll do. If you want to talk to me, just let me know."

With that Burns was gone.

McManigal was left sitting in the small room, brooding over the possibility of never again being with his wife and children. His career as a well-paid unionist bomber was over of course. Regardless of what would happen to him in court, he realized that he would never again be able to resume the life he had been leading.

Unlike J. J. McNamara, McManigal had no fanatical concern about the cause of organized labor. Unlike J. B. McNamara, he was not driven by a deep-seated hostility toward capitalist society. He had been roped into the conspiracy, he realized, but he also knew that he had lacked the courage to cut the rope, even as he lived many days of his life with dynamite at his side. But what could he have done? Quitting the union would have been suicide. Now, to remain loyal to it could be equally fatal.

Twenty minutes after Burns left the room, McManigal arrived at his decision. He stood up, took a long look around the small room, and then got the attention of the detective standing guard outside the door.

Seconds later, William Burns's telephone rang in his office. The guard at the other end spoke the words Burns had expected to hear.

"He says he wants to talk to you," the detective said.

"All right, tell him I'll be right over."

Burns, however, saw fit to let McManigal simmer awhile, and he attended to some paperwork, allowing an hour to slip by. Then the telephone rang for a second time.

"He wants to know why you don't come up," the detective said.

"All right," Burns replied, then remarked again, "tell him I'll be right over." But he made no move to leave his desk. Yet another hour passed, and the telephone rang again.

"Say, when are you coming up?" the detective asked. "This man's getting nervous."

Another hour passed before Burns arrived at Sergeant Reed's home. When he finally entered McManigal's room, he was, according to the detective, "ready to hug me," saying, "I know it's all up with me. You've got me right. It's no use me trying to conceal the truth any longer."

Shortly after midnight, that night of April 14, 1911, a stenographer arrived at the Chicago detective's modest home. Ortie sat across from Burns and in his soft, almost lilting, voice told his story from its beginning in the quarries of central Ohio to its end in a crowded hotel in Detroit, accompanied by the syncopated tapping of the stenographer's dictation machine. At times Burns would break in, prompting McManigal for more details, but the interruptions were infrequent, and McManigal's tale gushed out unhindered. Four hours later his voice and the stenographer's tapping ceased. For a very long moment, Burns blankly stared across the table at McManigal, who finally spoke again.

"I don't want to hang," McManigal said. "I just want what's best for my wife and babies."

Burns believed him. He would later write: "Preying on his mind all the time was the thought of his wife and children and their fate. He was genuinely disturbed about them, and had he been a single man I doubt whether he would have made the confession."

Chapter 27

The union's attempt to silence the *Los Angeles Times* had failed in more ways than one. Not only did the dynamiting not stop it from publishing, but its editorial voice raised against the unions was, if anything, more bellicose, more provocative, more defiant than ever.

In January, two weeks after Ortie McManigal's abortive attempt to demolish the Llewellyn Iron Works, it had editorialized: "Industrial freedom and closed-shop tyranny are utterly and hopelessly incompatible. They can no more exist under the same roof than a hawk and a pigeon can roost on the same perch; or a wolf and a lamb can lodge in the same corral; or a rattlesnake and a rabbit can burrow in the same hole. Indeed the last comparison is unjust to the snake, for he always rattles before he strikes, while the dynamiter is a silent and sneaking assassin. . . . There are two ways to deal with closed-shop tyranny. One way is to crush it, the other way is to be crushed by it."

On the other hand, defenders of the closed shop were referring to it as the soul of unionism. Without it, they declared, unions would be no more able to exist than inventors without patents. Even in the face of the overwhelming evidence of the plot coming out of San Francisco, many still suspected it was all part of a conspiracy to frame decent union men. There were also not a few angry workers who simply took the position that whatever the capitalist exploiters got, they deserved.

In the howl of this political storm, a few men attempted to speak reasonably. But they could hardly be heard over the noise of the angry conflict. One of the few was former President Theodore Roosevelt. On a visit to Los Angeles in March 1911, he surveyed the turbulent social landscape.

"Remember that this country can no more exist if it submits to brutal lawlessness that takes the form of murder than it can exist if it submits to brutal lawlessness that takes the form of arrogant organized greed," he told his audience. "This government is not and never shall be a government either of a mob or of the plutocracy. And it is just as much your duty as honest citizens to war against one form of evil as it is to war against the other." The words traveled no further than page sixteen of the *Times*. He was out of office; had broken with his handpicked successor, William Howard Taft; and was now just months away from launching a futile run for the White House again, this time on a third-party ticket with California Gov. Hiram Johnson as his running mate—like himself at the time, a "progressive" Republican-turned-independent.

Meanwhile, the Los Angeles District Attorney, John Fredericks, had printed fifty thousand wanted posters for the apprehension of the San Francisco suspects identified as Schmidt, Caplan, and Bryce. Across the top of each was the announcement that $25,000 would be paid in strictest secrecy for information resulting in their capture. At the bottom was detailed information about the suspects. Schmidt was described as a man whose distinguishing feature "is the absence of his left eye. He also has a weakness for Fernet highballs." Bryce, the notices said, was a man "with sallow complexion." Caplan was described as "the usual type of Russian Jew."

But when "Bryce"—that is, J. B. McNamara—was finally apprehended a few weeks later, not a word of his capture appeared in the press. Burns's elaborate scheme to keep the McNamara and McManigal arrests secret had been executed without a hitch. Even if local reporters had gotten wind of them, they would almost certainly have concluded that nabbing a couple of safe-cracking thugs in Indianapolis for a job they may have committed in Chicago was far from big news.

In Indianapolis, J. J. McNamara went about his normal routine, anticipating the usual newspaper clippings about the handiwork of his brother and McManigal.

But in Chicago Burns faced a logistical problem. McManigal's wife, he was now aware, would be expecting to collect the newspaper reports about the planned bombings in Detroit to send to Indianapolis. How was he going to keep J. J. in the dark long enough so that he and his men would have time to gather further evidence based on McManigal's confession and carry out an arrest? Burns's solution involved an elegantly elaborate ruse.

America in the spring of 1911, with all of its technical and legal potential and limitations, was a place where long-distance telephone calls were rare and connections unreliable; the telegraph was still the principal means of immediate long-distance communication. Criminals and police alike had only recently begun gravitating to telegraph and post offices, sending cryptic missives by Morse code or Western Union paste-up telegrams. The alternative was to dispatch them via the US Postal Service, which, although newly mechanized, still took days and sometimes weeks to process mail from sender to receiver. The legal landscape was equally primitive. Miranda rights were not even a concept, and habeas corpus procedures were honored more in the breach than in the observance. People were often arrested by private detectives, leaving little in the way of an official trail available to the public to scrutinize.

So William J. Burns, a private detective with absolutely no mandated authority, could oversee the apprehension of J. B. McNamara and Ortie McManigal without anyone—the press, the courts, the McManigal and McNamara families, their lawyers—*anyone* learning what was going on. All that was now required to continue to keep matters silent was one simple telephone call to Ortie McManigal's home. William Burns picked up the telephone in his Chicago office, asked an operator to connect him to a phone number with a HArrison prefix that Ortie McManigal had provided, waited for an answer, and, affecting a rough voice, asked, "Is this HArrison ####?"[11]

"Yes," Emma replied, "who is it?"

"Never mind who it is. You don't know me, and I don't know you, but I got a letter this morning with your number in it that I want to read to you." Burns changed the tempo of his voice, pretending to be reading: "'Immediately upon receipt of this letter' it says, 'call up HArrison ####, and tell the woman there her husband is all right. He and his friend were arrested for safe-blowing, but it was a mistake, the police let them go, and they're in Windsor, Canada, opposite Detroit, and they're all right.'"

"Good," Emma gasped. "Lord, that's good news to me. Good!"

Burns wasn't through, but the woman continued to gush with gratitude before he could continue.

"Just listen," Burns interrupted. He then went on, reciting from his apocryphal letter. "'Tell her to go to a certain party'—it doesn't say his name . . ."

"I know, I know," Emma replied. "Go on."

"'And get $500 from him, then go back home and wait until her husband sends for her, and in a day or two,' the letter says, 'he may write you himself.' That's all it says."

"Yes, yes. All right. I'll go right down tonight."

Another part of Burns's trap had been set. That evening, after arranging for the care of her two small children, Emma McManigal boarded a train for Indianapolis, with two Burns detectives following her every step.

In Indianapolis, meanwhile, another one of Burns's men, assigned to keep an eye on J. J. McNamara, reported to his boss that the union secretary-treasurer was betraying no sign of panic or even suspicion and was going about his business as usual.

Shortly after arriving in Indianapolis, Emma McManigal met with J. J. McNamara, who listened to the developments Emma had to report.

"That's funny," J. J. said to Emma. "I don't see why he didn't write me."

Otherwise, McNamara seemed perfectly satisfied, utterly unsuspecting, and went about his routine business as usual.

It was now time for William Burns to close the trap.

⌐⌐

Mayor Alexander was at home with his wife on the evening of Wednesday, April 12, when he received an unexpected visitor. It was E.R. Mills, superintendent of the Burns Agency's Los Angeles office, and he had extraordinary news: the *Los Angeles Times* bomber, along with a coconspirator, had been arrested in Detroit by Burns agents and were now being held in Chicago. Burns wanted the news kept secret until he could conduct additional arrests. The elated mayor instantly put in a telephone call to Police Chief Galloway and then to District Attorney Fredericks at their homes.

All of Alexander's mayoral business was put on hold the following day while he conferred with Deputy District Attorney W. Joseph Ford, who had been assigned to the case, as to how to set the city's legal machinery into motion.

Word of the discussions was whispered from one official to another, each aware that if the press picked up so much as a hint of their extraordinary conferences, J. J. McNamara might be tipped off. The grand jury was summoned to issue secret indictments, but reporters were informed that that they were meeting "to look into the subject of court stenographers."

Two days later, on April 15, Burns wired District Attorney Fredericks: "I have arrested and am holding in Indianapolis, Indiana, J. J. McNamara." The wire was untrue. But Burns wanted to have in his hands grand jury indictments on both McNamara brothers and Ortie McManigal, and extradition papers as soon as they could be produced.

He then followed up with a detailed summary of the evidence he had gathered against J. B. McNamara and McManigal, but conspicuously failing to mention any direct evidence against J. J. McNamara. The telegram referred to J. B. McNamara as "B," McManigal as "M," and Tveitmoe as "T." J. J. McNamara was referred to as "SECRETARY."

CAPTURED WITH B AND M TWELVE CLOCK DEVICES EXACTLY AS THAT FOUND AT LOS ANGELES ALL COMPLETE WITH FUSE ATTACHED STOP M STATES HE HAS BEEN WORKING WITH B UNDER DIRECTION OF SECRETARY NAMED ABOVE STOP WAS PRESENT IN JUNE 1910 WHEN SECRETARY GAVE FINAL INSTRUCTIONS TO B WHEN HE LEFT FOR COAST STOP M ACCOMPANIED HIM FAR AS CHICAGO FROM INDIANAPOLIS STOP HE TOLD ME THEY WERE GOING MAKE BIG CLEAN UP AT LOS ANGELES THAT THERE WAS PLENTY OF MONEY PUT UP STOP AFTER B REACHED COAST SECRETARY TOLD M HE RECEIVED LETTER FROM

B FROM FRISCO IN WHICH B SAID QUOTE IT NOW READS TIMES FOR NEWS IT WILL READ NEWS FOR THE TIMES UNQUOTE STOP WHEN M READ OF LOS ANGELES MATTER HE WENT TO INDIANAPOLIS TO SEE SECRETARY STOP LATTER SAID QUOTE SEE WHAT THOSE FELLOWS ARE DOING OUT THERE UNQUOTE M SAID QUOTE I WONDER IF THAT IS OUR FELLOW UNQUOTE SECRETARY REPLIED QUOTE IT WAS THE TIMES THEY WANTED AND GOT BY GOD THAT OUGHT TO MAKE THEM COME ACROSS UNQUOTE SECRETARY THEN DIRECTED M NOT TO COME TO HIS OFFICE TOO MUCH WAS BADLY FRIGHTENED AND WAS VERY NERVOUS STOP HE DIRECTED M TO RETURN TO CHICAGO AND KEEP UNDER COVER STOP WHEN B RETURNED TO CHICAGO FROM COAST SECRETARY HAD M TAKE B HUNTING IN WISCONSIN STOP THERE B TOLD M ALL DETAILS OF LOS ANGELES MATTER ALSO TOLD M HE REPORTED AT FRISCO TO TVI-ETMOE [sic] AND HE INTRODUCED B TO OTHER TWO FUGITIVES STOP LATER T ATTENDED CON-VENTION AT ST LOUIS MET SECRETARY AND TOLD HIM SEND WRECKERS BACK TO GET TIMES AUXIL-IARY PLANT BAKER AND LLEWELLYN IRON WORKS FOR CHRISTMAS PRESENT STOP SECRETARY THEN DIRECTED M TO PROCEED TO LOS ANGELES STOP HE CARRIED WITH HIM TWELVE QUARTS OF STUFF TEN QUART CAN AND TWO QUARTS IN VALISE STOP THIS WAS FURNISH HIM BY SECRETARY ALSO MONEY FOR TRIP STOP ON ARRIVAL HE INVESTI-GATED PLACES BUT WAS AFRAID TO CARRY OUT PROGRAM AND ONLY DID WHAT YOU KNOW OF THEN WENT TO FRISCO MET CLANCY OF FRISCO IRON WORKERS UNION AND TOLD HIM TO TELL T CHRISTMAS PRESENT HAD BEEN DELIVERED STOP IF THIS IS SUFFICIENT INFORMATION WIRE.

The telegram concluded with its most critical sentence: "AND FOR GODS SAKE DONT LET WORD LEAK OUT UNTIL OFFICERS LAND HERE WITH PAPERS STOP LOOKS GOOD STOP."

It looked very good indeed. And it looked good to the grand jury, which indicted the three coconspirators, and to Governor Johnson, who promptly signed an extradition warrant. Still, the veil of silence would have to be kept drawn until the legal papers arrived in Indiana and Illinois, which, in 1911, would take nearly eight days.

During that time Burns grew anxious as his bank account was slowly depleted. His operatives in Indianapolis who had been watching J. J. McNamara reported that the secretary-treasurer appeared to be growing suspicious, looking increasingly "pale and drawn and uneasy," as he still hadn't heard from his brother or McManigal, who were supposed to be in Canada. Burns could not make an arrest now and risk habeas corpus proceedings. He wanted to have the appropriate warrants in hand, arrest McNamara, have him arraigned, whisk him off to California, then search the union's offices for incriminating evidence.

In the meantime, Burns instructed McManigal to write a letter to his wife, saying, "Everything is OK." He then sent the note to his office in Detroit and had his agent there mail it to Emma so that it would have a Detroit postmark. Upon receiving the letter, Emma called J. J. by telephone and read him the contents. J. J. told her he could not understand why McManigal had not written to him directly. After all, they had agreed that in case of emergency, he was to write in care of a secret post office box number in Indianapolis listed in the name of Sandusky. Still, according to Burns's Indianapolis operative, McNamara appeared to be relieved after Emma's visit.

Besides, Burns was to say later in an interview in *McClure's* magazine, he was playing a hunch. "I was calculating that, no matter how worried J. J. McNamara might be about his brother and McManigal, he would not be in any fear for himself. He would suppose that the two men, if caught, would 'stand pat,' and trust that he would arrange for their legal assistance." McNamara, Burns believed, would never have even considered the possibility that one of the two men might confess.

On April 21, 1911, the California extradition warrants, duly signed by Governor Johnson, arrived in Chicago and Indianapolis, accompanied by an entourage of Los Angeles city and county law enforcement officers. Burns rushed by automobile to Indianapolis, while his son Raymond drove to Springfield, Illinois, to see that the midwestern governors sanctioned the requests. The following morning, Burns, accompanied by the California lawmen, visited Indiana Governor Thomas Riley Marshall, who approved the extradition papers on the spot and authorized a warrant for the arrest of J. J. McNamara. He handed the warrant to one of the Los Angeles police officers.

Now, at 5:45 p.m., while the L.A. officers and Burns waited at Indianapolis police headquarters, two of Burns's detectives, accompanied by two Indianapolis police officers, drove to the American Central Life Insurance Building, where McNamara was meeting with other union brass. A light spring rain was falling, and, as the men got out of the vehicle, one of the detectives told the driver to keep his engine running. He didn't want to waste time while he tried to crank up the engine when they returned.

On the fourth floor, an executive meeting of the Iron Workers was in session. One of the detectives named Gerber knocked on the glass pane of the door. The union stenographer, Mary Dye, appeared in the crack at the door, her face wrenching in alarm at what she saw. A split second later, the detectives and police pushed past her and flooded the outer office.

"Where is J. J. McNamara?" asked a detective.

"He's busy in a board meeting and cannot be disturbed," the stenographer replied.

Burns's men and the Indianapolis police rushed through the office and into the conference room. Inside, a large, highly polished mahogany table was ringed by the Iron Workers Union leadership from across the country, all standing at once, all shouting their outrage at the interruption. Among the leadership was none other than Eugene Clancy of San Francisco, Herbert Hockin of Detroit, and President Frank Ryan. The detective leading the pack spotted the man they were after at the end of the gleaming table.

"Is your name McNamara?" he asked.

"It is," J. J. said in a steady voice. He appeared pale but otherwise unshaken.

"Well, Mr. McNamara, the chief of police wants to see you at the station."

"What for?" McNamara asked, still maintaining his composure.

"You are wanted," the detective continued. "Will you come?"

"Have you got a warrant?"

"Yes, we have one at police headquarters."

McNamara looked around helplessly at his executive committee members, but there was nothing any of them could do for him and everyone knew it. J. J. approached Frank Ryan, leaned over, and mournfully whispered, "Shall I go with these fellows?"

Ryan nodded and said, "You had better go."

"I'll get my hat." He then crossed the room, closed the union's safe, and tossed a ring of keys on the conference table. "I just want to leave some keys here. Nothing wrong with that, is there?" He smiled at his colleagues and said, "I'll be back in time to make the motion for adjournment."

Two Indianapolis police officers accompanied Secretary-Treasurer McNamara to the door while Burns's men stayed behind, holding the chagrined union officers in their places. Ryan spoke first, asking why McNamara had been arrested, to which a Burns detective replied that they were not authorized to answer the question.

Ryan then asked them to leave the room so that they might be able to resume their meeting. They refused, and one of the detectives announced that none of them would be permitted to leave the room, either.

Ryan approached the telephone and attempted to get in touch with the union's lawyer, Leo Rappaport, who, as it turned out, did not customarily work on Saturday night. No one else in the room knew whom to call for legal assistance either, as the rest were all from out of town.

Shortly after McNamara was hauled off, the door to the conference room burst open again. In came William J. Burns, Indianapolis Mayor Schrank, Superintendent of the Indianapolis Police Hyland, and Chief Police Detective Holtz, followed by a bevy of reporters. Schrank, Hyland, and Holtz informed the union leadership that they were not there to free them nor to help them acquire legal counsel; they were there to facilitate the Burns Agency's search of the union's headquarters.

Burns gave nothing away. Followed by his ever-expanding entourage, he rushed into J. J. McNamara's office and took a quick look about, his gaze settling on the rolltop desk. In a dramatic thrust he lifted the cover, which clattered loudly, reached into the odd-size cubicles, and began hauling out their contents.

Hearing the commotion, Frank Ryan barreled into the room, sputtering, "Who are you that you have a right to come in these offices and search these apartments?"

"I am Burns," was the reply. "Do you know me?"

Before Ryan could respond, Superintendent of Police Hyland began reciting the search warrant in his hand while Burns continued intently gathering papers and ledgers.

"Ah, and who is Burns?" Ryan demanded.

Hyland responded that Burns was a private detective and that he had been invited to join the police in their search of the premises.

Meanwhile, in the next room, the union executives were finally told of the nature of McNamara's arrest. Each registered surprise at the news, with one remarking that someone had better go to the jail and arrange bail for their secretary-treasurer.

A more genuine sense of surprise mixed with foreboding was evident when they were told that McNamara was not being taken to jail in Indianapolis but was on his way to Los Angeles on charges related to the bombing of the Times Building and the Llewellyn Iron Works.

One of the union execs approached Ryan and whispered in his ear. Ryan entered another room and found Walter Drew, the much-despised attorney and spokesman for the National Erectors' Association, examining the union's checkbooks. More than any other corporate officer, Drew, who held the title of "commissioner" in the organization, had mobilized the resources of the great skyscraper builders to battle the Iron Workers and uphold the open shop. Now, here he was, an arrogant invader in the union's very headquarters, rifling through its checkbooks. In the eyes of the stunned union leadership, Drew's presence spoke volumes as to the innate bias of the investigation.

As the detectives began packing up all the documents in the secretary-treasurer's office, the office janitor, Harry Graff, walked in. He was dismayed by what he saw—papers and debris scattered everywhere—and asked what was going on. A Burns detective took the janitor aside and told him that they were in the midst of executing a search warrant. The janitor looked around at the mess, and images of the odd comings and goings of J. J. McNamara between his office and the basement late at night came to his mind. He had speculated about the furtive behavior of McNamara. Now he quietly sidled up to the famous detective and said, "Mr. Burns, do you want to search the vault in the cellar?" McNamara, Graff explained, had approached him a month or so earlier and asked permission to store some old union records there.

Without a moment's hesitation, Burns, his men, and the reporters who had now arrived at the scene dashed out of the office and down the stairs to the basement. Coming to the door, the superintendent of police prepared to wrench open the locked door with a crowbar when Leo Rappaport, the union attorney, suddenly appeared. The first words out of his mouth were a shout of protest that the detectives' search warrant did not authorize a search of the building's basement.

The police superintendent halted his work, saying he wanted to be "perfectly fair to everyone." He then deferentially excused himself, saying he would return to headquarters to obtain the proper authorizations.

—◆—

Burns decided to take advantage of the pause in the action at union headquarters to check out a tantalizing revelation in Ortie McManigal's confession. The bomber had claimed that J. J. McNamara had recently ordered that a massive quantity of stolen explosives be relocated to a barn outside of town owned by T. P. Jones. Burns had slipped McManigal's directions to Jones's property into his briefcase. Accompanied by part of his coterie of detectives and police, Burns hurriedly left the union offices, scrambled down the staircase, out the massive front door, and into the police car with its engine still running. He began reading off directions to the officer behind the wheel, while a convoy of police cars bristling with detectives and reporters formed behind them.

It was now early evening, and the police car, racing over the unlit country roads, clipped a pedestrian on the way. The pedestrian was not seriously injured, but the party was considerably delayed. By the time they arrived at the farmhouse, it was already night—a time when Jones rarely received visitors and hardly ever saw an automobile. Now, standing on his tiny porch, the farmer watched in rapt amazement as the misty cones of headlamps came rushing toward his farmhouse. Out from the first car hopped Burns, who abruptly approached the bewildered farmer, identified himself, and then told him that he was there to inspect the barn. Jones asked him to wait a moment, disappeared into his little house for a moment, and reappeared with a lantern. Then the entire party of detectives and police, led by the farmer, sloshed from the muddy road to the barn, which rose up behind the house.

At the door of the barn, Burns removed from his pocket the set of keys his men had taken from J. B. McNamara upon his arrest. Upon opening the broad barn door, he trained the lantern's light on a row of grain bins opposite the stalls. Next to them lay a huge box, the kind that might ordinarily have been used to ship grand pianos. It was stamped "Valley Gem," the brand name of a piano manufacturer owned by the Baldwin Piano Company of Cincinnati.

"Jones," Burns asked, "whose box is that? Whom does it belong to?"

"To J. J. McNamara," the farmer replied. The reporters busily jotted down the dialogue.

"What is it doing there?"

"Why, he has it to keep his books in."

"What sort of books?"

"Records—the union's old books."

Burns paused for effect, expanding the moment as the reporters' pens wiggled furiously against their notepads. One made a note of the fact that it was a strange sort of box to keep ledgers in—a piano box, all strapped and padlocked. Burns glanced at the reporters, then at the poor farmer. His timing was exquisite.

"Didn't you know there was dynamite in it?"

Jones gasped, "No!" and staggered, as if Burns's words had struck him in the solar plexus.

The reporters furiously transcribed the high melodrama.

As if he were at center stage, Burns now raised McNamara's keys in front of him. They gleamed as he held them in the soft lantern light and scrutinized each one to discern which might fit the padlock that fastened the piano box. As he did so, the farmer began pleading that he knew nothing about any dynamite. He nervously rattled off an account of how he had been paid a year's rent of $60 for the use of the barn, how he had been told that the box had been purchased at the Baldwin Music Store in Indianapolis; how he had been paid to buy sawdust and bring it to the barn so that it could be used for packing.

Burns tried the first key. It did not fit. Then another. And another. In the end the padlock was wrenched from the piano box and Burns thrust it open. Inside was another box—this too fastened with a crude padlock. This time Burns decided to ignore J. B. McNamara's keys altogether and wrench that one open as well, exposing fifteen sticks of dynamite and two quarts of nitroglycerin, all swathed in soft yellow sawdust.

The barn was full of knowing chuckles and low whistles. Burns let the party take it all in, the reporters recording the melodrama in vivid detail in their notepads. Then, in a voice that would have brought down the curtain at the local Bijou, he asked Farmer Jones, "What sort of books did you think they were going to pack in sawdust?"

❧

The evening's drama wasn't quite over. From Jones's farmhouse the Burns party dropped by J. J. McNamara's Indianapolis apartment on their way back to union headquarters. After searching the premises, it was decided that there was little in the way of evidence here, and Burns decided it was time to leave.

Then someone noticed the clock atop J. J.'s dresser. It was very small and somehow familiar, blithely ticking away: a New Haven Junior Tattoo alarm clock.

❧

It was past midnight when Burns and his party finally made it back to union headquarters in the American Central Life Insurance Building. By now Superintendent of Police Hyland had obtained the appropriate search warrant to inspect the basement storage area, and the means to do so in the person of a locksmith. The vault amounted to a narrow compartment in an alcove constructed of rough pine boards. Inside was a prosecutor's dream. Within the cool walls neatly stacked on shelves, Burns discovered seven packages of dynamite weighing some ninety-two pounds and a package containing percussion caps, long coils of fuse, and twelve Junior Tattoo alarm clocks, "similar," said the *Indianapolis Star,* "to those with which bombs are discharged."

Declared Hyland: "There's enough explosives there to have blown the center out of the town." He was exaggerating, but only slightly.

From the basement Burns led his men upstairs to the conference room where the Iron Workers executives were still cooling their heels, although it was now approaching two o'clock in the morning. Burns demanded the combination to the safe; the union leaders claimed they didn't know it. Ryan remarked, "McNamara is the only man who knows it, and you've carried him off, God knows where."

Burns asked the locksmith to drill through the lock and open it. But, after the discovery of the explosives stashed in the basement, the man was reluctant. After all, what if it was rigged to detonate if the lock was tampered with?

Superintendent Hyland suggested that he have one of his men round up a convicted safecracker. But Burns wanted to wait no longer,

"Well, I'll have to tackle it myself," he said, then knelt before the small safe, plugged a drill into an electric outlet, and began to apply it to the lock, as the onlookers stepped back. One of them, union attorney Rappaport, shouted from the rear of the room: "I protest. Are we living in darkest Russia?"

Burns turned toward Rappaport, scowled, bit his mustache, and returned to the task at hand. A moment later Burns, hearing the clink of the tumblers falling back, laid down the drill, and pulled the handle of the safe. As detectives began removing the ledgers and correspondence inside, Rappaport shouted, "Have we no rights?"

"Not under the circumstances," Burns coolly replied.

Now at three o'clock in the morning, he declared the search complete, and the union leadership was finally allowed to leave.

But Burns now discovered that he had in hand dynamite of an even more volatile kind than the cache in the basement—piles of correspondence from J. J. McNamara to members of his dynamite gang, stacked indiscriminately in the safe. Some of the letters contained warnings to the men not to include details of their work when writing to him. But McNamara had nevertheless retained all of these incriminating letters, meticulously filing them away in the safe, presumably convinced that no one would ever dare invade the sanctuary of a union's headquarters.

Burns rifled through the letters. In one, union organizer Ed Clark in Cincinnati had written about sabotaging an open-shop job in that city. "Joe, being so well known here, I do not think it advisable for me to buy any explosive," the letter said. "Could there be such a thing as you sending me from Indianapolis what I need?" A letter from Philip Dooley, a union official in New Orleans, referred to the cost involved in turning a trick at an open shop there. "Now, Joe, it will take about $250 to do any work. There is a few good fellows in this local at this time who can do the trick and get away with it." Another dynamiter, M. J. Hannan, wrote to McNamara, balking at performing a dynamite job aimed at assisting union local No. 23 in Scranton, Pennsylvania. "If No. 23 had a million, I would not do a job for them, as they don't know how to keep their mouth shut and I don't feel prepared to serve time." A letter from William C. Bernhardt told of an "accident" that had occurred at an open-shop construction project in Cincinnati, after which several union members had been arrested. A sympathetic police judge had let the men go, the letter said, but told Bernhardt, "For God's sake, don't bring that bunch around here any more or I'll have to do something."

McNamara had also diligently recorded the amount of cash he had removed from the union's coffers to pay his brother, McManigal, and others for their handiwork and expenses. He had jotted them down on the ledgers as "organizing expenses." He had then received a receipt from the men in return, and had filed each one away. It quickly became apparent that the dates for each of these withdrawals corresponded to dates of the explosions.

—◦—

Immediately after his arrest at 6:10 p.m., J. J. McNamara had been quietly rushed to Indianapolis police headquarters where, as he stood handcuffed to Los Angeles Police Detective James Hosick, Superintendent of Police Hyland read the extradition orders to him, informing him that the governor of Indiana had approved a request from the governor of California for him to stand trial for the dynamiting of the Times Building and the Llewellyn Iron Works. After being searched and booked, he was taken, still handcuffed, into the tiny courtroom of City Judge James A. Collins, who had never before held court on a Saturday. He had never before held court after 6:00 p.m. on any day of the week. The snap arraignment was over in minutes.

Judge Collins asked McNamara if he was the man named in the warrant, to which McNamara replied, "I am that man." Then, after a long pause, he summoned up his memories from law school.

"Judge, I do not see how it is a man can be jerked up from his business when he is committing no wrong and ordered from the state on five minutes' notice. You are going to let them take me without giving me a chance to defend myself. I have no attorney here and no one to defend me or to say a word for me."[12]

The judge appeared to ignore McNamara's statement and instead addressed one of the Indianapolis police detectives who had arrested him. "Officer, do you identify this man?"

The detective did so. Judge Collins then announced that he was not there to try a case and that according to Indiana law, he had no alternative but to turn the prisoner over to the officers of the state requesting extradition when extradition papers have been honored by the governor of Indiana. Although Indiana law required the court to give the defendant an opportunity and time to employ counsel, McNamara was given no such consideration.

Far from it, he was now effectively in the custody of the LAPD detective to whom he was handcuffed. McNamara was led first to the desk sergeant, who returned his personal effects to him, then ushered down the courtroom's back staircase, out the side door, and into a huge seven-passenger Owen motor car idling in the alley.

Packed with L.A. police, Burns detectives, a Winchester rifle, revolvers, and hundreds of rounds of ammunition, the car, capable of reaching the unheard-of speed of seventy-five miles an hour, rushed off in a squall of dust on a zigzag route cunningly mapped out by Burns to evade any union attorneys, process servers, or friendly unionist judges who might see fit to free J. J. McNamara on bail. Burns ordered the twelve-cylinder car driven at top speed and, if necessary, to plow through any obstacles in its path.

The first leg of the trip took them on an uneventful seventy-mile dash to Terra Haute, where they boarded a train to St. Louis, 165 miles away. In the Gateway City the party quietly made a transfer to a train bound for Hoisington, Kansas, 465 miles away, where another automobile was waiting to take them eleven miles south to Great Bend, where they boarded another train to Dodge City, eighty miles west. Finally, they boarded the Santa Fe Railroad's luxurious California Limited for the final 1,060-mile stretch to Los Angeles.

By extraordinary coincidence, once aboard the train, Burns and his men discovered it was also carrying his son, his detectives, Ortie McManigal, and J. B. McNamara. They would withhold that information from J. J. McNamara.

Chapter 28

Ortie McManigal treated the entire journey to California as one grand lark. He remained handcuffed to Chicago detective William Reed, who had been his host at his Chicago home and who had witnessed his confession. After McManigal boarded the train, he ordered a plate of ham and eggs and remarked: "We may as well get good and fat for the blowoff."

His behavior was so loose and jovial that he surprised everyone when at one point he suddenly lunged at Detective Reed, and with his manacled hands tried to grasp the detective's revolver. The other detectives joined the fray, shoving McManigal into his berth and shackling his hands behind him. Said McManigal: "I would have got off if I had gotten my hands on that revolver."

On the morning of April 23, news that the *Times* bombers had been arrested and were on their way to Los Angeles to stand trial was shouted by newsboys pulling wagons stacked with heavy Sunday papers down neighborhood streets.

"*Examiner, Times* pay-perrr!"

The *Los Angeles Times,* of course, had the report on its front page in an article datelined Chicago:

"The blackest page in the history of union labor was turned today when a high official of the International Association of Bridge and Structural Iron Workers was arrested on the charge of having engineered the dynamiting of the Los Angeles Times Building last fall," the article began.

"At almost the moment the official, John McNamara, Secretary-Treasurer of the union, was arrested in his Indianapolis office, a sinister little party slipped out of Chicago on a special train bound for Los Angeles. . . . One of the prisoners in the party that left Chicago was the mysterious

'J. B. Bryce.' . . . He proved to be none other than James McNamara, brother of the union labor official who for years has been head of the secret, red-handed wrecking crew in the employ of Secretary McNamara. . . . It is said in police circles here tonight that James McNamara has confessed, implicating high officials in labor union circles."

McNamara had made no such confession. Only Ortie McManigal, who was referred to in the *Times* article only as "the other prisoner."

"The arrests marked the end of one of the most thrilling criminal hunts ever recorded," the article continued. It then provided details of the hunt, which it said was conducted by "operatives of the William J. Burns National Detective Agency." It gave no individual credit to Burns himself.

On its editorial page, the *Times* commented that if the three suspects are "convicted and hanged, their deaths or the death of ten thousand like them, would not expiate their awful crime. But it will serve to warn the closed-shop laborites who inspired the assassins and the treasuries of whose organizations supplied the money to pay the expenses of their nefarious deed, that in attempting to carry [out] their ends by violence, they are butting against the bosses of the bucklers of society, and can gain nothing but bruises from the conflict."

Reaction from labor was immediate and unequivocal. In Washington, DC, AF of L President Samuel Gompers sounded the alarm: "How long are the American People going to stand for legalized kidnapping? . . . Up goes the curtain with a blare of trumpets upon the first act of a tragedy contemplating the assassination of organized labor. . . .

"From what I know of Secretary McNamara, my faith and confidence in his innocence is unshaken by the charges against him."

Socialist leader Eugene Debs one-upped Gompers's rhetoric: "Sound the alarm to the working class! . . . The arrest of John McNamara, international secretary of the Bridge and Structural Iron Workers, by a corporation detective agency has all the earmarks of another conspiracy to fasten the crime of murder upon labor union officials, to discredit and destroy organized labor in the United States."

Meanwhile, Earl Rogers, who had received the initial public acclaim for tracking down the original evidence and witnesses in the case in San

Francisco, had now resumed his principal occupation. When, on April 22, news of the arrests of the dynamite suspects was scattered throughout the *Times* and included the reaction of local figures, Rogers's remarks were notable for their absence.

Then, on April 25, details of Ortie McManigal's confession hit the front pages. At each stop along the route to Los Angeles, reporters would clamber aboard the train searching for the carriage that held the man who was now literally blowing up the dynamite conspiracy. McManigal enjoyed the attention. When a reporter asked him whether his leg irons bothered him, he crossed his legs awkwardly and remarked, "Not much. It's like a woman trying to learn to walk in a hobble skirt."

McManigal appeared relaxed throughout the journey. It must have seemed to him that whatever lay ahead for him could not possibly measure up to the peril in which he had lived since that fateful day when he had been spotted by Herbert Hockin.

As the train neared California, McManigal turned to Los Angeles Sheriff's Deputy Robert T. Brain and asked, "What do you think they will do to me if I turn state's evidence?"

Brain replied, "I am not in a position to tell you. Are you going to do it?"

"Yes," answered McManigal, "I'm going to tell."

"What are you going to tell?"

"All about it."

"You know what you are charged with?"

"Yes. I am charged with dynamiting the plant of the Llewellyn Iron Works."

"Did you do it?"

"Sure, I did."

"What did you get for it?"

"Two hundred dollars. That is the price for all such jobs."

"Do you know Bryce?"

"Yes, I know him."

"How long?"

"About a year and a half."

That was all McManigal was going to say for now. He told Brain he would tell the rest of his story when he arrived in Los Angeles.

Brain told him, "All right, Mac, I am not trying to coerce you. Do as you like about it. That's your right."

"When I get out there, I'll tell all about it."

When the train passed through New Mexico, the territory's last territorial governor, William J. Mills, came aboard to have a look at America's most famous prisoner. McManigal charmed the governor. By the time their chat was over, he was reciting his repertoire of off-color jokes to Mills. Later, as the governor was departing, he called out to McManigal, "If I can do anything for you, don't fail to call me."

McManigal called back, "All right, govie!"

Chapter 29

A massive adrenal rush, it would seem, had continued to keep William F. Burns on the move without sleep for two days following the arrests. Accompanied by two of his men, he returned to Union Station in Indianapolis, where he boarded a Toledo, Ohio-bound train, found his compartment, and promptly dozed off. Months of painstaking investigation and thousands of dollars of personal expense were finally, all at once, producing the most rewarding week in the life of the World Famous Sleuth.

For months his detectives had engaged in a relentless—and costly—surveillance operation. They had spent scores of days at the same hotels with J. B. McNamara and Ortie McManigal. They had followed the pair incessantly, relieving one another so they would not be recognized. They had examined hotel registers, visited dynamite makers, clock manufacturers, and wire factories, attended meetings of labor unions, and kept watch at factories where, they had been tipped, bombs would be planted. They had collected handwriting specimens, conferred with hundreds of police officers, and interviewed dozens of manufacturers who claimed that they had been threatened by union organizers. The operation had run smoothly, virtually without a hitch. And now, finally, it was all paying off.

In Tiffin, Ohio, outside of Toledo, in a shed belonging to Ortie McManigal's father, Burns found a prodigious dynamite cache—540 pounds. Splicing evidence to confession, Burns next visited the quarry where McManigal had said he had stolen the stuff, then paid a visit to the liveryman from whom McManigal had hired the horse and wagon to haul the dynamite away.

Back in Toledo he found a suitcase, soaked with nitroglycerin, that J. B. McNamara had checked at the train station a few days earlier, expecting to retrieve it on his return trip from Detroit.

Burns directed an operative to search J. B.'s home in Cincinnati, and there he discovered more alarm clocks and electrical devices—and another stack of incriminating letters.

He also found some letters that revealed more about J. B. McNamara than they did about the dynamite plot. One of them, neatly stashed away, was written by a Peter Curran and mailed from Chicago on June 7, 1909. Burns would later refer to it as a "classic."

"I received your postal and was glad to hear from you. I am still at the Rosena Hotel. The night clerk that was thur wen you were ther got into a sirkes girl's room and Miss Horton found it out and fired him. Jim and Eral is working at bumpers.[13] They can get pleanty orders if they can do them cheap anough. Everything is about the same around hear. Old Casper is moping around with the rat trap as usual. Mrs. Anderson have a very sore foot with roontisen. Mrs. Wright moved. I sean Willis and he gave me his address and said to send it to you wen I rote. 6817 So. Chicago Ave. It was very cold hear all spring. Have not much new to tell you lot of building gowing up. You must excuse me for not writing sooner. Let me now how you are getting along and how is your mother is and if you are tire of Cincinatia yet?

"Your truly

"Peter Curran

"Rosena Hotel

"corner 18th St. and Wabaush."

But as his train headed to California, J. B. McNamara held few warm thoughts, although he appeared relatively relaxed, rolling and smoking cigarette after cigarette, drinking from little tenth bottles of whiskey, and muttering to the Burns detectives, "We will never reach California. I know we are going into a ditch."

In the back of J. B.'s mind was an expectation bordering on conviction that, once word got out, his brother and the union apparatus would swing into action. The train would be stopped—perhaps at gunpoint, he imagined. Union lawyers and process servers would appear, and he and Ortie would be sprung from the illegal custody of the Burns Agency. He was totally unaware of the fact that his brother and McManigal were under arrest in different Pullman cars on the very same train, that McManigal had confessed, and that Burns had taken such a devious route to California that none of the union leadership or their lawyers could find them.

Within their field of view, the quarantined prisoners could see the crowds gathering at each train stop, hoping to catch a glimpse of the most famous prisoners in the world. Although they couldn't communicate with the crowds, both brothers independently sensed the popular support they would enjoy once they were sprung from the confines of the train. The sight made J. B. jovial, at times even cocky. "I'd blow up the whole damn country if I thought it would get us rights," he told his guards.

But as the train continued westward, the engine shrieking through the days and nights, J. B. began growing slowly but increasingly concerned about what was not happening. To distract his mind, he marked up the electric fan in his compartment to serve as a kind of roulette wheel. He and Burns detective Malcolm McLaren, to whom he was handcuffed, would switch the fan on, then wait for the blades to come up to top speed, then abruptly turn it off. The arrow that he had marked on the blade would then slow and slow until it stopped on one of the numbers on the screen of the fan. So the bomber and his guard passed the time as the western landscape fled by.

Then, shortly after crossing into California, the train stopped at the dusty desert town of Barstow. Yet another local reporter came aboard looking for an interview with the famous prisoners. A Burns detective led him to J. B.'s Pullman car, where he managed to strike up a conversation with the hungover bomber. During the course of that conversation, the reporter asked J. B. about Ortie McManigal's confession.

J. B. slipped into a prolonged silence.

The train moved on, steaming through the desert on its final leg, a sense of foreboding coming over him, the realization that his brother and the union would not be rescuing him, that he would be riding this train all the way back to Los Angeles. If Ortie McManigal was indeed cooperating with prosecutors, then all may very well be lost. With an overwhelming sense of dread, he now realized that he was in this alone, and that his very survival was at stake.

J. J. rode in a separate Pullman car accompanied by Detective Hosick and several of the Los Angeles and Chicago police officers who had arrested him in Indianapolis. Even to his captors, he cut a dashing figure. In stark contrast to his brother, he dressed like a banker and spoke like a gentleman, a composite that made for an air of serenity and dignity that prompted his handlers to treat him with deference. He was an astute enough lawyer to know intuitively what his first line of defense would be. When a reporter asked him about the circumstances surrounding his arrest, he replied offhandedly, "It's an easy thing to manufacture evidence, but I'll be riding back the other way without any shackles soon." Later he told a reporter for the *Chicago Examiner*, "As secretary, my duties were entirely clerical, not executive. I do not determine any policies. I have been editing the *Bridgemen's Magazine*."[14]

The Iron Workers chiefs had obviously contrived an official party line early on to be put into play in case of a crisis like this. Implicitly or explicitly, every leader in the union seemed to know the script. In Los Angeles, J. E. Timmons, the local organizer for the Iron Workers, said of J. J. McNamara: "He has always advised us to win our strikes by stick-to-itiveness and warned us never to use violence."

Timmons also recalled that when J. J. last visited Los Angeles, they went to a bar for a drink, and J. J. ordered lemonade. "He remarked that it was all right for others to drink if they wanted to, but he said he never used liquor himself."

It was true. While brother J. B. chain-smoked and drank his little tenth bottles of whiskey throughout the train trip, J. J. touched not a drop and appeared always to be the personable gentleman.

"We are two different personalities," he told a reporter who interviewed him. And, outwardly, so it seemed. Yet J. J. and J. B. McNamara were shaped by the same forces, and while their demons may have sought different outlets, they nonetheless took similar routes. On one thing they were in absolute agreement: The ends did justify the means, any means.

In Cincinnati, Mary McNamara got word of her sons' arrests from reporters who came pounding on her door. The poor woman's husband had been sent off to prison for raping their daughter. She had been forced to take sewing jobs in sweatshops to support herself and her children. And now this.

"How can I believe such things of my Johnny and Jimmy," she told the reporters. "Why, Johnny has been such a good son, the very best in the world, and I have always been so proud of him. . . . To appreciate the boy, one must know him. He is so clean, and strong, and fine. Wouldn't it be awful if they should hang my Johnny and Jimmy? Who can tell? They have hanged innocent men before, and only God knows what will happen to my two good boys."

Chapter 30

On the afternoon of April 22, 1911, Clarence Darrow, the world-renowned labor attorney, emerged from his posh Midway home in Chicago. His face was pale and deeply lined. As was frequently the case, he looked a disheveled mess. His suit was rumpled. Dried-up splatters of soup were visible on his jacket and tie. The tall man seemed even more stooped than usual, his posture betraying both his physical and mental woes at the moment. As he shambled down his doorsteps, Darrow was instantly accosted by a bevy of reporters who asked him to comment on the rumor that he had taken the McNamara case.

Darrow was out of temper, having recently returned from California, where he had unsuccessfully tried a mining case. Still more recently—in fact, earlier that day—he had driven up from Kankakee, Illinois, where he had defended the Kankakee Manufacturing Company's board of directors in a dirty little trial that he was also in the process of losing.

"The report that I have been retained to defend these men [the McNamara brothers and McManigal] is untrue," he announced to the reporters gathered on his front porch step in a voice that conveyed great fatigue. "I am not sure I could be induced to go into this case. It would mean a long, hard fight, and I'm getting too old for that sort of thing."

In recent years Darrow had achieved iconic status as "The Great Defender," the lawyer who had famously defended the cause of the beleaguered poor against the rich, exploited workers against the captains of industry. He had once been described by a close friend as having a superhuman capacity "to feel the pain of others," the pain of his lowly, socially and economically marginalized clients in particular. But now, at age fifty-four, Darrow was feeling and looking far older than his years. The defender of the downtrodden appeared mighty downtrodden himself.

Clarence Seward Darrow had begun his career as a corporate attorney for the railroads, only to "cross the tracks" and represent his former employer's employees who were attempting to organize. Changing sides from corporate lawyer to labor lawyer, however, meant a serious financial setback. Nevertheless, he embarked on a career of defending anarchists, Socialists, and, most notably, workers and union leaders, garnering courtroom successes that resonated with the American public in a way no other criminal defense attorney's cases ever had. To many, the trials often exhibited the epic scale of a David-and-Goliath showdown, with Darrow's resplendent oratory bringing jurors to tears, spectators to applause and making him an unlikely hero to millions of working Americans.

His first big client, Eugene V. Debs, president of the American Railway Union, owed Darrow his freedom for defending him during the Pullman strike of 1894. More recently, in 1907, Darrow had left his comfortable home in Chicago to successfully defend three jailed union leaders of the Western Federation of Miners who had been indicted for murdering the former governor of Idaho, Frank Steunenberg, using dynamite as the weapon of choice.

The trial had dragged on for months and had slowly drawn the life out of the Great Defender. His wife, Ruby, would later recall that he was so exhausted that he asked her to make a pledge to him "that if ever again he should be tempted or urged to go into another such terrific fight that I should refuse to go along, and that would keep him from taking such cases." Moreover, he met with Samuel Gompers, the president of the AF of L, and its executive committee, and told them about the pledge. It had provided him some relief, for the Steunenberg case had taxed both his wealth and his health. In the midst of the trial, Darrow had come down with a seemingly incurable infection that ravaged his left ear. Codeine injections given to him by Ruby had provided only temporary relief from a harrowing pain and made him so sleepy that he was barely able to function in court. Finally, in January 1908 he underwent mastoid surgery at California Hospital in Los Angeles. The operation proved successful, saving his life and preserving his dream of a long and early retirement. But then, hard on the heels of the operation, came devastating news of a different stripe.

While he was recuperating in Los Angeles, the virtually unregulated stock market had crashed, and this time it took Clarence Darrow's life savings with it. Warning signs of the market's volatility, which his wife, Ruby, had been privy to, had emerged during his long recovery. Fearing for her husband's health, however, she elected not to tell him. Better not to worry him about the precarious state of their most speculative investments, she thought. But had Darrow been well enough to keep on top of the situation, he would certainly have unloaded them before they became worthless.

Once it was too late, Darrow was finally told the full scope and nature of the catastrophe, and he was livid. In a pall of rage he shouted at his cowering wife, "Do you realize what you've done to me? You've thrown away my life savings, my dream of retiring. Now I'll have to begin all over again—be a slave to that irksome law work. We'll never be able to travel the world, write all those books! I'll never forgive you for this—never, never!" Lawyers were a theatrical lot in those days.

So it was that Darrow had returned to Chicago in 1908 in despair. He was weary of law, deeply depressed, nearly bankrupt, still in chronic pain from the operation, and alienated from his young wife of five years. He went back to work, but this time nakedly determined to put his own interests above all others'. Suddenly the man with the superhuman capacity to feel the pain of others was acutely attuned to his own, and relieving his general sense of depression did not stop with making fast money. In the spring of 1908, Darrow was introduced to a thirty-year-old social worker with literary aspirations and very long chestnut hair. Her name was Mary Field.

Twenty-one years his junior, Mary was even younger than Ruby and was everything she was not—beautiful, bohemian in her appreciation of literature and the fine arts, and radical in her politics. Most important of all, she blindly worshipped the legend of Clarence Darrow. Soon after having met they became lovers.

That her hero was taking on clients such as the Kankakee Manufacturing Company did not seem to have registered with the radical leftist sensibilities of Mary Field. Apparently she accepted Darrow for who he had once been, not for who he now was. Ruby was of a similarly accommodative mind. She suspected that her husband was seeking solace in the arms of another younger woman, a situation that she had tolerated with a certain sense of resignation throughout their young marriage.

Such was the melodramatic state of affairs in the life of Clarence Darrow on April 22, 1911. Earlier that day he had stood before a Kankakee court and argued on behalf of a large, corrupt, and defunct business against a group of small investors whose life savings had been wiped out by corporate fraud. While his infidelity threatened his marriage, his current work, which he had engaged in out of financial urgency, threatened his great name.

Shortly after having left the Kankakee courtroom, Darrow had learned the extraordinary news of J. J. McNamara's arrest. He knew at once that his old friend Gompers would be asking him for help. Indeed, from the moment the story hit the press, it was generally assumed that Darrow would defend the Iron Workers official.

The day after Darrow made his statement to reporters on the steps of his Chicago Midway flat, Gompers, along with several other members of the federation's executive board, walked up those same steps to pay Darrow a visit. For the moment the case was being handled in Los Angeles by Job Harriman, the Socialist candidate for mayor. Gathered in Darrow's library before a roaring fireplace, Gompers set before the group the panoply of charges that had been brought against the McNamaras and registered his belief that only a man of Darrow's legal skill could save them from the scaffold.

Darrow dismissed the idea of taking the case out of hand, saying that he had done his "share of the fighting." But Gompers and his associates persisted. The parallels between this case and the Stueunenberg case were readily apparent, they said, with both involving unreliable government witnesses, coerced witness testimony, extralegal means of extradition, all of which pointed to the unmistakable signs of a setup on the part of powerful antiunion forces designed to destroy the union cause by defaming it. Gompers and Debs were especially relentless in their appeal to Darrow: With all of the resources of the city and its business leaders mobilized against the McNamaras, no one else could free them, and if the McNamaras were convicted, the labor movement in America itself would be doomed. Gompers finally pulled out all stops. If Darrow continued to refuse to take the case, he would "go down in history as a traitor to the great cause of labor." The words struck home. Still Darrow balked.

If he did agree to take the case, Darrow finally indicated, there would be one condition that was not intended for public consumption. He told the AF of L leadership that he might come aboard for the staggering retainer fee of $50,000 plus expenses—money that would be raised by increasing the dues of union workers, those men and women who made anywhere between $2.50 and $4.50 for what was then generally a ten-hour day of work.

He could thereby appear to be the champion of the underclass while privately replenishing his retirement bank account. Yet Darrow warned that, ultimately, a real defense "against the powerful forces of society in the courts" would require a total expenditure of more than $350,000. Gompers claimed he could get it. Still, Darrow refused to commit.

Meanwhile, the news circulating through the streets of Chicago about the latest revelations in the case made the front pages daily, whipping up a public frenzy. Darrow recognized that this was the kind of landmark case that came about every few decades, one that would likely evolve into a historic courtroom epic.

Newspapers sympathetic to the labor cause editorialized that J. J. McNamara had been kidnapped and headlined that Indianapolis authorities had issued an arrest warrant for William J. Burns in connection with the crime. Indeed, three of Burns's colleagues had already been arrested earlier that day, including Walter Drew of the National Erectors Association, Assistant Los Angeles District Attorney W. J. Fox, and the chauffeur who had been behind the wheel of the Owen motorcar that had rushed J. J. McNamara to the St. Louis train station.

Furious labor leaders were also making the headlines, attacking the underlying murder charges as a "railroading" and "frame-up," and "high handed and infamous outrages." At his First Street office in Chicago, Samuel Gompers shouted at a reporter, "How long are the American people going to stand for legalized kidnapping?" A little later he added,

"The representatives of corporate wealth insistently seek to crush the movement of organized labor . . . [and] the men [who have] the confidence of the working people."

Deep within the impoverished neighborhoods of American cities in 1911, the accusation rang all too true.

Labor leaders had also adduced the motive of William J. Burns, and it too appeared to have credibility. Edward N. Nockles of the Chicago Federation of Labor aptly claimed that "The whole thing is a frame-up on the part of private detectives for the purpose of getting a big reward."

For his part, Burns predicted, "When the rank and file of laboring men in this country learn the truth of the evidence against these men, they will be with us to a man. . . . Laboring men do not stand for cold-blooded murder and anarchy."

Without agreeing to take the case, Darrow passed along some pro bono advice to union leaders: Present J. J. McNamara to the public as a kidnapped martyr, not an arrested criminal suspect. J. B. McNamara was to be ignored. Few knew much about him, but what was known wasn't particularly attractive. Ortie McManigal was to be vilified, his confession scorned as a fiction in a capitalist plot. The deaths of the men in the Times Building on October 1, 1910, were the result of a gas main explosion; the Zeehandelaar device and the bomb at the Otis mansion were so much planted evidence.

Reporters staked out Darrow's home, peppering him with questions about the case each day. On April 25 Darrow told them that he did not want it to appear that he was turning down the defense of the McNamaras because he believed them to be guilty. Far from that notion, he said. "Even if I thought them guilty I would defend them because I believe that anyone accused should have the benefit of counsel."

The next day he agreed to consult with the leaders of the Iron Workers union at their headquarters in Indianapolis. As he entered the building, he told reporters, "I am too old a man to take up McNamara's defense, a case in which capital and labor are necessarily arrayed." The union leaders offered him a suitable elixir: They firmly committed to the $50,000 retainer. If the case should spread into the following year, they would pay him an additional $50,000 plus $100 per day. He would receive up to $200,000 for additional expenses.

The following day, April 26, Darrow's tone changed. He now said that although he was no less reluctant to take on the defense of the McNamaras, "I suppose I shall be drafted to take this case in spite of my unwillingness. I would have much preferred that a younger and stronger man should have been chosen."

On April 27 Gompers, along with other AF of L officials, visited him at his Chicago home again. They turned up the pressure. But there was someone else who had to be convinced. He pardoned himself and left the room. Years later, Ruby would vividly recall the moment he walked into their bedroom. "Dee came to me in the back, wearily, sadly, taking my hand and conducting me to a seat beside him to break to me the news that he was asking me to break my pledge. . . . He explained that the men in the front room were saying that if he refused [to take the McNamara case] he would go down in history as a traitor to his cause. He asked me to lift my pledge and promise to go along to Los Angeles. I did not add to his dismay and dread of the situation. I offered no objections to having him do as he deemed necessary and best."

On April 28 Darrow received a telegram from Olaf Tveitmoe in San Francisco: "CALIFORNIA UNION LABOR WANTS YOU CHIEF COUNSEL LOS ANGELES CASES IMMEDIATELY STOP FULL CHARGE STOP FEE NO CONSIDERATION STOP WIRE."

Darrow responded: "WILL WIRE DEFINITELY TOMORROW GET NO ONE UNTIL CONSULTATION UNLESS ONE FIRST CLASS MAN IN SAN FRANCISCO OR LOS ANGELES STOP I KNOW THE COMPENSATION SATISFACTORY IT IS THE RESPONSIBILITY MAKES ME HESITATE."

Then, on April 29: "I have repeatedly said that I do not want to defend this case. It is purely a question of worry and work. However, it is impossible for me to believe that the men are guilty. They are entitled to a fair defense. . . . If all the elements behind the defense insist that I defend these men I will consider it my duty to do so."

On May 13, 1911, Job Harriman received the following terse telegram from Darrow: "Expect to start next week." Headlined the *Times*:

"Darrow Wires He Will Come At Early Date." The subhead read: "All Doubt Is Removed as to Arrival of Chicago Attorney to Defend the M'Namara Brothers by Receipt of Wire."

On May 25 Darrow arrived in Los Angeles to answer the call to duty. It would turn out to be the most tragic mistake he ever made.

The McNamara case would ruin him.

Chapter 31

Earl Rogers was in his Los Angeles office with his daughter, Adela, when the news arrived that Darrow would defend the McNamaras.

"Is there any chance that they are innocent?" Adela asked her father.

"No," Rogers answered.

"Do you suppose Mr. Darrow thinks they are?"

Rogers sat behind his desk, Adela would later recall, "rolling a cigarette, letting the first puff drift around his head, his face screwed up in disturbance, very thoughtful."

She was well aware that Darrow was one of her father's heroes, and that had something to do with his extended silence. Perhaps her father idolized Darrow because he often seemed to be linked to "A Cause." And perhaps, as she would write, he was "torn with concern for the man he so much admired. No one knew better than Earl Rogers all the difficulties of defending guilty clients." Yet that was what lawyers often did. In this country, "every person is entitled to a defense. It is not only the right but the duty of every lawyer to defend." The words had been spoken by Clarence Darrow.

In any case, Earl Rogers never answered the question.

Darrow's soon-to-be clients were scheduled to arrive at the Santa Fe train station in downtown Los Angeles at 3:00 p.m. on April 26, 1911. Los Angeles District Attorney John Fredericks, however, had grown concerned that union operatives might move to spring the prisoners or that they might attempt to escape into the crowd of spectators expected to gather at the downtown station. As a precaution, he arranged to have

The Llewellyn Ironworks, showing the minimal damage that resulted from Ortie McManigal's bombing on Christmas Day, 1910. It would eventually prove to be enough, however, to send J. J. McNamara, who ordered it, to prison for nearly nine and a half years.

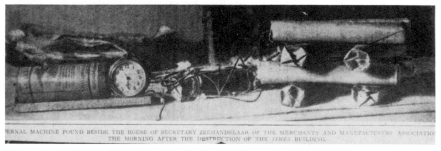

ERNAL MACHINE FOUND BESIDE THE HOUSE OF SECRETARY ZEEHANDELAAR OF THE MERCHANTS AND MANUFACTURERS' ASSOCIATION THE MORNING AFTER THE DESTRUCTION OF THE *TIMES* BUILDING.

The unexploded Zeehandelaar bomb. It would reveal clues that would help lead to the capture of the dynamiters. COURTESY HUNTINGTON LIBRARY, ART COLLECTIONS AND BOTANICAL GARDENS

Attorney Earl Rogers. In an era before Hollywood stars, he was the closest thing to one. Dapper, handsome, with a remarkable court record, it was seemingly inevitable that the city would turn to the nationally famous Rogers to help track down the dynamiters.

Burns (left) followed by reporters.

Clarence and Ruby Darrow.

No. 140   Times 3   Charge $ Paid $ 135

Wanted By Party of men 16—24 foot Launch
for 10 Days cruise around Bay and Tributaries
best of Refs

JOHN GRAY, 689 E. 22d st., Oakland.

MISCELLANEOUS WANTS

WANTED—By party of men, 16 by 24 foot
launch for 10 days to cruise around bay and
tributaries; best of reference. Box 1885, Call.

DRESS SUITS, tuxedos, Prince Alberts and other

The *Pastime/Peerless*. Although it effectively hid the dynamiters' cargo, its unusual design attracted attention everywhere it went. COURTESY HUNTINGTON LIBRARY, ART COLLECTIONS AND BOTANICAL GARDENS

The contents of the safe at Iron Workers headquarters in Indianapolis, including a suitcase said to belong to J. J. McNamara, the components for several infernal machines, and a revolver "to be used only if confronted by a guard." COURTESY HUNTINGTON LIBRARY, ART COLLECTIONS AND BOTANICAL GARDENS

The Valley Gem piano box stored in Farmer Jones's barn containing a half ton of "union records."

J. B. McNamara arriving at the train station in Pasadena and covering his face as he hears Lena Ingersoll shout, "It is Bryce!" FROM THE *LOS ANGELES HERALD* COLLECTION, COURTESY

MCNAMARAS WORK
IN JUTE FACTORY

Dynamiters Pass a Sleepless
Night; Wake in Darkness
to Begin Long Grind.

Behind the thick walls of San Quen-

As the trial got under way with the selection of a jury, the *San Francisco Chronicle* published photographs of some of the prosecution's key witnesses.

A distraught Emma McManigal leaving Los Angeles County Jail after failing to convince her husband to recant his confession. COURTESY LOS ANGELES PUBLIC LIBRARY

Jurors playing cards and (below) their temporary living quarters.

With J. B. McNamara seated to his right, Darrow questions a prospective juror.

Samuel Gompers posing with the McNamaras in their prison cell. "They impressed me with their sincerity."

Mr Samuel Gompers,
C/o American Federation of Labor Convention,
Atlanta, Ga.
Sincere

Fraternal Greeting to the Officials and Delegates to the Atlanta, Georgia, Convention of the American Federation of Labor. ~~Permit us to~~ May your deliberations redound to the continued advancement of the great Labor Movement.

Permit us to sincerely thank the Federation officials you and through them the representatives of affiliated organizations and Departments for their untiring efforts in our behalf.

J. J. & J. B. McNamara

A letter to Samuel Gompers presumably intended for publication in the program for the AF of L's 1911 convention.

Los Angeles Cal
Dec. 4. 1911

I, J. B. McNamara defendant in the case of the people against McNamara and others having heretofore plead guilty to the crime of murder desire to make this statement of facts concerning the same:—
And this is the truth on the night of ~~Oct~~ Sept 30, 1910, at 5.45 p.m. I placed in ink alley a portion of the Times Building a suit case containing 16 sticks of 80 per cent Dynamite set to explode at one oclock the next morning it was my intention to injure the building and scare the owners. I did not intend to take the the life of any one. I sincerely regret that those unfortunate men lost their lives, if the giving of my life would bring them back I would freely give it. In fact too in pleading guilty to murder in the first degree I have placed my life in the hands of the state.

J. B. McNamara

J. B. McNamara's handwritten confession (with a little help from attorney LeCompte Davis).

A ribbon worn by a member of the McNamara Protest Committee.

One of the dozens of demonstrations staged throughout the United States by organized labor on behalf of the McNamaras.

Vaudeville performers staged fund-raisers for the McNamara defense.

COURTESY ARCHIVES AND RARE BOOKS LIBRARY, UNIVERSITY OF CINCINNATI

The McNamara brothers, appearing in court for their sentencing. PHOTOGRAPH BY THE *LOS ANGELES HERALD,* COURTESY THE LOS ANGELES PUBLIC LIBRARY

J. J. McNamara, who directed the most destructive campaign of industrial sabotage in US history and who plotted to bring the city of Los Angeles to its knees, would wind up—a number.

Attorneys Jerry Geisler and Clarence Darrow as they await the jury's verdict in Darrow's second trial. PHOTOGRAPH BY THE *LOS ANGELES HERALD,* COURTESY THE LOS ANGELES PUBLIC LIBRARY

The reconstructed Times Building, which opened two years after the bombing.

them taken into custody separately at the Pasadena and South Pasadena train depots. Burns concurred and instructed his men and the LAPD officers on the train to expect serious trouble upon their arrival, issuing orders that "the prisoners will be surrounded with a cordon of men armed to the teeth."

All the while, Burns was growing increasingly alarmed over certain aspects of the case. Throughout the journey he had consistently read accounts expressing outrage over his tactics, and he was now worried that the initial public sentiment was tilting dangerously in favor of the McNamara brothers. Taking a page from Darrow's playbook, he called ahead to inform certain trusted members of the press that two of his prisoners would be arriving shortly at the Pasadena train station. He then called the Los Angeles Police Department to have them escort Lena Ingersoll to the train station to identify her former lover and boarder, J. B. McNamara, in front of the reporters.

The train pulled into Pasadena at 2:05 p.m., and the manacled and cuffed men, surrounded by a bevy of armed guards, prepared to detrain. The drama was choreographed just as Burns had instructed, with Lena Ingersoll seated next to a female investigator for the district attorney's office in an open-topped automobile that had been drawn up next to the one in which J. B. McNamara was about to be driven to jail. Lena wore a heavy veil and a large swooping hat that obscured her face. As planned, J. B. appeared in the door of the Pullman, looking "like the 100-pound man described in the official circulars," wrote a *Chicago Daily Tribune* reporter. He paused before the pool of journalists, descended, and then stepped up and into a waiting police car. Just then Lena Ingersoll swept back the veil and shouted in a voice audible to everyone present: "It is Bryce!"

J. B. instinctively shrank away from Lena's gaze, attempting to cover his face with an unbound hand, presenting to the dozens of reporters—nearly all of whom had been reporting for the past six months on the mysterious J. B. Bryce—an unintentional but very convincing picture of guilt.

With J. J. McNamara still onboard, the train then moved on to its next stop, South Pasadena. A few reporters who had been alerted had gathered at the tracks to see the by-now-famous union official disembark.

"His manner was so dignified and impressive," noted *Chicago Daily Tribune* reporter John Gray, who observed that the officers accompanied him "almost as a dignitary, rather than a prisoner." He did not look like a bomber who had been arrested, but rather a magazine editor and attorney who had been kidnapped. J. J. McNamara tipped his hat to the crowd, and he was off to jail.

There, in the booking office, he would encounter his brother. He looked away. The two did not speak.

Three days later, J. B. McNamara was taken from his cell in the county jail and, along with ten other prisoners, taken to the visitors' room. A teenaged boy, accompanied by a deputy district attorney, was waiting for them. He glanced at the lineup, pointed directly at J. B. McNamara, and remarked, "That's him."

Corroborating Lena Ingersoll's identification of McNamara as the man who called himself Bryce was Trevor McCachren, a bellboy who worked at the Argonaut Hotel in San Francisco, who remembered J. B. as the man who never allowed him to help with his heavy luggage. Pointing at J. B., whose face flushed, McCachren said, "I know this one. He is Jim Bryce."

Chapter 32

There was a conspicuous reason for the American Federation of Labor's promise-him-anything approach to the Great Defender—his victory four years earlier in the Haywood-Moyer-Pettibone case, a case that had threatened the very survival of the labor movement. It was also the case that had lifted Clarence Darrow into the ranks of international celebrities.

The Haywood Affair, as it had come to be known, began on December 30, 1905, when the antilabor ex-governor of Idaho, Frank Steunenberg, was murdered by a dynamite bomb planted at the entrance to his home. James McParland of the Pinkerton Agency was assigned the task of hunting down the bombers, and soon arrested one Harry Orchard. During the course of "a rough interrogation," Orchard confessed and claimed that his accomplices in the Steunenberg murder were Charles Moyer, president of the Western Federation of Miners (WFM), his sometime bodyguard, "Big Bill" Haywood, and another man affiliated with the WFM, George Pettibone. McParland promptly had the three men arrested in Denver and hauled off to Idaho without so much as a hearing. Laborites across the country were outraged, denouncing McParland as a kidnapper. But Orchard's confession seemed damning. Even labor-friendly President Roosevelt weighed in by labeling the union men "undesirable citizens" well before their trial even began. Thousands of working people responded by wearing buttons proclaiming: "I am an undesirable citizen."

The trial began in May of 1907, with Clarence Darrow heading the defense. It would now be Darrow's moment. In his closing arguments, while denouncing Orchard as a man who had acted as a vigilante and had accused the union leaders in an effort to escape the gallows, he nevertheless seemed to advocate the use of "any means necessary" to achieve labor's ends, passionately declaring, "I don't care how many crimes these weak, rough, rugged, unlettered men . . . are guilty of. I know their cause is just."

It was said that Darrow could voice the most unorthodox and unpopular views, yet still win over his listeners. A friend once remarked, "With his gifts as a speaker and writer and with his winning personality, there is no office in this country Darrow could not have obtained if he had been politically ambitious and practical. But then, he would not have been Darrow."

But perhaps he felt justified making such improvident admissions before the jury in the Haywood trial because he knew what its verdict would be. Enemies and friends alike suspected him of having bribed the bailiff and several jurors during the proceedings. His fellow attorney, Charles Erskine Scott Wood, became convinced that Darrow had no scruples when it came to defending his clients. In the end Darrow won an acquittal for Haywood, and later the freedom of Moyer and Pettibone. (Some historians have suggested that jurors voted for acquittal because they feared retaliation from union thugs if they did not.) At the age of fifty, Clarence Darrow found himself the hero of millions of working Americans.

So it was that, nearly six years later, Darrow finally shook hands with Gompers and the other union leaders and agreed to take the McNamara case. "Hard as it was to give them a 'Yes,'" he would later write, "it would have been harder to say 'No.'"

But shortly after accepting the case, Darrow regretted having done so.

Arriving in Los Angeles on May 25, he headed straight from the station to the county jail to meet his new clients. He did not ask them whether they were innocent or guilty. "In all of his cases," Ruby Darrow was to say later, "Mr. Darrow tried not to know, because he could do better work if he was allowed to presume his clients innocent and go along on that assumption."

But as Darrow pored over the evidence against the brothers, he saw that the prosecution had built a seemingly watertight case against them, complete with forensic results, a battalion of eyewitnesses, incriminating correspondence, union ledgers, matching dynamite, nitroglycerin, and clocks—all topped off and corroborated by a devastating confession by one of the principal bombers. He may have not asked the brothers about their guilt, but at one meeting with them at the county jail, he blurted out, "By God, you've left a trail a mile wide!"

Chapter 33

It was as if the country had suddenly become mobilized for civil war. From the moment the prisoners arrived at county jail, throngs of outraged demonstrators all over the United States took to the streets to protest. On May 1, 1911, May Day, more than twenty thousand banner-carrying protesters—6 percent of the city's entire population—paraded around the Temple Street jail. It was the biggest political demonstration Los Angeles had ever witnessed. The AF of L had designated the day "McNamara Day" and had distributed McNamara lapel buttons to union members across the country, showing a picture of J. J. McNamara with the word "Kidnapped" in red letters below—and the words "Justice for the McNamaras AF of L" above. In cities all over the country, the American labor movement displayed a solidarity that was virtually unmatched in its history. Only the American Federation of Musicians refused to support the McNamaras; the president of the Los Angeles local, C. L. Bagley, was convinced that the brothers were guilty.

While all the rallies were going on, Samuel L. Browne, chief detective of the district attorney's office, paid a visit to J. B. McNamara in the county jail and, over his vigorous objections, took his fingerprints. He then sent copies to San Francisco to be compared with those left at various locations by Bryce, including the particularly clear ones left on the *Pastime*.

Four days later, on May 5, the McNamaras made their first appearance in the packed courtroom of Judge Walter Bordwell for their arraignment. At 3:30 in the afternoon they were marched across the "bridge of sighs" connecting the county jail to the new Hall of Justice. Prosecutor W. J. Ford opened the routine proceedings.

"You are John J. McNamara? That is your true name?" Ford asked.

"I am," he replied, his voice barely audible.

He turned to the other prisoner.

"James B. McNamara? That is your true name?"

Ford's booming voice now filled the courtroom. "The grand jurors have indicted you for murder," he said and began reading from the indictment, charging that the two men and their accomplices did "willfully, unlawfully, feloniously and with malice aforethought kill and murder one Churchill Harvey-Elder, a human being." He then began ticking off the names of eighteen other men who had died in the *Times* holocaust, dramatically emphasizing the word "murder" as he read each count from the lined legal document. J. J. McNamara appeared visibly upset. He clasped his hands behind his back tightly. He stood rigid throughout the proceedings, looking away from the accusing prosecutor. J. B., by contrast, the man accused of being the actual perpetrator, appeared almost indifferent. He held his black derby hat behind him, sometimes strumming a light tattoo on the rim with his fingers. Every seat in the 150-seat courtroom was filled, and fifty persons waited outside in the hallway.

Ford then handed each man a copy of testimony from 183 witnesses who had appeared before the grand jury, a volume that exceeded three thousand pages. Judge Bordwell asked both sides to refrain from making the testimony public.

He then set June 1 as the date on which the men would enter pleas. In the meantime, they would continue to be held without bail.

The proceedings thus concluded, the two prisoners were ushered back to their jail cells. The formalities had been dispensed with.

⚊⌒⚊

Word that Clarence Darrow was on his way to California to defend the McNamaras was greeted with a roar of approval from labor leaders, Socialists, and working men and women across the country. Reporters who gathered around him hung on his every word as he expounded on the proposition that the two brothers had been framed. He would prove it, he told them.

But many defenders of the McNamaras went further. They contin-ued to maintain that the bomb had been planted by General Otis's own henchmen. In New York City, American Federation of Labor leaders organized what they called a Monster Rally, attended by thousands, to coincide with Darrow's departure to the West Coast. The Socialist Party of America promised its full support, which was considerable with its four thousand local organizations and media outlets that included ten daily newspapers and one hundred weeklies. Darrow's former client, Bill Hay-wood, and the radical Industrial Workers of the World (IWW) called for a general nationwide strike in support of the McNamaras to take place on the day their trial began.

One of those who had taken notice of Darrow's entry into the case was his erstwhile bohemian paramour, Mary Field. Mary had moved to New York, where she instantly fell into the circle of the Great Defender's literary and Socialist friends, including the novelist Theodore Dreiser and Max Eastman, who would become editor of *The Masses*. At that time, neither was well known. Another of Darrow's friends, union organizer Mother Jones—"the most dangerous woman in America," as she was sometimes called—soon became a close friend of hers. In no time she was writing for small, radical publications, eventually becoming the coeditor of the *American Magazine*.

After announcing that he would take the McNamara case, Darrow's Chicago office was flooded with interview requests and letters from admirers, detractors, labor leaders, and his legion of friends. One of the letters that eventually found its way onto his desk was from Mary in New York. In it she explained that she would be covering the McNamara trial in Los Angeles for *American Magazine*. To her it was the story of the century.

Darrow wrote back immediately, asking her not to come to Los Angeles. Her presence, he knew, would hurt Ruby. Moreover, he expected that once he got out there he would be followed by detectives for the prosecution. If they learned of anything untoward going on, they would immediately attempt to exploit it, and, he argued in his letter, he and Mary couldn't allow themselves to jeopardize a capital murder case.

When Mary received the response, her independent streak revealed itself in spades. She was a highly regarded journalist, a serious writer, she wrote back, who had no intention of passing up the trial of the century. Not for Ruby, not for Darrow, not for anyone else.

A few days later the Darrows boarded the train in Chicago for Los Angeles with a retinue of reporters in tow. All seemed right with the world that day at Northwest Station in Chicago. Darrow's career was suddenly and unexpectedly in its ascendancy once again; he was smiling, so happy to have Ruby at his side. For three days on the train they were surrounded by friends and admirers.

There was no welcoming committee to greet Darrow in Los Angeles, only Anton Johannsen, the San Francisco labor leader and benefactor of J. B. McNamara's coconspirator, David Caplan. From the train station he was escorted directly to the L.A. County Jail to meet his new clients. Darrow saw at once the stark contrast between the two. J. J. presented himself as the polished, innocent secretary-treasurer he had always claimed to be. As always, J. B. was another matter. After a month of incarceration his language was more profane than ever; J. B. looked every bit the part of the feral unionist bomber. The brief meeting informed Darrow's pretrial strategy. In discussing the case he would focus on J. J.; J. B. would be studiously ignored.

From the jail Darrow headed to the offices that had been rented for him in the Higgins Building at Second and Main Streets, where he began the process of assembling his legal team, selecting his colleagues not so much because of their legal expertise but for their stature. His resident expert on all things California was Le Compte Davis, a conservative former assistant district attorney who had previously worked as an attorney for General Otis. He also hired Joseph Scott, the city's leading Catholic attorney, who, Darrow hoped, would help swing any Catholic jurors in favor of his Catholic clients. Also on his team was the labor attorney Cyrus McNutt, a former Indiana Supreme Court justice. Finally, there was Job Harriman, the Socialist candidate for mayor (whom Davis, years later, described to a reporter as "idealistic" and "likable," but "not too much of a lawyer").

Harriman was an original thinker with ambitious plans for a political party that rarely attracted a majority of voters in municipal elections. In order to do so, he had strenuously argued, Socialists needed to wed themselves to organized labor, although a large block of the party saw unions and their leaders as uncommitted to the principles of class struggle and opposition to the capitalist system. By standing for solidarity with the unions, Harriman had been all but banished from the party's leadership; but now, with the groundswell of nationwide support for the McNamara brothers, his comrades recognized the political opportunity the case presented for their party and nominated him to run for mayor of Los Angeles. A few months earlier, the Republican reformer Hiram Johnson, General Otis's archenemy, had won the governorship. If Harriman won the L.A. mayor's seat, Otis's dream of a union-free Los Angeles would be all but dead.

Meanwhile, the McNamara trial and the elections were becoming braided together in a most extraordinary way. The trial was expected to get under way in October, which would likely be followed by the primary for the L.A. mayoral election scheduled for October 31. A verdict was expected shortly after the primary, which would in turn be followed by the general election on December 5.

Harriman would spend the summer and fall of 1911 campaigning, and remain cocounsel in name only. But as such he had irrevocably tied his political fortunes and those of the Socialist Party to the outcome of the McNamara trials.

The brothers, of course, began harmonizing their proclamations of innocence the moment they arrived at their cells at the L.A. County Jail in downtown Los Angeles. In model penmanship J. J. McNamara wrote out a statement on April 26 and handed it to Leo Rappaport in the visitors' room, who in turn had it typed up, copied, and distributed to the press, where it appeared unedited the following day—even in the *Los Angeles Times*. It also appeared in virtually every union bulletin in the country—and was addressed to union members:

A MANLY FRATERNAL GREETING

To the Brotherhood of Organized Labor in California and the United States:

In this second attempt to crush and discredit the cause we represent, I realize fully the desperation of the enemies of labor arrayed against us, but I am of good heart, for it will fail.

That I am innocent of any infraction of the law in word or act needs no emphasis from me, for the truth is mighty and will prevail right speedily, and for it I shall contentedly wait.

I send to all brothers and friends of union labor the world over my earnest and affectionate greetings, with the assurance that there is no villainy or conspiracy possible of which we are afraid.

I am also confident that it is not asking too much of the public to suspend judgment in these matters until opportunity for a full and fair defense has been afforded.

John J. McNamara

Never had such volatile understatement been set so adroitly to paper. Within days, letters and telegrams of support from outraged workers began turning up at the Los Angeles County Jail by the sackful. Many were written on the letterheads of union locals.

William Dobson, secretary of the Bricklayers, Masons and Plasterers' International Union of America, wrote: "To my mind, our would-be destroyers believe that by the sudden and swift removal of able and successful leaders from our midst, the surest method of our annihilation has been found, and I believe that in the person of John J. McNamara they found a leader whose powers for bringing victory to the cause he represents have proved so great that his removal from his field of operations was the only means by which the progress of his organization could be temporarily retarded."

Letters of profound sympathy and support arrived at the home of Mary McNamara, the brothers' mother. After visiting J. J. in jail, J. E. Timmons, head of the Iron Workers local in Los Angeles, wrote to her on April 28, saying that "he looks and feels well and is quite brave and cheerful and feels sure that he will be acquitted. . . . He sends his best love to you and asks that you do not worry as everything will come out all right." The family priest, the Rev. M. J. Fitzpatrick, wrote two weeks later to the McNamara's younger brother Robert, "Although I cannot say much to soften the anguish that I know must be weighing down your poor mother's heart at the prospect of her boys being under such a serious charge, still I would fain say one word of comfort in her hour of trial. God is good and He will see justice done in His own good time, and I would urge you therefore to have confidence in His Justice and pray that He may set all things straight."

But no one wrote more frequently than Herbert Hockin—often as many as three chatty letters a week, keeping J. J. apprised of the union's affairs and what it was doing in his defense. "Relative to the toilet set that was sent you. I mailed you that myself," he wrote in one letter. In another: "Say Joe, do you ever hear from Clancy? I have not had a scratch of a pen from him since he left headquarters. . . . I cannot understand why he does not write me." In another, he urged him to send a column to be included in *Bridgemen's Magazine.* "If I do not receive it by tomorrow, I will be unable to publish it." By now Hockin was not only the temporary editor of *Bridgemen's Magazine* but he was also acting secretary-treasurer of the Iron Workers Union, temporarily, at least, replacing the man he had betrayed. He had also formally entered into a plea bargain with the Los Angeles District Attorney's office to testify for the prosecution at the McNamara trial—and any subsequent trials involving Iron Workers officials—in exchange for a light sentence for his own role in the union bombings.

Chapter 34

Despondent and out of sorts, Earl Rogers found himself walking by the Los Angeles County Jail with Adela one day in June 1911. Inside those walls were the men suspected of killing their young friend Churchill Harvey-Elder. But as the forty-one-year-old father and his seventeen-year-old daughter approached the building, they happened to see a throng of adoring women gathered around J. B. McNamara's jail cell window. The sight appalled Adela. When she saw one of the girls blowing kisses at the window, she ran after the young woman and "got into a hair-pulling match." Her father separated the girls and told Adela she was "too old for [that] anymore." (But if she had looked inside the barred windows, she might have been even more appalled—floral arrangements overflowed J. J.'s cell on the third floor and J. B.'s in the basement and now decorated the usually bleak corridors outside, all sent by adoring women.)

Shortly after the arrival of the McNamara brothers, Rogers had learned that D. A. Fredericks no longer wanted to retain him as a prosecutor in the case. Fredericks had set his sights on the governor's mansion and wasn't about to share the spotlight with anyone, certainly not the grandstanding Earl Rogers. On the same day that Fredericks said that he would not hire additional assistants, the Merchants and Manufacturers Association disclosed that Rogers was no longer representing them and that the organization would leave the case exclusively in the hands of the D. A. So Rogers would be relegated to the status of spectator at the Trial of the Century—if he decided to attend the trial at all—while Fredericks would be doing what Rogers had been expecting to do: cross-examining troublesome defense witnesses.

Meanwhile, Clarence and Ruby Darrow found immediate quarters in a posh suite at the Alexandria Hotel in downtown Los Angeles. As Darrow began preparing his legal battle plan, he determined that the first order of business ought to be organizing an effective counteroffensive against the *Times*, General Otis, Burns, and the prosecution. At the same time a second campaign was to be launched extolling the virtues of J. J. McNamara. Within days of the McNamara brothers' arrival, red, white, and blue banners inscribed with SAVE THE MCNAMARAS were swinging from "barber poles, cars, front porches, and were displayed in store windows," noted Adela Rogers.

In addition to the thousands of buttons featuring J. J. McNamara's image, the AF of L now began distributing similar stamps. However, they began confusing sorting machines at the post office, causing the US postmaster to issue a decree noting that by law no stamps resembling US postage stamps may be affixed to letters on the address side. The AF of L quickly responded to the order by designing an octagonal-shaped stamp. However, that too was rejected by the Postal Service, which warned that any letter displaying it on the address side would automatically be sent to the Dead Letter Office.

Darrow immediately drew on a network of union and pro-union publications that he had at his disposal, just as he had during the Haywood trial. Eugene Debs's weekly Socialist publication, *Appeal to Reason*, alone boasted a national circulation of more than four hundred thousand. And Debs had already expanded distribution throughout Los Angeles with headlines that implicated the capitalists of that city in a vast, murderous conspiracy.

"Sound the alarm to the working class!" Debs wrote as if he were shouting from a campaign platform. "There is to be a repetition of the Moyer-Haywood-Pettibone outrage upon the labor movement. . . . Be not deceived by the capitalist press!" In Los Angeles, the capitalist press, of course, was General Otis's *Times*, which was waging its own propaganda campaign in the spring and summer of 1911 with headlines such as "Declares Men Sure to Hang," over a subhead of "Burns Sure of his Evidence." Another announced: "Unionite Plots Quickly Squelched."

Darrow's tactic was simultaneously easy to pull off and elaborately contrived—and exhaustively field-tested during the Haywood trial. Drumming up support for his defendants by accusing the victim of complicity in the crime had worked in Idaho four years earlier. In the *Times* case, the victim, as personified by the blustering, widely scorned General Otis, made for an easy target.

At just what point Darrow also decided to engage in witness and juror tampering is unclear. He would later admit that from the very beginning he realized his clients were guilty and that his case was, in his own word, "hopeless." No matter, he would add, "It is a lawyer's business to save life."

So why did he not do what countless criminal attorneys have done in the past when faced with such circumstances—broker a plea bargain with the prosecution? The answer, almost certainly, was that things had progressed too far. The entire American labor movement was committed to proving the McNamaras innocent. The careers of its leadership hung in the balance. And there was that $50,000 retainer Darrow had received from them—money he desperately needed after being nearly financially ruined a few months earlier. No, he would now have to employ any means necessary to get his clients off.

He realized at once that his most challenging obstacle was Ortie McManigal's confession, for it was broad in scope, minutely detailed, and utterly convincing—particularly his account of the events surrounding the Christmas Day bombing of the Llewellyn Iron Works for which J. J. McNamara was charged. Was there the possibility that McManigal also represented the prosecution's Achilles' heel? Perhaps, he must have thought, if he could only convince McManigal to retract his confession and to cooperate with the defense, then a reasonable doubt could be raised about the testimony of Burns's other witnesses, and the detective's abundant evidence would thereby become undermined.

To execute such a coup Darrow knew that he and his team had to hit McManigal ruthlessly where he was the most vulnerable, and Darrow knew where that was. Emma McManigal had been steadfastly proclaiming her husband's innocence ever since learning of his arrest. She was also known to be faithful to the cause of organized labor. Her cooperation alone, Darrow recognized, was significant, as Burns himself had gone on record calling Emma "one of the most important witnesses against J. J. McNamara." Burns was aware from Ortie's confession that she had often been the conduit between her husband and union officials, including J. J. McNamara.

Darrow had identified another point of vulnerability for the hapless McManigal. The former bomber, Darrow learned, had been raised by his grandfather and his uncle George Behm in the wake of his mother's death thirty years earlier. McManigal was understood to be still close to Behm, a staunchly union railroad engineer living in Portage, Wisconsin. Thus Darrow's scheme entailed squeezing McManigal between his wife and his surrogate father. It may not have been legal, and certainly not ethical, but Darrow was out to win a monumental case, as his friend and mentor Erskine Wood had foretold, using "bribery where safe, perjury where safe."

In early June, Darrow returned to Chicago, where he had arranged to confer with Samuel Gompers. His most important meeting, however, was with Emma. To his great delight he discovered that he wasn't going to have any difficulty whatsoever in convincing her to cooperate, for she had made it clear just how desperate her life had become. No money had been coming in from her husband. Their savings had dwindled to almost nothing.

"Do I need help?" she rhetorically asked a reporter shortly after the meeting with Darrow. "Well, I'll get along and take care of the children until my husband gets clear of this trouble—for he will; I know he will."

And Darrow, flush with a virtually unlimited expense fund, knew exactly how to help the impoverished wife. First, Emma was brought into his inner circle and made to feel cared for and safe. Darrow invited her to his Midway flat, which must have appeared palatial to Emma, who was about to be evicted from her comfortable Sangamon Street home for failure to pay her modest rent.

Darrow's familial company and cocounsels were all contrast to the aggressive Burns detectives. Darrow played the part of Emma's savior, and played it well. Completely convinced of his good intentions and the inevitability of his success—he had never lost a significant case involving a working man—Emma was sure that Ortie would come around. Their future together, she now believed, lay with the tall, eloquent man—the celebrated Great Defender—who had offered to represent him for free.

To Darrow's further delight, Emma also agreed to talk to Ortie's uncle George Behm. With little prodding the old man came down to Chicago from Wisconsin and was invited to Darrow's home where he gladly agreed to accompany him to Los Angeles, meet with Ortie in his cell at the L.A. County Jail, and explain to him exactly what he needed to do with his confession.

In mid-June Darrow was off to Washington, DC, where he again met with the executive council of the AF of L to develop a broader strategy for defending the McNamaras. From DC he took a train north to New York City, where he was regaled with a Monster Rally held in his honor on the day of his departure. Back in Chicago he gathered up his legal staff, his wife Ruby, Emma McManigal and her two children, her neighbor friend Sadie McGuire and her daughter, and George Behm. Together they headed to the Northwestern station while a parade of eighty thousand working men and women marched through downtown Chicago in a show of support for J.J. McNamara. Brimming with confidence and newfound vigor, and surrounded by a throng of cheering unionists who had arrived at the station to give their hero a proper send-off, Darrow headed for the West Coast for the second time to defend the working class from what he was now calling "an antilabor plot."

Three days later, on June 26, 1911, the ever-expanding Darrow entourage arrived in Los Angeles on the Santa Fe Limited, whereupon Clarence and Ruby moved into their new temporary home at the Rampart Apartments on the corner of Sixth Street and Rampart Boulevard. Darrow immediately began making arrangements with attachés of the Los Angeles District Attorney's office for Emma to talk privately with her incarcerated husband, who was saying that he "wanted one more chance to plead with her to return to me, and to remain by my side during the trial." But Darrow had something very different in mind when he began drafting a document for Emma to present to Ortie to sign—one stating that "in the future, union labor attorneys only should be permitted to see him."

The document also declared that Ortie was retracting his confession.

Chapter 35

With the help of the Burns agency, Ortie McManigal had managed to turn his jail cell on the second floor into a fairly cozy nook. In one corner he had set up exercise equipment that he used each day and which had helped him bring his weight down to 158 pounds. On a desk lay a set of mechanical drawing instruments. On the walls of the cell he had hung photographs and copies of paintings. One of them showed President Lincoln with his son Tad. There was a picture of Lord Cornwall surrendering to Washington at Yorktown. And there was a collection of photographs of famous actors and actresses, including Joseph Jefferson, who had died five years earlier, perhaps the most famous comic actor of his day. Among this collection was also a picture of a cowboy holding a revolver at arm's length above the motto, "Live so you can look every man in the eye and tell him to go to hell."

He received frequent visits from District Attorney Fredericks and other members of the prosecution team. It was Assistant DA Ford who had brought him the news that Darrow was escorting McManigal's wife, Emma, to California to see him. McManigal and Ford, who were about the same age, had struck up an intimate friendship and often talked about their families. McManigal's children, Evelyn and Walter, were six and five, respectively. Ford, McManigal had learned, had three children: Jack, who was four; Robert, three; and Margaret, one. But in recent weeks Ford's lovely twenty-eight-year-old wife, Maud, had developed peritonitis, a painful infection of the lining of the abdominal wall, and was being treated at Clara Barton Hospital. However, she was not responding to medication, and indeed, there were more times than not when it was McManigal who was working to boost the spirits of the prosecutor.

McManigal was elated, of course, to hear the news that Emma would be coming to see him. But Ford then warned him about what lay in store. He told McManigal that Darrow had persuaded Emma to support the McNamaras and that she had been brought to California for only one purpose—to persuade him to repudiate his confession.

Ortie didn't believe it. His wife, he was sure, "would remain true to me in my hour of need."

Ortie McManigal was sitting in the grand jury anteroom when the door opened. His heart pounding, he immediately stood up when he saw Emma and asked, "Dear, is it you?"

He had expected his wife to come toward him, but Emma inexplicably sauntered to the opposite side of the room. Deeply puzzled, he approached her and took her in his arms, and together they sobbed for a long while. When they separated, Emma sat at the table, and then stated rather coolly, "I have only fifteen minutes to stay with you."

Ortie understood and immediately began to beg Emma, "Come back to me and leave the labor attorneys."

"Darrow's my friend," Emma replied.

McManigal took his wife in his arms again and began beseeching her to cooperate with the prosecutors and "when [you get] to the stand to tell the truth."

Emma refused. She continually repeated that "the union attorneys would get you out on bond immediately if you would consent to see them and denounce the attachés of the district attorney's office."

He tearfully shook his head while Emma maintained her resolve. She then produced the document Darrow had drafted, which, she said, would bring them together again.

"As soon as you sign it, steps will be taken by Darrow to get you out on bond," she told him. "A check for four figures will be placed in my hands immediately." Darrow would send the entire family back to Chicago and get him a good-paying job, and this whole nightmare would be over. He recognized at once that it was all nonsense. The DA would have him hauled back to California to stand trial for conspiracy to commit murder, a capital offense.

"I'd give up my life for you and the babies if necessary," Ortie sobbed, "but not for the McNamaras."

Emma remained unmoved.

Ortie then attempted to explain that he was in no position to back out, that he had already signed a sworn statement and had to see this matter through. He desperately caught the attention of one of the sheriff's deputies in the room and asked him to explain to Emma the position he was in. But Emma plugged her ears with her fingers, closed her eyes, and began yelling for Ortie to just sign the document.

Furious, she shouted, "If you don't sign it, you'll never see me again." McManigal was stunned.

In the silence that followed, Emma pushed the document and a pen before Ortie. Completely broken, he took the pen and the document and did as his wife instructed. He then asked to see his children, who were just outside the anteroom in the foyer. Emma merely stood and hurried from the room, where she was immediately surrounded by the tall, pale-faced figures of Darrow, Harriman, Davis, and the bodyguard they had provided for her. Ortie could see his children milling about in the hallway, but for now would be denied their company.

He could hear Emma screaming outside the door, then heard her collapse, followed by a commotion from those around her. He put his head in his arms and wept. "A peculiar feeling came over me that I was unable to fathom," he said later.

A few minutes after he was led back to his cell he called for Gallagher and asked him to summon DA Fredericks and Assistant DA Ford.

"They have poisoned her against me," he told the prosecutors when they arrived. Then McManigal told them about the document he had signed. Fredericks and Ford were outraged—not so much with McManigal but with Emma and "the unionite lawyers" in their brazen attempt to solicit perjury from their star witness. They then drafted another document rescinding the one Emma had just had him sign, and set it before the hapless bomber. McManigal paused, then signed this document as well, glumly conscious that he was also signing away his marriage and his children.

———

The very next day Emma was scheduled to appear before the special grand jury. Darrow explained to her that in a grand jury hearing he would not be permitted to be in the room with her, and that she was to answer none of the questions. Emma was terrified at the prospect of not having Darrow at her side. She nevertheless rose to the occasion and remained silent in the face of Fredericks's and Ford's questions. For the second time in as many days, the prosecutors were again furious with their star witness's wife and asked Judge Bordwell to cite her for contempt. The judge promised to consider the request but would ultimately decline, concluding that the husband-wife relationship enjoyed its own privilege of confidentiality.

Emma left the courtroom in tears, with Darrow and Harriman waiting for her when she emerged. They were escorting her when, as chance had it, she and Ortie met in the hallway. Both broke down as Ortie attempted to embrace his wife. And Emma fainted. When she came to she found herself being carried away by Darrow himself.

The pressure was taking a toll on Emma's health, but her ordeal was only beginning. The following night she and her friend Sadie took the children to dinner at the Lankershim Hotel and immediately found themselves under the surveillance of Burns detectives. After supper, Emma and Sadie led the three children out to the automobile, scurrying along in an attempt to elude the detectives. They jumped into their own automobile, engaging in a race through downtown Los Angeles in which "corners were rounded at a terrific speed," as the *Los Angeles Times* reported, "the detectives tearing along behind in their wake." The women raced through the unfamiliar city to their West Sixth Street apartment, where they ran inside with their children and locked the door—only to discover that the detectives had rented the adjacent apartment. Indeed, the entire building was soon surrounded by shadowy figures guarding doors and windows all around the perimeter of the building. Within minutes reporters were also descending upon the neighborhood.

Emma immediately called Darrow's office and spoke with Harriman, who arrived minutes later, passing through a gauntlet of detectives and reporters, to calm his prize witness. To the newsmen on hand, Emma "appeared worn and nervously run down from the excitement," but Harriman reassured her that he and Darrow had detectives of their own watching Burns's operatives to make sure nothing happened to her or the children. Such was the paranoid state of the pretrial universe, with everyone spying on everyone else, each side heavily bankrolled and able to hire dozens of detectives. The situation so unnerved Emma that she checked into Pacific Hospital in downtown Los Angeles, where she was treated for anxiety.

Although his scheme to invalidate McManigal's confession was in an advanced state of unraveling, Darrow could not have been more pleased with the national hoopla surrounding his clients. By late June prosecutors were clearly on the defensive, as the momentum of public sympathy for the McNamaras continued to build. The defense was equally effective at keeping Emma's hospitalization in the papers, garnering sympathy as she played with aplomb the role of the distraught, faithful wife.

Darrow was on the offensive in the courthouse as well. At the July 6 hearing, he challenged Judge Bordwell's impartiality in a maneuver to quash the indictments against the brothers. Bordwell, who indeed was a firm supporter of the MMA, was having none of it. Six days later he overruled the motion and set a trial date of October 11, 1911.

In his jail cell, Ortie McManigal got the word and winced. It would be Emma's thirty-second birthday.

⁓

William J. Burns also felt besieged as Gompers appeared to mobilize public opinion against him.

In late April he had received a death threat by mail. Within a few days the text of the message was circulating in newspapers nationwide:

"You arrested the McNamara brothers illegally and they are innocent. I am the guilty one. Your operatives hunted for me in the west. Ever since the Los Angeles job I have been in New York.

"Tomorrow I sail at 10 a.m. for Europe and will remain there until the trouble is over. I will be kept informed of the progress of the trials of the McNamara boys and McManigal. If they are convicted, I will kill you as sure as your name is Burns. Your son Raymond will meet the same fate. I am an all around machinist and a clockmaker. I can make any kind of explosive without anybody's aid."

The letter was allegedly written and signed by Matthew Schmidt.

As improbable as the message seemed, it could nevertheless prove corrosive to public opinion. Could Matthew Schmidt, who was known to have purchased the dynamite used in the *Times* bombing—and who was still on the loose—have been the actual perpetrator? And the news was only growing worse.

On June 16 Burns was formally indicted by an Indianapolis grand jury for the methods he used in capturing J. J. McNamara, which meant submitting to the indignity of a formal arrest and putting up his own $10,000 bond—every step of which was chronicled in the press. By the end of the month, the depiction of Burns's methods in the press had so concerned the detective that he began to adopt a conciliatory tone toward his adversaries.

"If Mr. Gompers will just sit down with me, at his convenience," Burns said, "I am certain I can convince him this is strictly a criminal case and does not concern organized labor. If need be, I will even show him evidence that cannot be made public as yet."

Gompers dismissed the gesture out of hand, reiterating his accusation that Burns's evidence against the McNamara brothers had been fabricated and planted and that McManigal's confession was "trumped up."

For a time Burns's mood seemed to edge into gloom. "This detective business," he told a reporter, "loses its glamour when one actually gets into it, you know."

And yet he was still being hailed by large blocks of the public, his name lauded. Shortly after the arrests former President Theodore Roosevelt himself wired Burns with congratulations: "ALL GOOD AMERICAN CITIZENS FEEL THAT THEY OWE YOU A DEBT OF GRATITUDE FOR YOUR SIGNAL SERVICE TO AMERICAN CITIZENSHIP."

The approval he was receiving from the district attorney's office in Los Angeles was equally effusive. Assistant District Attorney W. J. Ford was now carrying most of the load of the case.[15] Ford told a *Chicago Daily Tribune* reporter, "I cannot give Detective W. J. Burns too much praise for the careful and thorough way in which he has worked up his case." Several weeks later, as Darrow's propaganda began to resonate in the national media and the attacks on Burns became more vicious, Ford struck a combative note in defending the detective, remarking, "I don't think even a bribed jury would dare acquit [the McNamara brothers] now."

The statement was designed to stick in the craw of the man who, he reckoned, would be willing to perform any shady tactic necessary to save his clients. Before the year was out, even many of Darrow's friends would be wondering if the assistant district attorney hadn't been uncannily perceptive.

Chapter 36

His name was Bert Franklin, and he knew his native patch of Southern California like his own backyard. He had been a guard at the Los Angeles County Jail, where the McNamaras were now spending their days, and had gone on to work for District Attorney John Fredericks, leading numerous criminal investigations—many with Samuel Browne, the detective who had worked hand-in-glove with Earl Rogers in San Francisco in the wake of the bombing. For five years he had served as deputy investigator for the US Marshals' L.A. office. Now, in the summer of 1911, Franklin had been hired by LeCompte Davis of the McNamara defense team to investigate "every prospective juror." He was assigned to learn "what their feelings were toward union labor, their feelings and opinions regarding the *Times* explosion, their opinion as to whether the McNamaras were guilty." He would work out of his own office and be paid in cash directly by Clarence Darrow.

Bert Franklin knew hundreds of citizens of the then small city of Los Angeles as if they were part of his extended family.

On October 5 he and Darrow met at a downtown cafe. As they chatted, Darrow took from his pocket a list of potential jurors given to him by Judge Bordwell. "It's about time to get busy with the jury," Darrow said.

As they carefully combed through the names, Darrow asked Franklin if he knew any of them personally. Franklin said he did. Incredibly, he knew twenty-six of them. Darrow was impressed. One of the men was George H. N. Lockwood, a former policeman and jail guard, whom Franklin described as "a man I had the utmost confidence in . . . a man of character and sterling integrity and that our friendship was such that if he could not accept it, it would go no further." Clearly "it" was money. Another man on the list was an elderly carpenter, Robert Bain. Franklin had known Bain for twenty years and understood that Bain was "hostile to unions." Franklin was also aware that the prosecution knew of Bain's hostility, and that the old carpenter would likely be an acceptable juror in their eyes. What Franklin knew and prosecutors did not was that Bain was having financial difficulties. Like so many in L.A., Bain had played the real estate game—and lost. Now he and his wife Dora were making ends meet by taking odd jobs, he as a carpenter, she as a maid, physical work that they were hardly fit to carry out at their age.

"Do you think you could get him?" Darrow asked.

Franklin replied, "Yes."

That was all Darrow needed to hear. The next day Franklin dropped by the Higgins Building, where they discussed fees. Franklin would receive $5,000 for each juror, $4,000 to be paid to each juror who voted for acquittal with $500 to be paid up front. He would retain the remaining $1,000. Darrow handed him $1,000 in cash to be used in his approaches to Bain and Lockwood.

Darrow had also brought with him to L.A. another Bert, Ruby's younger brother, Bert Hammerstrom. He was assigned to conduct undercover work under Darrow's chief investigator, John Harrington, whose job was to track down and "persuade" witnesses not to testify for the prosecution. A number of detectives were working for Harrington in this capacity, including Larry Sullivan, who was prepared to use all manner of approaches to bring "trustworthy" witnesses into the fold for the defense. Darrow had hired Sullivan on the recommendation of his old friend and cocounsel in the Haywood case, Charles Erskine Scott Wood, and Sullivan appeared to fill the bill, having, like Darrow, no qualms about doing whatever it took to prevail in court. One of the potential witnesses Sullivan was looking to visit was George Phillips of the Giant Powder Works. Phillips had told the grand jury that he could identify the man who had purchased the 80 percent dynamite from him on September 10, 1910.

Nevertheless, as the summer of 1911 wore on, Darrow became increasingly alarmed at the mountain of evidence and testimony the state had been able to procure. Through his spy system, he had learned about evidence that had not been made public. Fingerprints left all over the *Pastime*, for example, turned out to match J. B. McNamara's. To Darrow the prosecution's case looked rock-solid.

But then so did the PR campaign that the unions and the Socialists had mounted on behalf of the McNamaras. Newspaper surveys had Job Harriman leading Mayor Alexander in the mayoral contest, which few thought possible in a city that decidedly had been under the thumb of General Otis and the M&M before the notorious arrests.

Darrow and the defense had a second, unexpected problem as the summer advanced: money. The hundreds of thousands of dollars that the AF of L had promised to raise had yet to materialize. Indeed, Darrow had seen only $80,000 of the $250,000 to $300,000 he had expected to have at his disposal for expenses (apart from his fee of $50,000). And everyone—cocounsels, detectives, landlords, clerks, even witnesses such as Emma McManigal and Uncle George—seemed stubbornly unwilling to do anything on behalf of the McNamaras without being paid in advance. When some staffers were not, they became turncoats, accepting money from Burns and the DA to act as spies for the prosecution.

"There is no way to try this case with a chance of winning without a great deal of money," Darrow appealed to Gompers. "The other side is spending it in every direction. They have all the organized channels of society, the state's attorney, grand jury, police force, mayor, manufacturers association. . . . No one will do anything without money. It is a tough game and I want you to understand it." Gompers got the message and promised a vigorous new fund-raising campaign.

In the meantime, the McNamara brothers and McManigal whiled away their time in their cool cells at the Los Angeles County Jail. According to the union-friendly *Los Angeles Record*, J. J. McNamara spent his summer in autodidactic pursuits, reading "high-class, educating literature" having to do with "education and character building, through the proper control and exercise of his intellect. . . ."

Meanwhile, in the absence of alcohol, J. B. seemed to be in the midst of a monastic spiritual odyssey, his hell-raising temperament having quelled itself to the extent that he had taken to making yarn mats for the other prisoners and even jailer Gallagher and his assistant.

"They both seem to be as contented as any prisoners I have ever had in here," Gallagher told the *Record* reporter.

Outside their barred windows steadfast supporters continued to gather, many of them women, to keep "the McNamara boys" company— fond evidence of the grassroots devotion that they enjoyed. Gompers even announced plans to have the upcoming Labor Day declared "McNamara Day," to support the brothers' defense fund, which by late July (as Darrow had discovered) was all but depleted.

"Funds must be provided to ensure a fair and impartial trial," he declared. "The great need of the hour is money with which to meet the heavy drains incident to the collection of evidence and other necessary expense."

Ortie McManigal, on the other hand, lay in his cell, heartbroken by Emma's behavior and the sense that unionists now regarded him as a traitor. Not a single supporter lingered outside the window of his cell. His Uncle George had visited him just once in his attempt to get him to flip for the defense and then, after having failed, had gone to the newspapers, saying, "When I visited him in the jail, he seemed to be in fear for his life after the trial and said he feared he might be shot by some union men or by detectives. He seemed to be either doped or crazy."

McManigal was neither. He had reached a very rational conclusion when he sobbed to reporters, "My wife has sold herself for a few thousand dollars of union money."

One could conclude too that McManigal had sold his testimony in exchange for a greatly reduced sentence, but it was in exchange for truthful rather than perjured testimony—and he was about to pay a reprehensible price for it.

In late July Darrow enlisted McManigal's Uncle George Behm to intensify the psychological pressure on his nephew. On the Sunday after Emma's ploy had failed to bring Ortie around, Uncle George took McManigal's five-year-old son Walter for a walk on the sidewalk in the field of view of his father's cell. Seeing the boy for the first time in months,

McManigal called out to Behm: "Hey. Uncle George, bring over the boy and let me see him."

Behm refused and led the boy up and down the street in front of the jail. "I was sweating blood to press Walter's little warm body," he would later relate. "[Uncle George] understood the torture he was putting me through—for he is a father himself."

Behm then headed to Darrow's office and told him of his tactic.

"I didn't take the boy over [to McManigal]," Behm told Darrow upon his return. "I didn't pay any attention to the hollering."

"That's right, goddammit," Darrow said, revealing a ruthless resolve. "Tease him and then he will come across."

Desperate as he was for the company of his child, McManigal never would. And he knew who was behind the plots to "torture" him.

"Attorney Darrow," he would claim a few days later, "whose brain has schemed all the treachery that my poor wife and my uncle have practiced upon me, will stop at nothing in his fight for the McNamaras. . . . He has broken up my little family and robbed my wife of her womanly sympathy and love."

McManigal had made a friend in Burns detective Malcolm McLaren, who had taken him into custody in Chicago. In response to the continuing flow of denunciations appearing in the press about McManigal, McLaren told reporters that he believed McManigal to be "thoroughly penitent" and that "when called upon to testify he will convince all as to his honesty."

In late July, Ortie's Uncle George was notified that he too would be required to appear before the grand jury. Although grand jury proceedings are conducted in secret, Fredericks informed the press that the summons was an attempt to "put an end to alleged wholesale tampering with State witnesses by delegations and attorneys employed by labor unions."

Darrow and LeCompte Davis brought Behm to their offices at the Higgins Building and coached him on what to say—which was to say nothing at all. On July 31 the old man displayed his mettle to DA Fredericks and Assistant DA Ford by answering each of their questions with the refrain, "That has nothing to do with the case." Frustrated to no end, Judge Bordwell ordered Behm to testify again three days later, but when he returned, the old man still managed to keep his answers vague and short enough not to incriminate either himself, Emma, or anyone else associated with the McNamara defense. The judge cited Behm for contempt and ordered him to post bail of $2,000.

But by this time, Uncle George and Emma had grown weary of spy-infested, subpoena-happy Los Angeles. On August 10, a week after giving his grand jury testimony, Uncle George, Emma, Walter, and Evelyn boarded a train back to Chicago, leaving the McNamara defense fund a few thousand dollars slimmer than it was when they arrived.

Later that week, the AF of L executive committee voted unanimously against sponsoring further parades throughout the country, "or any demonstration that would necessitate the expenditure of money," in an effort to funnel any surplus funds to the McNamara defense. The sale of the "Kidnapped" buttons and stamps with J. J. McNamara's face on them was reinaugurated. Donations, however, continued to trickle rather than flow in to defense coffers, and in at least one instance they evaporated altogether, when the money donated by the Cooks, Waiters and Waitresses Union in Medford, Oregon, was embezzled by the organization's financial secretary.

But Darrow's principal money problem stemmed from the fundamental reality that his clients were guilty, that no evidence whatsoever could be produced to support their defense, that no witnesses whatsoever could be produced to counter the prosecution's. At the same time, he was being paid an enormous amount of money to produce an acquittal. As a result, he had come to depend on the two Berts and Sullivan to see to it that as little of the prosecution's evidence as possible ever reached a jury.

He also brought onboard John L. Harrington, a morbidly obese attorney who was an associate of Olaf Tveitmoe and an employee at the Asiatic Exclusion League's San Francisco chapter. In July 1911 Harrington tracked down David Caplan's wife, Flora, just after she had been subpoenaed by Fredericks and had Anton Johannsen spirit her away in a chauffeur-driven car to Reno, Nevada (at a cost of $200), where they boarded a train for Chicago. Harrington then called on Lena Ingersoll and her husband, both of whom were scheduled to be called as witnesses to identify J. B. McNamara as J. B. Bryce. At Darrow's behest, Harrington arranged a meeting with the estranged couple at the Fairmont Hotel in San Francisco, where he offered them $5,000, it was later charged, to "procure the absence of Mrs. Ingersoll from the State, and agree to provide the automobile for that purpose."

Mr. Ingersoll expressed an interest in the proposition, while Lena refused outright. Harrington replied that her continued refusal might anger some unionists and that she might arrive at her "little home" one day to discover that it had been destroyed by dynamite. Terrified by Harrington's threat, she fled San Francisco for L.A., where she approached Fredericks and Ford with the matter and began life anew in Southern California under an alias.

Suborning witnesses was proving not only expensive but, to Darrow, essential. Larry Sullivan approached Michael Gilmore, a clerk at the Giant Powder Works, to ask a favor of George Phillips, the man who had sold the dynamite to J. B. Bryce. Sullivan solicited Gilmore to persuade Phillips to alter his testimony in a very specific manner: to testify that the man who had introduced himself as Bryce had been missing a finger. Since J. B. McNamara was in possession of all his digits, the testimony would prove exculpatory.

Sullivan offered the witness money in exchange for such perjured testimony; he likewise intimated that Phillips's life might be in danger should he decline to cooperate. Both back-channel attempts backfired, however, when each witness went to Fredericks and Ford with accounts of their meetings with Sullivan.

On September 18 Fredericks issued a warrant for John Harrington's arrest on charges of witness tampering. Harrington was nowhere to be found.

Meanwhile, Darrow also enlisted Bert Hammerstrom to track down one of the prosecution's most devastating witnesses, Kurt Diekelman, the clerk at the Hotel Baltimore who had registered J. B. McNamara and chatted with him on the evening of September 30, 1910, hours before the explosion at the *Times,* when J. B. had asked for a late checkout; Diekelman could put him in Los Angeles on the day of the crime.

After some checking around, Ruby's brother found Diekelman in the small town of Albuquerque in the New Mexico Territory working as a waiter. Diekelman would later recall that Hammerstrom told him: "We are trying our best to save J. B. He is innocent. Don't you think it would be right for you to consider the least doubt there is and be on our side?" Diekelman recalled telling Hammerstrom that he didn't think there was any doubt at all, whereupon Hammerstrom told him, "Now you are a valuable witness to us, and whatever your price is, we will give it to you." He then asked Diekelman if he was familiar with Rector's restaurant in Chicago. When Diekelman replied that he was, Hammerstrom said to him, "Well, I think Mr. Darrow has an interest in that. How would you like to be assistant manager there?" Hammerstrom then offered Diekelman and his girlfriend an all-expenses-paid trip back to Chicago, together with cash. Finally the young man accepted. But Chicago also happened to be the headquarters of the Burns Detective Agency, and within a few days he was tracked down by Burns detective Guy Biddinger, who convinced him to return to Albuquerque and make himself available to testify in Los Angeles when the time came.

The alternating trend of good news for Darrow on the public relations front followed by bad news from his investigators only intensified as the summer waned. On Labor Day 1911, which Gompers had indeed proclaimed "McNamara Day," fifty thousand organized workers, including an estimated five hundred women, paraded down Fifth Avenue in New York, led by marchers carrying a banner reading WE DEMAND JUSTICE FOR J. J. MCNAMARA. Behind the banner eight men carried a large American flag to collect silver dollars thrown into it for the McNamara defense fund. At Fourteenth Street the parade was halted briefly after a man raced up to the flag carriers and said that his diamond ring had slipped off his finger as he threw in the coin. The flag was set down and the pile of silver dollars was raked over until the ring was found.

In Los Angeles thirty-five thousand men and a few women marched through downtown, many wearing McNamara KIDNAPPED buttons. The three-mile-long parade snaked through downtown, past the jail on Temple Street, where the marchers removed their hats as they passed. Suffrage rights activists also participated, as the women's vote was central to Harriman's campaign. Women would be voting in the Los Angeles mayoral election for the first time in history. Of course the candidate himself addressed crowds of supporters all through the day.

Meanwhile, Gompers had crossed the country to deliver his McNamara address in San Francisco, before a throng of tens of thousands, then took a steamer to Los Angeles to speak to an equally massive crowd. Accompanied by Darrow and LeCompte Davis, he also met with the McNamara brothers in their cell, where he was photographed with them.

"They impressed me with their sincerity," Gompers would later relate. "As I was parting with John J., I remember he took my hand and said, as near as I can remember: 'Take this message to the laboring men of the country. This is a damnable put-up job and we are innocent.' I saw no reason for doubting their word."

On September 17 newspapers were reporting that Ortie McManigal's confession had been corroborated in the most devastating fashion possible—by photographs he had taken of "buildings and bridges destroyed by dynamite." Prosecutors alleged that he'd taken the pictures to be developed at the Willis-Shores Photo Supply Company in Indianapolis in October 1910 with the intention of using them as a receipt in exchange for payment from J. J. McNamara. Equally devastating corroborative evidence had been unearthed in the union books, which had three meager but unmistakably clear expense entries for the photos:

"October 11, O. E. McManigal, $1.26

"October 15, O. E. McManigal, $0.63

"October 17, O. E. McManigal, $1.42"

The amounts matched the Willis-Shores Photo Supply's sales tickets.

Further evidence indicating that union higher-ups were privy to the dynamite campaign surfaced in the union books in the form of cryptograms: "Peoria (Ill.): Halley's Comet passed this way the other night and found union men on the job." "Detroit (Mich.): A large noise was heard in this vicinity last night, which woke up some people."

Despite the crushing weight of the evidence against him, J. J. McNamara was reelected secretary-treasurer of the Bridge and Structural Iron Workers' Union at its convention in Milwaukee a week later. A certificate ratifying his election was forwarded to him at the Los Angeles County Jail.

As the trial's scheduled opening date approached, it was announced that the brothers would be tried separately, with J. J. being tried only for his complicity in the Christmas Day Llewellyn Iron Works bombing. The case against J. B. for the bombing of the Times Building was by far the stronger of the two, and should he be found guilty, he could be hanged. DA Fredericks announced that J. B. would be tried first for the murder of only one of the victims of the bombing, Charles J. Haggerty, a machinist whose body was found nearest Ink Alley.

As the trial commenced with the selection of the jury, Darrow began doing all he could to pack the twelve-man panel with individuals friendly to the cause of Labor. His constant objections to potential jurors who were not caused frustrating delays that tried the patience of Judge Bordwell. Darrow was unapologetic, asking each prospective juror, "Do you take the *Los Angeles Times*?" "Have you the opinion that labor unions as they exist are proper, or that they are inimical and a menace?" "I presume you are aware of the bitter warfare going on between organized labor and capital?" "Are your sympathies with organized labor or not?" If a candidate juror did not express outright union sympathy, prosecutors and Judge Bordwell were in for a withering series of objections from Darrow. If the jurors claimed union sympathy, the objections of course emanated from Fredericks and Ford.

The tortuous jury selection process was accompanied by a mounting surge in popularity for Job Harriman, who, by October, appeared certain to win the primary election and go on to become Los Angeles's first Socialist mayor.

By fall it had become clear to a variety of business and political leaders in L.A. that it would be in their best interest if Harriman were stopped. The best way to do so, everyone knew, was to see to it that his clients, the McNamara brothers, were found guilty. Nevertheless, the protracted jury-selection process made it appear inevitable that the general election would take place sometime before testimony got under way.

On October 14, 1911, Emma McManigal, who was now back in Chicago with her "father-in-law" George Behm, made news by filing for divorce from Ortie in an Illinois circuit court in an attempt, prosecutors suspected, to circumvent rules barring a wife from having to testify against her husband. In her filing Emma alleged "cruelty and infidelity." She also denounced Ortie as a "conspirator with the rest of the McNamara prosecution" and alleged that Ortie had entered into an agreement with William Burns to receive immunity, along with a large share of the reward upon the conviction of the McNamara brothers. She went on to claim in her divorce papers that she was summoned to Detective Reed's home on the night her husband confessed and that there William Burns and his operatives promised her that if she came to California and backed up her husband's accusations against the McNamaras they would secure a home for her and release Ortie immediately. When she visited her husband in jail, she said, she was confronted by a detective, her husband, and another man and when she refused to answer their questions, she was threatened with physical violence. The men, she alleged, also threatened her with imprisonment if she did not verify her husband's statements, the suit alleged. A prominent, high-priced lawyer was now representing her and had prepared the divorce documents—none other than Clarence Darrow.

Chapter 37

Darrow was playing a losing hand, and he knew it. Moreover, by the fall of 1911 he realized that he was now caught between the two great forces of the American Left: radical socialism as represented by Socialist Party leader Eugene Debs on the one hand, and moderate unionism as represented by Samuel Gompers and the American Federation of Labor on the other.

A great many of the Socialists who had been so instrumental in drumming up national support for the McNamara defense truly did not care if "the boys" were guilty or not. Many in fact believed that they were and that the case was being mishandled by Darrow. What they wanted above all else was a trial that would serve as a political platform to highlight the desperate plight of the working class, what Emma Goldman had hoped would be "a proud avowal of their acts and an intelligent analysis of the causes that had compelled them to resort to violence." But such a pleading would, by necessity, be predicated on the understanding that J. B. McNamara would be found guilty of murder—the penalty for which was death by hanging. Moreover, the Socialists were not paying the bills. The defense was being funded by the AF of L, a relatively conservative organization that had publicly renounced industrial violence vigorously and repeatedly. And Samuel Gompers had been assured that the McNamara brothers "were as innocent as newborn babes." The bottom line was clear: The AF of L was not going to destroy itself by condoning, rationalizing, or explaining away the use of industrial terror.

Mainstream union leaders in the United States in 1911 were less interested in revolution than in securing labor contracts that offered a fair wage for an honest day's work. To accomplish their ends they understood that they had to abide by the rule of law and, if they found the laws unjust, to challenge them in the courts, relentlessly.

"I was in a terrible crisis that I faced almost alone," Darrow would later write of the autumn of 1911. But if he felt isolated, it was because he had by now detached himself from the band of lawyers he himself had assembled to try the McNamara case. Although he received little credit, it was actually LeCompte Davis who had taken over the actual day-to-day legal chores associated with the case, something Darrow himself later conceded.

"Of course, I realize that I have been sometimes called the chief counsel in that case," Darrow would say later. "Perhaps my associates deferred to me in some things, but I was not familiar with the codes of California. Davis, being an old-time criminal lawyer, was really relied on more than myself." And Davis had already reached the conclusion that, barring some miracle, the McNamaras would have to plead guilty in order to avoid the gallows. He had begun to prepare for that eventuality.

Job Harriman was deliberately kept out of the loop, as the massive public support he was receiving as L.A.'s first Socialist mayoral candidate was largely based on the general belief that his opponent was in cahoots with those attempting to frame the McNamaras.

As October waned, the trial was being billed nationwide as the great showdown between capital and labor, the "epoch-making event in the history of the industrial war in the United States," as Emma Goldman called it. It was, the headlines proclaimed, the great event of its time, the "greatest trial in all of American history." But the screaming headlines were like the bellow of the carnival barker. Disappointment was in store for all who entered the tent, as the humdrum process of selecting a jury dragged on for days, then weeks, and continued throughout October, throughout November.

It was Davis who now questioned the prospective jurors.

Davis: "Are any of your sons in any way connected with organized labor?"

Z. T. Nelson, a farmer, sixty-two: "Not that I know of."

Davis: "Do you belong to any labor union or any branch of organized labor?"

Nelson: "No."

Davis: "I presume you are aware of the bitter warfare going on between organized labor and capital?"

Nelson: "Yes."

Davis: "Are your sympathies with organized labor or not?"

Nelson: "I am not prejudiced against labor unions as an organization."

Davis: "Well, do you believe labor unions as you understand it to be carried on here in California are a menace?"

Nelson: "It is hard to answer. I don't think an organization should be held responsible for the acts of one lawless man."

And so it went, day after monotonous day, one featureless prospective juror after another.

As a result, the Los Angeles mayoral primary took over center stage, the trial's political corollary. When the ballots were counted on the night of November 1, Job Harriman led with a commanding plurality—but not a majority. A runoff election between him and incumbent Mayor Alexander was automatically scheduled for December 5, 1911.

L.A. business leaders were stunned. General Otis and the *Times* dismissed the results editorially as "an unusual trend of political perversity toward the Socialist candidate whose campaign has been made on the most extravagant misstatements of municipal notions and purposes."

But privately the business community was in a state of panic— fearful not only over the city's political future but over the potential outcome of the trial itself. If Harriman won the runoff general election, then this laborite coalition could make its influence felt in the courtroom. After all, the new mayor would be cocounsel for the McNamaras.

As a result, DA Fredericks was prepared to take extraordinary steps. First he began hiding "dictographs," primitive bugging devices, in Darrow's office in the Higgins Building. Next he began embedding his own people in Darrow's team, hoping to get a better handle on what the defense was up to. Finally he publicly accused Darrow of coordinating

Harriman's campaign with the McNamara defense out of his clients' defense fund (which, as it turned out, proved to be true—and, at the time, entirely legal).

In fact, given the weight of the evidence against the McNamaras, Darrow increasingly regarded Harriman's campaign as his lifeline. But it could only save him if he could delay the trial until after the election. The prosecution accurately surmised what Darrow was up to and daily began leaking more incriminating evidence against the McNamaras to the press, slowly and surely eroding support for the defense.

In a whispered voice, the Great Defender began to share his sense of impending doom with a few of those closest to him, most frequently, of course, with Mary Field, who wanted to see the trial go forward for the same reasons Emma Goldman did. Erskine Wood wanted it to go forward as well, but only because he thought the Haywood affair had emboldened the most radical elements in the labor movement to adopt terrorism as an acceptable means to their ends. The McNamaras and the bombing of the *Los Angeles Times,* Wood believed, were the end results of Big Bill Haywood's plot to murder a former governor of an American state. Terrorism was not only counterproductive to the cause of organized labor, Wood argued, but shameful. And now the working men and women of America were about to pay the price for it.

Chapter 38

Even before Judge Walter Bordwell's gavel signaled the start of the trial on October 11, 1911, the McNamara case had already become the most expensive municipal courtroom proceeding in American history. By the time it ended, each side had spent the equivalent of $10 million in today's dollars. And most of those funds had been doled out for espionage, bribery, and other semi-legal shenanigans representing unconscionable misconduct even by the rough-and-tumble standards of 1911. Corruption was everywhere, on both sides of the case.

When the first venire, or panel of jurors to be considered, was drawn, it was impossible not to notice that it included the names of an unusually large number of L.A. business leaders, many of whom had dealings with the *Times*. Other ploys were less subtle. On the afternoon of October 23, 1911, Harry Chandler decided to take a walk through downtown Los Angeles near the new Hall of Records. During the walk he "just happened" to come across B. W. Clark, one of the veniremen who had been tapped for the trial. Chandler told Clark that he hoped he would "qualify as a juror." Little more was alleged to have been said, but when Clark brought the encounter to Judge Bordwell's attention the next day, Bordwell promptly ended his tenure as a venireman. No charges were brought against Chandler in spite of what appeared to be an attempt at influencing a potential juror. Darrow, of course, claimed to be outraged—although, it would turn out, he had little right to be.

Earlier in the month, on October 5, 1911, Bert Franklin dropped by the home of prospective juror Robert Bain, a member of the jury pool that he had recognized on Darrow's list. He knocked on the front door, but no one answered. He then came around to the side of the house and knocked on a window. Bain's wife, Dora, was in her nightgown and refused to let him in. She did recognize Franklin as a friend of her husband's, however, and opened the window to ask what he was doing there while Bob was at work. Franklin said he would explain if she would just open the door. Inside the house, Franklin pulled out his bulging wallet. Mrs. Bain could see that it held hundreds of dollars in cash.

"Do you think you can change a $50 or $100 bill?" he asked slyly.

Mrs. Bain laughed. "I haven't seen so much money since I was a cashier."

Franklin then reached in the wallet and pulled out nearly all of the cash. Holding the bills in his hand, he began asking her questions about their house—how much had they had paid for it? Dora told him they had bought it years ago for $1,800 and paid $15 per month on the mortgage.

"Well," Franklin said, "I think I can help you. I think I can put you and Bob in a position to pay for your little home and live easy for the rest of your lives."

"How's that?" Dora asked.

"I know that Bob has always been honest. I can put him in a position to make it easy for him." Franklin hesitated, and then added: "You know what I mean?"

"No," Mrs. Bain responded. "Unless you want him to do election work."

"No, not that. You know that Bob has been summoned on the jury?" Franklin now got to the point. Dora and Robert would receive $4,000 if she could persuade her husband to vote for acquittal in the McNamara trial, as "they are trying to railroad those guys." Moreover, "there will be plenty of testimony to prove they are innocent and he need not have any conscientious scruples." Franklin then offered Dora the $400 that he had withdrawn from his wallet as a "down payment" on the promised funds. He would provide an additional $100 promptly; the remaining $3,500 would be delivered upon her husband's vote for acquittal.

Dora Bain stammered. Her husband was a proud veteran who took his civic duties seriously, she said. She nevertheless accepted the money and agreed to speak to him.

Franklin returned the following day, October 6, and found the seventy-one-year-old Bain at home alone; Dora was attending a lodge meeting.

"Did you talk to Dora about our discussion?" he asked. Bain nodded.

Franklin looked at him earnestly. "Bob, you and I are poor men and must provide for our old age. I can tell you how to get some money if you are a juror in the McNamara case. No one will know about it." He then described how there was bribery on each side and that he "had a perfect right to accept money." He told Bain that he was employed by Clarence Darrow and repeated the offer he had made to Dora—$500 now, $3,500 more after he voted to acquit.

Bain said that he feared that he "would not be accepted as a juror on account of my age." Well, said Franklin, if that proved to be the case, he'd still be $500 ahead. "You take that money and help us out. The money is not mine. It belongs to Darrow. You will not be the only one. Darrow has $20,000 for reaching jurors."

Once again, he reached for his wallet, withdrew some bills, and laid them on Bain's dining room table. He then told Bain that he believed detectives from the district attorney's office had been following him and that he planned to drive to San Bernardino that evening to throw them off his trail.

Before doing so, he stopped at the First National Bank, where he deposited a $1,000 check that he had received from Darrow. He then wrote out a check to himself for $500, handed it to the teller, and received $500 in cash.

On November 4 Franklin paid a visit to the ranch home of another prospective juror, George N. Lockwood, whose name he had also recognized on Darrow's list of veniremen. It was late at night, and when there was no answer to his knock at the door, he began pounding on it thunderously. The noise, however, failed to waken Lockwood, but it did his wife, who was sleeping next to him. She came to the front door and shouted out to the unwelcome visitor. Franklin shouted back that he needed to speak to her husband, that the matter was urgent. Lockwood finally came to the door, complaining about the late hour.

"I want to see you about the McNamara jury," Franklin told him. "Can I talk to you about it?" Lockwood recognized Franklin and let him in.

"You and I have gone along through life together," Franklin began. "Here's a chance for you to make a little money by using your head. There's $2,000 in it for you and probably $2,500 in it if you serve as a juror." Five hundred dollars would be his right away, given to him by a third party, before even entering the jury box, as "earnest payment" on voting for acquittal.

Then, perhaps to ease Lockwood's mind, Franklin added, "I have fixed two members of the permanent jury in this McNamara trial and I am going to get a couple more before I am through." (The remark was an exaggeration; he had only approached Bain.) Lockwood again expressed interest and asked him to return the following day at a more reasonable hour. The appointment was set for early the following evening. In the morning Lockwood arose and immediately informed the district attorney about his late-night visitor's proposal.

When Franklin returned the following evening, three police detectives monitored their meeting, one perched on top of a water tower and two inside the house manning dictographs. Lockwood asked how he could be sure that he would receive the money if he delivered the vote. Franklin proposed that the entire $4,000 be held by a man they both knew, Charles "Cap" White. He would arrange for the three of them to meet at the corner of South Los Angeles and Third Streets in downtown L.A. on the morning of November 28, at 9:00 a.m., at which time he would turn over the $4,000 to White. He then drove to White's home and offered to pay him $100 to act as a "stakeholder."

Meanwhile the defense and prosecution continued to slog it out over the selection of jurors in a trial that would take place in L.A.'s new Hall of Records, which was "but a stone's throw from the scene of the explosion," as the *Chicago Daily Tribune* duly observed. After rejecting nearly every talesman on grounds of harboring one sort of bias or another against labor unions, Darrow mysteriously accepted one who was believed to be hostile to them. In the midst of the process, he questioned Civil War veteran Robert Bain after asking him what he would do if he "had to give a verdict without hearing the evidence."

"I would not do it," Bain replied. Inexplicably, that seemed to be good enough for Darrow.

—◆~—

The proceedings would continue to drag on for nearly two months, with Robert Bain sitting with only five other men in the jury box. Although little was getting done, the courtroom was filled beyond capacity each day. Toward the front of the room were seated US senators and congressmen, "captains of industry," California society, labor leaders, prominent political figures of the right and left; in the back stood men and women wearing McNamara buttons, some pinned to grimy and ratted clothing, their eyes ablaze with incandescent hatred of the men responsible for the prosecution of J. B. McNamara, the skinny man incessantly chewing gum at the defense table. Mary and Sara Field managed to gain admission to the courtroom on behalf of their respective publications, each proud in her own way of her special affiliation with the tall, gloomy figure dominating everyone's attention even as he sat aloof from most of the proceedings and LeCompte Davis questioned the prospective jurors.

Darrow, however, was enjoying none of it. A parade of witnesses was set to testify, twenty-eight of whom could identify James B. McNamara as J. B. Bryce. The witnesses included Kurt Diekelman, the clerk who spoke with J. B. on the day of the bombing at the Baltimore Hotel; the taxi driver in San Francisco; George Phillips and Manuel Cortez of the Giant Powder Works; a survivor of the explosion who had seen J. B. enter Ink Alley the night of September 30; others who had seen him casing the building earlier; and of course there was Ortie McManigal and J. B.'s erstwhile lover, Lena Ingersoll. And they were just the vanguard. Prosecutors had registered a grand total of eight hundred witnesses, from explosive experts to former friends, nearly all of whom they were prepared to call, although none, save McManigal and Lena Ingersoll, was currently in Los Angeles.

Once again, lack of funds threatened to cripple the defense. Hence, Gompers announced a resolution requiring one week's pay from "every paid officer of a labor union in this country" to "swell the McNamara defense fund." The resolution was roundly adopted at an AF of L convention in New Orleans, with the leadership stopping short of calling for a direct appropriation of $50,000. But Darrow needed an immediate infusion of cash. The appropriated wages, he surely knew, would be a long time in making the long, slow, circuitous journey to Los Angeles.

Meanwhile, General Otis was doing his level best to thwart the defense in his own unique way. Concerned about the booming public support for the McNamaras and worried that the evidence discovered in Indianapolis might be blocked from coming to California, Otis had contacted the most powerful ally he had—no less a man than the president of the United States, William Howard Taft. Otis and Taft were men of their time, each of them fitting the stereotype of the American tycoon that Charles Coburn would play in movies in the 1940s—corporeal profiles, walrus mustaches, and washed-out eyes. Both were conservatives in the recently ruptured Republican Party, both enemies of the "Progressives," chief of whom was the "Mad Messiah," Teddy Roosevelt, the man whom Taft had served under as vice president. And now, as the trial was about to begin, Otis invited Taft to come out West for a long talk about this matter that so affected the business community. Ever accommodating of a wealthy, like-minded Republican, Taft sent word back that he would be arriving on October 16; he and General Otis could meet at President Taft's sister's home in Los Angeles.

The presidential train steamed first to San Francisco, and then south through the night to L.A.. But then, at the outskirts of Santa Barbara, the train screeched to a halt. It huffed on the tracks at the El Capitan Bridge spanning a gully. The president was alerted that thirty-nine sticks of dynamite had been spotted by a watchman tucked among the bridge's wooden spars. In remarkably short order the explosives were cleared and the president's train continued on its way.

When vague reports of the apparent attempt on the life of President Taft hit the streets the following day, liberal newspapers across the nation expressed skepticism. Since the arrests of the McNamara brothers and Ortie McManigal in April, the phenomenon of industrial terror had all but evaporated. Reporters and editors speculated that perhaps this most recent dynamite incident had been contrived by General Otis himself in order to call the commander-in-chief's attention in the most dramatic fashion possible to the danger of unionist violence.

If such was the case, it apparently worked. The day after the president's arrival, he and General Otis met at Mrs. William Taft Edwards's beautiful Los Angeles home and, over brandy and cigars as they sat among the extravagant flora of the terraced patio, talked about the McNamara case.

Otis had been in touch with Walter Drew, the head of the National Erectors' Association, who had inspected the papers in J. J. McNamara's desk and in the basement vault on the day that Burns and his men had arrived to place McNamara under arrest. That evidence, he realized, was crucial to the prosecution's case. But it remained in the hands of Indianapolis authorities, who, it seemed, had no intention of turning it over to District Attorney Fredericks or to anyone else in Los Angeles. But they did imply that they might return it to the union.

"Well, Joe, I suppose you are getting a little anxious as the time approaches for your trial," Herbert Hockin had written on Iron Workers' letterhead to J. J. McNamara in prison on September 30. He then attempted to soothe his anxiety. "I see by the papers this morning that Baker, the prosecutor, says he is going to return our books to us next week. The paper also states that there is no possibility of the books being taken to California."

Learning of the prosecutor's plans, Drew dashed off a letter to US Attorney General George W. Wickersham asking that the federal government intervene and take possession of the evidence.

"A large number of letters were found of most incriminating character," he wrote. They included "letters from J. J. McNamara to local union officials, including members of the Executive Board, regarding explosions contemplated and also letters from such officials to him, clearly showing that explosives were carried from Indianapolis to different sections and used in pursuance of an understanding between the officers at headquarters and those stationed in different localities. The testimony of the witness McManigal that he was assisted at different times by these local officials is fully corroborated by these letters."[16]

Drew sent the letter on October 6, 1911, just five days before J. B. McNamara's trial was due to begin. But Marion County Prosecutor Frank Baker was insisting that the evidence must remain in Indianapolis pending the prosecution of the McNamaras locally. Although Baker had initially cooperated with L.A. prosecutors, he now refused to do so. To find out why, Drew planted spies in the DA's office. They reported back that the Iron Workers had bought him off. "They own him body and soul," the detectives reported to Drew. And now he received word that Baker was planning to return the seized documents and other evidence to the union.

"The return of this evidence means, of course, its absolute loss to any prosecution, Federal or State, to which it might be material," he wrote to Wickersham.

And indeed, on October 18, Iron Workers attorney Leo Rappaport asked the court to issue an order directing Baker "to surrender immediately to [McNamara] any and all such documentary evidence belonging to said defendant."

It looked like McNamara would get it too. Assistant US Attorney General William Harr had advised his boss not to intervene, noting that the city's case appeared to rest "entirely upon the confession of McManigal" and that the authorities in Los Angeles "merely wished to use the Federal Government for the purpose of pulling their chestnuts out of the fire."

President Taft listened as Otis and Oscar Lawler, representing the Merchants and Manufacturers Association, laid out the troubling scenario. Otis wanted the president to federalize the case. After all, he observed, the bombing of his newspaper had been part of a national criminal conspiracy. Therefore, while the County of Los Angeles's case moved forward, the brothers could and should be charged by a federal grand jury for separate crimes. So should any number of higher-ups.

President Taft gave General Otis everything he had asked for. Nine days after the president's departure, it was announced that a federal grand jury would be convened in Indianapolis to begin investigating the case.

The defense vainly attempted to counter such awesome displays of political power by harnessing the relatively new innovation called moving pictures for propaganda purposes. The union decided to commission the production of a film to boost the McNamara defense. It would be titled *A Martyr to His Cause*. But although the subject of the "picture drama" was imprisoned in the city that would one day become the movie capital of the world, not a single film company existed there yet. Instead the film would be shot in Dayton, Ohio, by the W. M. Seely Company, and of course it would use an all-union cast and crew, the first such all-union film in history. The budget was $3,142.19, and the plan was for a single print to be struck and then transported city by city to union halls across the United States, beginning in Dayton on October 26, 27, and 28. Tickets were to be printed by the Building, Metal and Label Trades. If all went well, the union hoped, perhaps theaters would also show it along with their regular vaudeville acts.

The fifteen-minute film made no mention of the *Times* bombing or indeed of any bombings whatsoever. Instead the two-reel silent film began with a seventeen-year-old J. J. McNamara leaving home and promising his mother and father to "be a good boy and to play fair in all that he does." We see the young man's dangerous work as an ironworker. He is further portrayed as an industrious, God-fearing family man who loves his country and his church. The film then shows how manufacturers and corrupt judges act in cahoots to oppress workers "contrary to the laws and traditions of our republic," something that the young man was to become aware of as he rose to the rank of foreman and then secretary-treasurer of his union. The film then shows detectives led by a fat, mustachioed chief breaking into union headquarters while its leaders are holding a regular meeting and spiriting away John McNamara to a jail cell across the country.

A copy of the screenplay was recently discovered by labor historian Philip S. Foner in AF of L files. These are the final two scenes:

"HIS MESSAGE TO ORGANIZED LABOR

Scene 19: Cell. Mac, seated in his cell, is writing. As he finishes, flash on sheet the following:

"TO THE BROTHERHOOD OF ORGANIZED LABOR:

[There follows in text McNamara's declaration of innocence, which he released after being incarcerated in Los Angeles.]

"(Back to picture) Mac with head bent low, reads the paper, then dissolve into:

"Scene 20: The home fireside. Close-up of mother alone, weeping over a letter from her son."

The film hit Cincinnati, the McNamaras' hometown, during the same week that J. B.'s trial opened in California. (J. B. barely received a mention in the film.) It reportedly drew fifty thousand people during the six days that it played there. The "specially designed" tickets were sold for 5 cents apiece, with 4 cents of that amount going to the McNamara Defense Fund. Posters for the movie showed a near-naked J. J. McNamara wearing a loincloth and holding a sword, while cannons labeled "vindictiveness," "politics," "money," and "intolerance," took aim at him. "See the Only Original Moving Pictures of the McNamaras Including Their History and the Actual Scenes of Their Arrest," the posters said. Even in those days, movie posters were not to be trusted.

In Detroit police attempted to shut down the showing of *A Martyr to His Cause* not because of anything in the film itself but because of the lecture that accompanied it, delivered by Max L. Corrigan, former business agent of the local actors' union. Police Captain Alfonso Baker, head of theater censorship in Detroit, charged that the lecture violated the city's law against stirring up class hatred.

But another harsh critic of the film was J. J. McNamara himself. When he was told about it, he fired off an indignant letter to the producer, W.M. Seely, demanding to know why he was not consulted about the script. Seely wrote back apologizing.

"We have depicted the principle [sic] events in the affair as near as is [sic] was possible [sic] to get them from your friends," he said. "Now it will be posible that I could ad [sic] something to this picture of interest and will gladly do so if you will submit me some suggestions."

The film turned out to be a huge success at union halls in the first three cities where it was screened. By the end of November, one labor leader was predicting that it would earn as much as $100,000. Unfortunately, at the same time, further showings of the movie had to be canceled when the entire justification for it became moot.

It no longer exists.

Chapter 39

He was a compact figure, always crisply dressed, always managing to place himself at the nexus of the great social events of his day. So it was natural that he would find his way to Los Angeles in the autumn of 1911.

At the dawn of the twentieth century, Lincoln Steffens was a waning media superstar, one of those writers who had become famous by exposing the ugly underbelly of American urban life—writers Theodore Roosevelt called "muckrakers." His books *The Shame of the Cities* (1904) and *The Struggle for Self Government* (1906) had both proved to be enormous commercial and critical successes, making Steffens a hero to millions of working Americans and the left-wing literati. In 1910, just before leaving for Europe, he had covered the Mexican revolution for *American Magazine*, the very publication for whom Mary Field was now working. (In 1919, after returning from Soviet Russia following the Bolshevik revolution, he would make his famous remark, "I have seen the future, and it works," an observation that endeared him to America's radical socialists and earned him ridicule from everyone else.)

Now, in early November 1911, it was announced that the veteran journalist would be coming to Los Angeles to cover the Trial of the Century. Union activists paid the news scant attention, while Darrow, Debs, Harriman, and Gompers welcomed what they thought would be a conduit to more popular support, someone who could articulate to a readership of millions what the labor movement was up against in the McNamara trial.

What none of the labor stalwarts understood when the little man stepped off the train at Sante Fe station in downtown Los Angeles on November 6, 1911, was that he had already concluded that the McNamara brothers were, as Darrow himself had been quietly whispering to trusted friends for several weeks now, "guilty as hell."

During the summer and fall of 1911, Steffens had been living in Europe, preparing to expose the graft and economic inequities that had created the squalor of many modern, industrialized European cities—just as he had done in America to such great acclaim. But as the summer wore on, he began reading about what was happening in Los Angeles. In July he had dinner in a Paris restaurant with his old friend from the San Francisco graft trials, William J. Burns, who had sailed across the Atlantic to squeeze in some consulting work. Burns gave the journalist a primer on the case against the McNamara brothers. By the end of dinner, Steffens realized that the story of the day was happening in his home state and every journalist worth his salt was there covering it.

Steffens returned to New York, where he asked his radical-thinking editors and publishers to send him to Los Angeles. When he told them his angle, they were shocked: to "show why labor was guilty and what lay behind their acts of violence."

His editors were instantly sold on the provocative idea. The five-foot-four journalist purchased a transcontinental train ticket and arrived at Darrow's L.A. office four days later, finding his old friend, the Great Defender, in a state of emotional chaos.

"At three o'clock he is a hero for courage, nerve, and calm judgment," Steffens would later report, "but at three-fifteen he may be a coward for fear, collapse, and panicky mentality. He is more of a poet than a fighting attorney; his power and his weakness is in the highly sensitive, emotional nature which sets his seeing mind in motion in that loafing body. . . . His face was ashen; he could hardly walk; he was scared weak and did not recover for an hour."

With his trademark directness, Steffens asked Darrow if he could meet the McNamara brothers. Intimately aware of Steffens's pro-labor background, Darrow had no reason to refuse him.

The very next day Steffens descended into the Los Angeles County Jail, where the brothers sat together in a single cell, waiting for the meeting. They had been visited by so many renowned supporters—from politicians to journalists to labor leaders—but this little man with the tiny gold-rimmed spectacles and fastidiously groomed goatee was a giant in their eyes. Here was the man who could potentially sway public opinion like no one else in America, and they, like Darrow, had every reason to believe he was on their side.

One of the first statements out of Steffens's mouth, however, astounded them. Steffens wanted to write a series of articles that would be syndicated nationwide, titled "Justifiable Dynamiting." The articles would simply and directly assume that they were guilty, and, incredibly, Steffens wanted "the boys" to help him. The McNamaras sat across from one another in shocked silence while Steffens kept talking.

"It's a doubtful experiment and a risk for you," he said, "but it's got to be done sometime. Why not now? Why not help me dig up on the side, while the legal case is going on, the case of Labor against Capital as a parallel, as a background to the case of California versus the McNamaras? I might be able to show why you turned to dynamite."

J. J. McNamara could hardly believe what he was hearing. "Have you seen Darrow about this?" he asked.

According to Steffens, J. B. McNamara was less astounded, saying, "If you could do what you propose I'd be willing to hang." Then he turned to his brother and said, "It's for this that we have been working, [J. J.], to force attention to the actual conditions of labor. He means to go and get the actual cases of blacklisting that have made it impossible for discharged men to ever get work. Why wouldn't I risk my life to get that told? It's what I've been risking my life for right along." (The words of course are undoubtedly filtered through Steffens's pen.)

The meeting ended without a commitment to cooperate. And yet the fact that the brothers would entertain such an extreme proposal in the midst of a capital murder trial is a measure of just how unsettled they had become by the case Burns had established against them.

Steffens now smelled the scoop of his career coming together. In the days that followed, he traveled to his native San Francisco, where he approached Anton Johannsen with the same proposition that he had put to the McNamaras. Johannsen was flabbergasted—until Steffens explained to him what the San Francisco labor leader already knew: it would be better to have the motives behind the bombings explained to the world in a series of rational articles by someone like himself rather than have them horrifyingly delineated by DA Fredericks in a trial the McNamaras were almost sure to lose.

Steffens quietly shopped his proposal to other prominent figures in San Francisco, one of the first of whom was the City Club president, Meyer Lissner, a progressive, Jewish Republican who was a natural ally of Governor Hiram Johnson and a sworn enemy of the openly anti-Semitic General Otis. Lissner also detested Harriman and saw a change in plea by the McNamaras as the death knell to the Socialist candidate's mayoral campaign.

By now Darrow had also concluded that he had been backed into an inescapable corner. He might have been able to pound Ortie McManigal and the San Francisco crowd on the witness stand, but the transfer of the incriminating documents from Indianapolis had doomed whatever trace of hope he had of saving the McNamaras from "the rope."

LeCompte Davis, an old L.A. legal hound, had early on reached the conclusion that victory for the defense was impossible and that the best that could be hoped for was a hung jury—and even that was a dubious possibility. (Davis almost certainly was aware of the bribery shenanigans but no doubt was pessimistic that they could be pulled off.) He arranged to meet Darrow for lunch one afternoon and was surprised to find Lincoln Steffens seated next to him. Steffens described his plan to have the McNamaras plead guilty under his byline. Davis promptly rejected it, indicating that he would like to begin delicately sounding out District Attorney Fredericks on a plea bargain. After all, he considered him to be a close friend. Darrow gave him his blessing.

The first meeting between Davis and Fredericks did not go well. Davis started off by suggesting that the defense had the upper hand.

"You know, you will never be able to convict J. B. McNamara with the jurors that have now been selected," he remarked.

Fredericks responded, "Another jury will be chosen before the trial begins." After all, he pointed out, the prosecution (and the defense) still had the right to invoke a peremptory challenge even on a hunch that a juror might be biased.

A second meeting proved to be more productive. This time Fredericks led off, saying that he was willing to "join hands in securing clemency for the McNamaras." The remark took Davis aback. He had not anticipated such a generous concession—certainly not so quickly. But to Fredericks it was all principally a matter of economics. The trial had already become a costly drain on the resources of the city—it would become a far greater one if it continued. To his knowledge, no one in California who had agreed to plead guilty to a capital offense had ever been sentenced to death.

The only question that remained, it seemed, was whether Davis could sell a plea bargain to the McNamaras and the unions and whether Fredericks could sell it to General Otis and the business community.

When Steffens was informed of the meeting, he told Davis and Darrow that he knew just the man who could act as an intermediary with both the labor and business communities: E. W. Scripps, the liberal newspaper baron and mutual friend of his and Darrow's. By 1911 the burly but sickly Scripps had amassed a fortune some estimated to be worth $50 million, mostly through his chain of liberal newspapers and a vast, tentacled wire service, just as his fellow contemporary Californian, William Randolph Hearst, had done. Darrow and Steffens arranged to meet him at his sprawling two-thousand-acre ranch outside of Miramar, just north of San Diego, on the weekend of November 19.

There the three talked about the desperate state of the defense, Darrow expressing grave concern that the two men might be executed for committing an act that they believed would better the condition of the working man. J. B., he remarked, had no intention of killing anyone. He had placed the dynamite in Ink Alley in order, as he would later put it, to "scare the employees of the *Times* and others working in nonunion shops; what is now too generally done by racketeers, and called a 'pineapple'" (an apparent reference to using a hand grenade for the purpose of sabotage and intimidation). He said that he would do all in his power to prevent the two from dying for a cause. But the prosecution's case was overwhelming, he conceded. A courtroom victory just didn't seem to be in the cards. They talked freely. Darrow was amongst friends, men with a similar philosophical outlook.

Between hearty rounds of brandy, bourbon, and coffee, Scripps went inside to his study and returned with a draft of an editorial he had already written about the war between Capital and Labor, titled "Belligerent Rights in Class Warfare." The assumption upon which it was based shook Darrow.

"We, the employers, have every other weapon," the millionaire publisher read, "we have the jobs, to give or withhold; the capital to spend, or not spend, for production, for wages, for ourselves; we have the press to state our case and suppress theirs; we have the Bar and the Bench, the legislature, the governor, the police, and the militia. Labor has nothing but violence and mob force."

Darrow saw where Scripps was going as he likened the McNamaras to John Brown, their acts part of a morally just social cause, but their approach unacceptable to a country bound by the rule of law.

"Working men should have the same belligerent rights in labor controversies," Scripps went on, "that nations have in warfare...."

"I wish the people of Los Angeles could see it that way," Darrow said. "I believe it would be to the best interests of the community and also right and just to get rid of this case without shedding any human blood. I wish I could make a settlement."

But to Darrow's mind, asking the court for clemency based on the assertion that the McNamaras had acted to advance a social cause seemed futile. Even Theodore Roosevelt had recently commented in *The Outlook* magazine, where he was now associate editor, "All we are now concerned with is the grave and vital question of fact, whether or not the accused men have been guilty of murder, and of murder under circumstances of peculiar foulness and atrocity." Roosevelt was surely speaking on behalf of a sound majority of Americans, regardless of their political outlook, who saw the event first and foremost as a heinous crime.

The next night Darrow and Steffens left Scripps's ranch and took a train back to Los Angeles, where they had breakfast together at the Van Nuys Hotel. The conversation began anew.

Steffens would later claim that he remarked to Darrow at the time that he believed he could convince the business community of Los Angeles that a settlement would be in their best interests. The assertion is hard to buy. Steffens not only had no influence with businessmen in Los Angeles; he was despised by them—in particular by General Otis. In his newspaper and magazine articles at the time and in his autobiography later, Steffens would claim that he acted as an intermediary in the case. His claim was later swallowed whole hog by several of Steffens's admirers. There is, however, no record that he talked to a single Los Angeles businessman about it.

But Steffens had continued to cultivate his relationship with the McNamaras. If a plea bargain could be negotiated, Steffens felt confident that the brothers would provide him with an interview that would be splashed on the front pages of newspapers all over the world under his byline. And they had confided to him that even they had come to realize that there was little hope for their acquittal and that their real hope was to be able to use the witness stand as a platform to tell the world why they had acted as they had. As for the deaths, J. B. McNamara had said, "We'll count our dead with [theirs] any time."

The person doing the hard legwork with the business community was actually LeCompte Davis. Unlike Steffens, Davis had developed strong ties to leading business figures in Los Angeles, most especially to Harry Chandler and General Otis, for whom he had once worked. When Otis heard about the proposed plea bargain, he was thunderstruck. He was well aware of the evidence in the case. To him it was open and shut, and there was not the slightest reason to consider leniency.

But there was, Davis responded. The city was one week away from a mayoral election in which the outcome was as certain as the outcome of the court case. A Socialist would be elected to the city's highest office, and not just any Socialist but one of the principal legal defenders of the McNamaras. An admission of guilt by the two men would disintegrate Job Harriman's election chances and guarantee the reelection of Mayor Alexander. Moreover, he told the general, should the McNamaras be sentenced to death after having consistently and forcefully proclaimed their innocence, they would become martyrs in the minds of millions of workers, and labor unrest might rise to revolutionary proportions in the city and elsewhere.

It was a bitter pill that Davis presented to the general. And he swallowed it.

The deal that Davis had proposed was that J. B. McNamara would confess and receive whatever sentence the court might impose, with the exception of capital punishment, and that all charges be dropped against J. J. McNamara and everyone else connected with the case. The business leaders now took the settlement deal to District Attorney Fredericks. To their annoyance, Fredericks refused to accept it.

In a slim book titled *Bombs and Bribery*, writer W. W. Robinson published an account of a meeting between Fredericks and Otto F. Brant, general manager of the Title Insurance and Trust Company. Brant, who was accompanied by Harry Chandler, recalled that when he described the proposed settlement to Fredericks, the DA replied that he "most emphatically" rejected it, adding, "I am of course willing to settle this matter, but it will have to be on a different basis than that." Brant then suggested that the proposal be set in writing. Thomas Gibbon, part owner of the *Los Angeles Herald*, drew up the document. Again Fredericks balked, saying, "Those men are both guilty and I will be able to convict them. I of course would like to avoid the necessity of going through with this long trial, but I cannot and will not accept the terms proposed."

On Sunday, November 19, Darrow, together with cocounsels Davis, McNutt, and Scott, Steffens and Fremont Older, paid a visit to the McNamaras in L.A. County Jail. Darrow, as he himself would later write, "pointed out the impossibility of winning, or even trying the case, the number of indictments, the strong feeling, and the evidence in the hands of the State." The defense, Darrow added, "had no evidence of any importance that we could offer." J. B. McNamara, Darrow claimed, could not be put on the stand "for he would not be able to sustain himself on cross-examination." Davis then explained that efforts had already been under way to arrange a plea bargain in J. B.'s case, but that the district attorney would not agree to his proposal that the charges against J. J. and the others connected with the case be dropped. Darrow said that he wanted to propose a life sentence for J. B. and a ten-year sentence for J. J. for his part in the bombing of the Llewellyn Iron Works—a sentence that would likely be reduced to five years with good behavior. A plea bargain of this order, he felt, was within the realm of possibility.

Steffens joined in. If the district attorney and the business leaders of Los Angeles accepted such a deal, it would go a long way toward achieving a détente in the growing strife between labor and business and set the stage for compromise elsewhere. It could bring love and brotherhood to Los Angeles. (Darrow thought Steffens's remarks were all, as he would later put it, "nonsense," but he held his tongue.) J. B. was unmoved. He was willing to take whatever sentence was meted out to him, he said, but J. J. must go free. If the secretary-treasurer of the Iron Workers Union was forced to plead guilty, it would have a devastating effect on the American labor movement, he argued. Besides, shouldn't Gompers, Ryan, Tveitmoe, and others in organized labor be brought into the discussion? And what about Darrow himself—wouldn't guilty pleas by himself and J. J. destroy him professionally?

"I told him I had no right to consider myself and they needn't bother about that part of it," Darrow later said in an interview. "Neither did I think Labor had any right to be consulted, as far as a lawyer's duty was concerned, and I didn't think they should sacrifice their lives when something better could be done."

It is likely that investigators for the district attorney's office listened to the entire conversation. The *New York Times* later discovered a piece of wire dangling from an upper window of the McNamaras' cell on the third floor to an unoccupied cell on the second floor. When a reporter asked DA Fredericks if it was true that a dictograph device had been used to listen in on the McNamaras' conversations, Fredericks replied, "There should be nothing unusual about it. There's just a round disk attached to the window shade. . . . and then there's the wire leading to some other place."

The brothers agreed to discuss the proposed settlement between themselves, and the others left. All, that is, except Joe Scott. As a prominent Catholic layman, he had been brought into the case as cocounsel as part of an effort to ecumenicalize the defense team. (He also had close ties to local government and business, serving at the time as a member of the Los Angeles Board of Education and president of the Los Angeles Chamber of Commerce.) Scott was also a man who wore his religion on his sleeve, and on this Sunday he thought it might be appropriate to suggest to his Catholic clients that they seek spiritual guidance in making their decision.

Despite his respected position among the city's elite—several years later he would be called "Mr. Los Angeles"—Scott could understand, perhaps better than his colleagues, what psychological and intellectual motives inspirited the McNamaras. He himself had left England as a young man because "there was no room for a man of my blood and faith in England in those days, no chance at all." In America he had married a Jewish woman, later writing, "I come from a persecuted people myself, and I have not much to say for the man and woman who only resent persecution of himself or his or her people. The Jewish people have been misunderstood. Did you ever know how it feels to be misunderstood?"

Now, on leaving the McNamaras, Scott ran into the prison chaplain, Father Edward Brady. As it turned out, Brady had been visiting the McNamaras regularly and told Scott that he was trying to find a copy of an old prayer book that the brothers often used when they were children. Brady remarked that they had strayed from their faith and that the prayer book might return them to it. With Scott's help a copy of the prayer book was found and Father Brady brought it to them. Scott would later claim that delivering the prayer book to the McNamaras was what it took to bring them around. They sent word to Darrow that they would agree to his proposed settlement.

As Darrow would later recall in an interview: "J. B. agreed to plead guilty and take life, all of us expecting that the time would come when his sentence would be committed or he would be pardoned. We had a separate conversation with J. J. and he was willing as he had been before to accept . . . a sentence of ten years, but of course he wanted us to get him off entirely. We agreed to do that. His case was not on trial, and we left the jail with the understanding that the J. B. case would be disposed of [first]."

DA Fredericks would later claim that he received a visit from Darrow and Davis, who argued that they couldn't plead J. J. guilty because he had become a symbol for labor and a guilty plea would crush the union movement.

"He'd better do it now," Fredericks said he replied, "because Mrs. Bain is sitting out there in the next room and is about ready to come through."

"Bain?" Darrow asked.

"You know Bain, who is on the jury. You know all about him."

Neither Darrow nor Davis said another word, staggered by Fredericks's calculated remark. But a short time after they left, the DA received a telephone message from Darrow, saying that they had talked to J. J. McNamara and that he had agreed to change his plea to guilty.

November 23, 1911 was Thanksgiving, and the newspapers reported the makings of the McNamara brothers' sumptuous jailhouse feast: ripe olives, celery, mushroom cocktail, oxtail soup, roast turkey, macaroni, green peas, candied sweet potatoes, mince pie, raisins, nuts, and cigars. In what can only be imagined as a truly incongruous affair, the brothers hosted a remarkable Thanksgiving banquet. As one reporter described the scene: "Tables were improvised in the trustees' room and the accused men ate heartily of the luxurious fare. Flowers were sent by labor union admirers, and the prisoners altogether passed the best day since their incarceration." Through the initial courses there was a sense of equanimity. After all, they no longer faced the overwhelming likelihood of J. B. being hanged. That fact, of course, went unmentioned, but obviously the two men realized that they had more than most to be thankful for on this holiday.

Some time after midnight that night, Otto F. Brant of the Title Insurance and Trust Company received a telephone call from his old friend, Harry Chandler. After his Thanksgiving dinner, Chandler informed him, LeCompte Davis had gone to Fredericks's home and had made final arrangements for the confession. In an interview with southern California historian W. W. Robinson nearly a half century later, Davis would justifiably boast, "I saved the lives of the McNamara boys. It was my greatest victory. I was the man."

Chapter 40

No one had told Bert Franklin, the man who had been placed in charge of investigating potential jurors, about the proposed settlement. Now, on a sunny Tuesday morning, just days after it had been negotiated, Franklin set off on a casual stroll through downtown Los Angeles. Franklin's purpose this morning was to pay the agreed-upon bribe to potential juror George Lockwood.

First he stopped at a saloon and had a few shots of whiskey while he looked about to see if anyone had been following him. He was anxious, as he knew the city to be crawling with the DA's spies, and he was now carrying $4,000 in cash, given to him by Darrow.

By the time Franklin had finished his whiskey, it was already a minute or two past the agreed-upon rendezvous time of 9:00 a.m. He paid his tab at the saloon, and after walking outside, removed two rolls of cash from his pocket. He now clenched them in each fist. As he approached the corner of Los Angeles and Third Streets he spotted Lockwood and Charles "Cap" White, the man who was to hold the bribe money until after the verdict was delivered, waiting for him. Next to them on the street corner, Lockwood noticed, a man had pulled up on a motorcycle that had mysteriously quit on him. At the very same moment, he glanced down Third Street and saw Franklin.

Franklin wasted no time. With one hand he discreetly handed Lockwood a wad of bills amounting to $500 and, with his other, handed White a wad of larger-denomination bills amounting to $3,500. (Testimony regarding the actual denominations of the money is conflicting.) The men quickly stuffed the cash in their pockets and were about to turn away when the motorcyclist stood up and appeared to motion to someone. With that, Franklin, the veteran investigator, swore, then told the two men not to look around.

"Let's get out of here," he remarked and began walking toward Main Street.

Franklin had seen that his old friend and former colleague, LAPD detective Samuel Browne (the same Samuel Browne who had accompanied Earl Rogers to San Francisco and had located the *Peerless/Pastime*), had witnessed the entire transaction from behind a nearby building. Then the scene became downright bizarre.

Loping down the opposite side of Third Street came the tall, agitated figure of Clarence Darrow himself, the lanky hair tossed to the side of his large forehead, the gray, deeply lined face illuminated by the morning L.A. sun. Seeing Franklin, he crossed the street waving his hat.

According to various news accounts, Darrow arrived at the corner of Los Angeles and Third Streets just in time to realize what was happening, to witness the bribe being executed, and to see that Franklin, Lockwood, and White were loosely surrounded by several men. Just as Darrow stepped onto the sidewalk, Detective Browne stepped in front of him and warned, "Don't talk to this man, Mr. Darrow. He's under arrest."

"My God, Browne. What is all this?" Darrow asked.

"You ought to know what it is," Browne replied. "It's bribery." Then he turned to Franklin, his old friend, and said, "Bert, I want you."

"What for?" Franklin asked.

Suddenly three other detectives closed in on the trio. The man with the broken-down motorcycle abandoned it and took two of the men by the arm just as DA Fredericks himself appeared with several assistants from behind a building. LAPD Detective George K. Home thrust an automatic weapon against Franklin, just as White attempted to dodge behind a telegraph pole.

Lockwood and White kept their hands thrust deep in their pockets, refusing commands from the detectives to reveal the evidence. White shouted, "I demand to know what this outrage means. I want to know my rights."

"You'll get them," Browne replied.

"What does this mean, Browne?" Franklin asked again.

"Bert, you have been an officer long enough to know what it means."
Lockwood remained silent. He knew he was there as bait.

Browne and his detectives marched the men about a half mile to the
offices of DA Fredericks on the eleventh floor of the Hall of Records.
When they finally removed their hands from their pockets, Browne
would later relate, the bills "clung to their fingers."

Darrow had come along too. Although he had not been arrested, he
nonetheless recognized not only his professional but legal peril. The Trial
of the Century was in progress, and he had just been caught at the scene
of a bribery of potential jurors.

"It was a 'plant,'" Darrow's cocounsel Joe Scott later announced in a
familiar refrain to the press, "and before we get through we'll know who
did it, and I believe Mr. Fredericks will be as much surprised as anybody."

The surprise would be on Scott himself. The bribery plot was being
run out of Franklin's office. Darrow had been funneling funds for it that
he had received from Tveitmoe in San Francisco without informing Scott
or his other colleagues. He had confided in several friends and associates
that he might attempt to suborn witnesses and jurors as a last resort. Each
time his confidant had inveighed against such a strategy. Each time Darrow had responded, "I guess you're right."

Who can comprehend why Darrow had allowed himself to walk into
a trap on that late-November morning? The most likely explanation is
that a glitch had developed in the settlement deal and that had distracted
him, occupying his attention and preventing him from warning Franklin.
Or perhaps he felt that there remained the possibility that the deal might
come undone. If so, a sympathetic juror could prove to be an invaluable
bit of insurance. Yet if Fredericks's account of how he had told Darrow
about Mrs. Bain is to be believed, Darrow's decision to wait until the
last moment to intercept the payoff at Third and Los Angeles Streets
seems downright sloppy. Several newspaper accounts claim that Darrow
remarked aloud, "They're on to us, Bert," as he approached the corner.

Watching the arrests swiftly being executed before his very eyes must have sickened him. It must also have dismayed even Samuel Browne, the detective who pulled off the sting. Browne understood that he had the goods on his old friend Franklin, but it gave him no sense of pride or accomplishment. He told reporters that "It was hard to arrest Bert Franklin. He has been a personal friend of mine for years, and my daughter was soon to have attended his daughter's wedding."

Nothing was mentioned to reporters of Darrow's presence at the scene of the arrests that morning. However, Browne advised reporters to expect additional dramatic developments.

"This is not the big smash," he told them. "That will come in court just a little later."

Reading Browne's words, the Great Defender realized that it was now only a matter of time before he, too, became a victim of the unfolding catastrophe.

Later that afternoon, ashen-faced and dispirited, Darrow made his way back to the Hall of Records and posted $10,000 bail for Franklin's release. As they left the building, both men appeared utterly distraught. Franklin, a man who had served nobly for eight years as an investigator for the United States marshal and the L.A. district attorney, realized he had disgraced himself in his hometown, and Darrow knew he had been caught smack-dab in the middle of a transaction he thought could deliver him from his private hell.

Two days later an article appeared on the front page of the *Times*, "Seek Identity of Higher Ups," and subheaded, "Cutting Deep into Alleged Attempts at Bribery." The piece claimed that the DA would be looking to "trace the supposed corruption fund to its first source and lay bare the methods ascribed to someone connected with the defense of the McNamaras."

That someone, Darrow of course knew, was himself.

"The first thing that entered my mind," he would say years later, "was as to whether it would be possible to carry out this settlement [after Franklin's arrest], and if not, whether it would be possible to save these men's lives. I was shocked and broken up over it."

The arrest of Bert Franklin and Darrow's entanglement in the matter had made finalizing the McNamara settlement not only critical but urgent. Should the trial proceed, it would surely be brought to the court's attention that there had been an attempt to corrupt the jury, thus all but ensuring that J. B. would hang.

Chapter 41

On the morning of Friday, December 1, 1911, Lincoln Steffens awoke in his hotel room near the beach and took a long, bracing swim in the Pacific Ocean. He emerged from the frigid water, strode across the sand, and had breakfast, exhilarated by the belief that his articles about his role in the settlement of the McNamara trial were soon to become a national topic. His hope had been to "put the ancient controversy between labor and capital on a new and clearer basis forever," and at this moment of exquisite calm he must have felt that he had succeeded. But as Steffens biographer Justin Kaplan would later note, he also began to sense that morning "an undercurrent of premonition," and as the day progressed, "downright fear."

At the same time Steffens was having breakfast, Darrow was leaving his office at the Higgins Building, where he wended his way through the crowd of people in the street wearing their McNamara buttons and carrying their "Harriman for Mayor" placards. He headed toward the Hall of Justice and entered the courtroom where the jury-selection process was now in its seventh week. He took his seat at the long defense table, his head bowed. He picked up a pencil and, as he began examining the sheaf of papers in front of him, began chewing on it and rolling it in his mouth. The lines on his face seemed to have deepened; those near his mouth were twitching. Joe Scott sat next to him, looking as grave and dejected as Darrow. LeCompte Davis untypically also seemed worn and distant. Cyrus McNutt and Job Harriman were not present.

A side door opened and deputies led J. B. McNamara in. He walked to the defense table and took his usual seat next to Davis. Across from them,

District Attorney Fredericks and chief deputy Joe Ford were engaged in animated conversation.

A moment later Judge Bordwell entered the courtroom. He strode to the bench, adjusted his glasses, and in his usual firm voice, opened the day's proceedings.

"People versus McNamara. The defendant is in court?"

To the surprise of the crowd in the courtroom, Fredericks rose and asked for a continuance until 2:00 p.m. "I cannot tell Your Honor the reasons," he said, "but must ask you to accept my word that they are of the highest importance." The attorneys adjourned to the judge's chambers where they submitted the plea agreement that they had negotiated.

Bordwell sat back in his chair and sighed as he considered the bargain. After all the annoyances the defense had put the court through in the course of jury selection, and the alleged bribery of three potential jurors, he would seem to have lost all patience. What came next startled Darrow.

"Ten years isn't long enough for John J. McNamara," the judge said. "He'll have to take fifteen."

It had been difficult enough getting the brothers to agree to a plea bargain that required J. J. to accept a sentence of ten years; now there would be no chance whatsoever of a commuted sentence of two or three years. Since Darrow could not accept the change in terms on J. J. McNamara's behalf without consulting him, he returned to the county jail with the news. J. J. was crushed. Nevertheless he understood that he had no choice, and Darrow was soon back in the judge's chambers to tell him the defense had agreed to the additional five years.

When court reconvened, it was clear that despite Fredericks's request for a continuance earlier in the day, reporters and spectators had suspected no significant development in the case. Outside, despite the late-fall date, the L.A. sun was growing hotter and the usual crowd of courtroom hangers-on grew restless as they waited for the courtroom to be unlocked so that they could cool off inside. The doors opened and the spectators filed in.

They looked on as the defense attorneys arrived, appearing haggard and beat. They began talking among themselves when the inner door of the courtroom opened and, led by a phalanx of plainclothes lawmen, in walked both J. B. and J. J. McNamara. J. J. had not attended the proceedings previously, and his appearance in court caused a stir. The brothers, both of them chewing gum, took seats near their lawyers, looking positively jaunty—as if they had just got off work and were dropping by the courtroom before heading down to the local saloon. J. J. flopped into a chair next to Darrow and draped an arm over the back of his chair. He was smiling his usual half-smile even as he chomped on his chewing gum. J. B. McNamara took a seat next to Davis and Joe Scott. Scott slapped him on the back, then put an arm over his shoulder. J. B.'s eyes darted around the room.

Bordwell entered the courtroom and repeated his ritual opening:

"People versus McNamara. The defendant is in court?"

Fredericks once again stood and addressed the bench, "Your Honor, the defense wishes to address the court."

LeCompte Davis then rose and made the statement that would shake the labor movement for a generation: "Your Honor, the defendant is in court. In the case, People versus McNamara, that is now on trial, may it please the court, after a long consideration of the matter and final consultation between counsel for the defendant, we have concluded to withdraw the plea of not guilty and have the defendant in this case enter a plea of guilty."

There was a long, stunning pause, and barely a murmur—as if no one could quite believe what had just been said. A baby began crying in the rear of the courtroom. Its mother stood up and hustled it out the door. J. B. stared straight ahead. Then Davis continued: "And we intend to pursue a like course with reference to J. J. McNamara, in the case of the people against him, wherein he is charged with having placed dynamite at the Llewellyn Iron Works."

From the hallway behind the courtroom, the cradles of telephones could be heard being lifted as reporters raced one another to phone in the news to their city desks and telegraph operators.

Fredericks now stood and asked the clerk for the file documents in the case, flipping the pages of the complaint while the hubbub in the back of the room was silenced by the bailiffs. Now, looking directly at J. B.

McNamara, he said, "J. B. McNamara, will you please stand up." The thin, ghostly pale man seated next to Clarence Darrow rose.

"Do you now wish to withdraw that plea of not guilty?" Fredericks asked.

His answer, "Yes, sir" was spoken in a voice so low that most of those in the court did not hear it.

"Are you ready to plead?" Fredericks asked.

"Yes."

"To this indictment No. 6939, charging you with the crime of murder, do you plead guilty or not guilty?"

"Guilty," J. B. answered. At the same moment another baby cried out at the rear of the courtroom.

A moment later Fredericks asked J. J. if he wanted to change his plea from "not guilty" to "guilty" to indictment No. 6944 charging him with the dynamiting of the Llewellyn Iron Works.

"I do," J. J. answered.

"J. J. McNamara, this is the time agreed upon for you to plead to the same. Do you want to plead guilty or not guilty?"

"Guilty, Your Honor," J. J. said. The baby wailed again as the words left his lips.

"Three little boxes concealing telegraph wires were prepared for the developments," the *New York Times* reported, "and less than two seconds after the word 'Guilty' left the mouth of each defendant, the news was being flashed forth across the land."

Darrow sat slumped in his chair, his eyes closed, as the judge set sentencing for December 5, 1911, election day.

The moment Bordwell uttered the words "Court adjourned," all hell broke loose. The prosecutors assisting in the case bolted out of the courtroom to District Attorney Fredericks's office, where a victory spread had been laid out. As Fredericks pushed through the army of frantic reporters, a correspondent shouted with respect to J. B. McNamara, "Why did he confess?"

"He confessed because he was guilty and that's all there is to it," Fredericks shouted back. To another reporter he said, "I don't want a pound of flesh. I look at this from two viewpoints. As a lawyer I wanted these men to plead guilty because they were guilty—because the evidence we gathered showed them guilty beyond any doubt. But as a man I want to say that if I can recommend a less severe punishment than death or be merciful in any way and at the same time rid union labor of its desire to use violence to obtain its ends, I want to do that thing."

Other reporters managed to put the question directly to J. B. himself, who replied that he had done so to save his brother Joe's life. And then, inexplicably, he added: "J. J. is not in on this deal. . . . I don't care what happens to me. . . ." And then he was gone, soon to be put away for the remainder of his life.

Another reporter asked Darrow why J. B. McNamara confessed. Darrow responded in a voice betraying tremendous fatigue:

"He was counseled to confess," Darrow said, "because that was the best thing he could do in the opinion of counsel. I will say now that there was no other reason or motive in it. I've studied this case for months. It presented a stone wall."

A reporter asked, "Why didn't you wait until after Tuesday's election? Don't you know this will hurt Job Harriman's chances to be elected mayor?"

"I know," Darrow replied forlornly, "but we could not take any chances. Maybe the state would have backed out of the agreement. Lives were at stake and I think we saved them." Darrow's eyes welled with tears. He appeared utterly defeated. "They had it on us. The county had a complete case. Every loophole was gathered in by the state."

In the midst of the cacophony, Burns detective Malcolm McLaren approached Fredericks and said, "There's just one thing I want to ask you, and that is that you do all you can for McManigal."

Fredericks paused, raised his right hand, and said, "I promise you I'll do all in my power for him."

There was one remaining bit of business for the court. Jurors and prospective jurors were led back into the courtroom, where Judge Bordwell informed them about what had just transpired. They immediately burst into applause.

The final session of the McNamara trial had lasted less than twenty minutes.

Darrow made his way to the doors of the crowded courtroom and was about to leave when he noticed a throng had gathered on the courthouse steps, silently waiting in gloomy silence. Darrow stared back for a long moment. At his side was Billy Cavanaugh, a policeman and an old friend. Cavanaugh was now alarmed.

"Come with me," he said, taking Darrow by the arm.

"No, Billy," Darrow would later remember saying. "I shall go down the street with the crowd. I have walked with them to the courthouse when they cheered me, and I shall go back the way I came."

So he did, Darrow would later recall, descending the stairs and then parting a sea of "sullen faces, and threatening gestures" as he was assaulted by "hard and cruel words." The crowd pushed in around him, whereupon a man spat in his face. Cavanaugh and Darrow pressed on through the mob—he could see Harriman and McNamara badges on the walkway, the courthouse lawn—every few yards someone yelled, "Traitor!" Miraculously, no one in the mob assaulted him. As they moved down the block, the crowd thinned, and soon they broke free as they hustled toward the Higgins Building. The city was suddenly transformed. Evening was gathering and the gas lights just coming on, revealing the litter of Harriman buttons that had been torn from the lapels of thousands of McNamara supporters. Thousands. Here and there were badges with J. J. McNamara's portrait and the word KIDNAPPED over the picture, others with the portrait of Harriman, reading MCNAMARAS NOT GUILTY! VOTE FOR HARRIMAN.

Chapter 42

Job Harriman learned of the news from a newsboy shouting the headlines of an extra edition on a street corner. He was thunderstruck. As he headed back to his campaign headquarters, he realized that the confessions would cost him the election. But for the time being he would stoically keep up appearances, telling reporters who were inundating his offices, "The trial has nothing to do with local issues. I was not called into conferences because the other attorneys said they did not want the local situation brought into it."

Furious Harriman campaign workers knew better. Several claimed loudly that the plea was part of "a plot to destroy socialism" by destroying Harriman.

Harriman was equally furious. "Why wasn't I informed?" he asked Darrow when he met with him later that day. Darrow replied that no one had the heart to tell him.

Reaction to the news throughout the country was swift and severe. In St. Louis, Socialists and members of the Typographers Union Local No. 8 telegraphed a resolution calling for both McNamara brothers to receive the death penalty. Likewise, the Chattanooga Typographical Union drafted a resolution that "required" the McNamara brothers "to pay the maximum penalty for their crime." In New York the outrage was directed at Darrow, with the Central Labor Union of Brooklyn proposing that the $190,000 given to the defense team thus far be turned over to the relatives of the victims. The Grand Rapids Typographical Union Local No. 39 denounced the McNamaras as "archfiends." And in Norfolk, Virginia, the Typographical Union Local No. 32 declared "the confession of the McNamaras was the greatest blow dealt union labor in twenty years."

Lincoln Steffens would finally write his self-serving article about the settlement, putting himself at center stage. But there was no scoop, no interview with the McNamaras. Steffens told how, although the McNamaras were not set free, the principle of the Golden Rule had eventually won out and that as a result there might now emerge a reconciliation between capital and labor that could prevent further violence. He said that he himself had had several conversations with Judge Bordwell about invoking a spirit of conciliation in sentencing the McNamaras. Perhaps the judge might say something like this: "Labor and Capital both stand convicted here today, the one of direct crime, the other of inciting labor to crime."

Finally, he asked, "What are we Americans going to do about conditions which are breeding up healthy, good-tempered boys like the McNamara boys?"

The *Chicago Daily Tribune* had an answer for him: "We are going to teach them that murder, whether by the footpad [street robber] or by the labor agitator, is more than a misdemeanor." In another column the paper accused Steffens of suffering from "an excess of mildness." Theodore Roosevelt dealt Steffens's message the most cutting repudiation: "It seems to me that Steffens made an utter fool of himself," he said.

Samuel Gompers appeared thoroughly outraged, not so much at being deceived by the McNamaras but by Darrow's neglect in consulting him. The AF of L had paid the celebrity attorney his $50,000 retainer and for its money had unexpectedly been rewarded with two guilty pleas. Gompers's greatest concern, however, was the larger political impact of the confessions.

"I am shocked beyond expression at the news," he told one reporter. He went on to tell another that "This unexpected self-confession is nothing more than a failure of two individuals to live up to the high principles of organized labor, and cannot reflect just condemnation upon the cause of labor as a whole."

Burns would now revel in schadenfreude. "I feel I have gained a great personal victory in the McNamaras' confessions," he said, "especially after men occupying such exalted positions as Samuel Gompers have repeatedly charged me with 'planting' the dynamite at Los Angeles."

Then Burns fired a shot across the bow of the AF of L when, referring to himself in the third person, he told another Chicago reporter, "Burns is still on the job. We've got the evidence—overwhelming evidence—to prove just who was concerned in this entire matter and we'll get the men before we quit."

"That means the men who employed the McNamara gang that blew up the Los Angeles Times Building?" the reporter asked. "Do you know them?"

"We know who they are," Burns said. Then he reminded the reporter that Matthew Schmidt and David Caplan were still at large. Those he was ultimately after, however, were the men higher up.

His comment got the attention of Frank Ryan, the current president of the McNamaras' union.

"Much has been in the newspapers concerning an investigation of the 'higher ups,'" he told the *Indianapolis Star*. "If I am in the class, I welcome such an investigation as I have nothing to fear therefrom."

He had a lot to fear therefrom. For authorities were beginning to tighten a net around Ryan and, for that matter, nearly every official of his union.

And once again it would be Ortie McManigal who would be the instrument of their downfall. A short time after the McNamaras' guilty plea, Fredericks visited him in his jail cell to bring him the news.

He would not have to testify against them, after all, Fredericks told him. McManigal showed no signs of relief, let alone elation. His agreement to turn state's evidence had cost him everything—his wife, his children, his freedom, his good name. And now Fredericks was telling him that it was all in vain.

Or was it? Fredericks told him that the federal government had asked that he turn over the evidence that he had intended to produce in the McNamara trial to them. The US attorney general, he said, was planning to pick up the case where he had left off. Burns had already discussed it with federal prosecutors and was prepared to produce further evidence of complicity that could involve not only Iron Workers officials in Indianapolis but also figures in the highest ranks of the AF of L. McManigal's testimony would likely be required in the forthcoming legal proceedings. Meanwhile, Fredericks continued, he would recommend to the court that McManigal be released from prison after his testimony was no longer needed. He could make no promises, but he felt confident that his recommendation would be favorably received.

Ortie wasn't buying it. A few minutes later, when reporters inevitably arrived and asked him, "What's next?" he replied, "Oh, I suppose I'll get mine." Then, laughing, he added, "I ought to get something for all I did. I think I might be given anywhere from one year to life."

Then McManigal's fatalistic attitude turned to exasperation. "I haven't seen my wife since she left here. Darrow promised her a life's living if she would desert me, and she took him up. . . . All I want to have is my children, but I don't suppose I can have them if I have to go to prison."

At nearly the same moment, half a continent away, a reporter was ringing the doorbell at Emma McManigal's home, the same doorbell that her husband and J. B. McNamara had once used to test their infernal machines.

"I am done with Mr. McManigal. . . . He is nothing to me," she said. "The shock of his admission to such a crime was almost more than I could stand. . . . I have not heard from my husband since I filed my application for divorce. And I do not care whether I ever hear from him again."

In Cincinnati reporters brought the news of the guilty pleas to the McNamaras' mother, Mary. Unlike the movie about them, the real drama did not end with the mother grieving by a fireside after receiving a letter from her innocent son. But there was grief aplenty. More grief than any one woman ought to have ever experienced. Her husband had deserted her. Her daughter had been raped by him. One of her sons had been incarcerated in a home for wayward boys and was now looking at serving the rest of his life in prison. And another son, the source of her greatest pride, would now be sent away too. It was more than she could take in.

"I know my boys are innocent," she said senselessly.

General Otis was one of the few who seemed satisfied with the plea bargain. "If today's result leads organized labor to the performance of its manifest duty, namely, the expulsion of lawbreakers, dynamiters, and murderers, the greatest possible good will have been done for lawfully organized labor." Not that the general could be confused with anyone who had the advancement of organized labor at heart.

And in a prison in Boise, Idaho, Harry Orchard, the man who confessed to murdering twenty-five men, including ex-Governor Steunenberg, and who had been called a liar in court by Clarence Darrow for saying that he had received his orders to do so from union leaders, felt vindicated at last. The confessions, he said, were "the only way the whole country could be convinced that some of the labor leaders have been engaged in wholesale assassination."

On Monday, December 4, LeCompte Davis visited J. B. McNamara at L.A. County Jail. He withdrew from his heavy, well-worn briefcase a yellow legal pad on which he had drafted the confession that he would submit to the court on the day of sentencing. They discussed its wording.

> *Los Angeles Cal*
> *Dec. 4, 1911*
> *I, J. B. McNamara defendant in the case of the people against McNamara and others having heretofore plead [sic] guilty to the crime of murder desire to make this statement of facts concerning the same. And this is the truth on the night of Sept 30, 1910, at 5:45 p.m. I placed in ink alley a portion of the Times Building a suit case containing 16 sticks of 80 percent Dynamite, set to explode at one o'clock the next morning it was my intention to injure the building and scare the owners I did not intend to take the life of any one. I sincerely regret that these unfortunate men lost their lives, if the giving of my life would bring them back I would freely give it. In fact in pleading guilty to murder in the first degree I have placed my life in the hands of the state.*
> *[signed] J. B. McNamara*

Davis handed a pen to McNamara, who, in his immaculate handwriting, copied the text onto a separate sheet of paper, botching the final sentence.

Davis duly delivered the confession to DA Fredericks. No similar confession would be forthcoming from J. J. McNamara.

At 10:00 a.m. on December 5, 1911, James McNamara was brought into the courtroom to be formally sentenced. He wore a white tie against a dark suit, and his face appeared very pale. His shackled brother stood at his side. Darrow sat next to Lincoln Steffens and the brothers in morbid silence.

DA Fredericks rose, addressed the court, picked up the copy of J. B. McNamara's confession and read it aloud. He then handed it to the bailiff, who passed it on to the bench. Judge Bordwell then asked J. B. if he affirmed the truth of the statement. J. B. said that he did.

"The court desires to ask you one question, and one only, Mr. McNamara. . . . Did you seek to purchase . . . dynamite of a higher degree of percentage?"

J. B. did not answer right away and, according to one reporter, "seemed to lose his composure."

"No, Your Honor," he lied. "No sir."

"You did not?"

"No sir," he lied again.

Judge Bordwell was apparently unimpressed. "I say that a man who under these circumstances would place a dynamite charge of that quantity in such a building, in which you, as a printer, knew gas was burning in many places, and in which you knew there were scores of human beings toiling, must have had no regard whatever for the lives of his fellow beings. He must have been a murderer at heart."

J. B. blanched. Indeed, he appeared to be on the verge of collapse.

"Counsel on either side," Bordwell remarked, "is aware of the usual custom of granting some degree of consideration to a defendant who has pleaded guilty—not on the ground of mercy, but on the ground of service to the State. This defendant has pleaded guilty. By doing so he has settled for all time in the minds of many what would have been regarded as a doubtful question."

And with that the judge sentenced J. B. McNamara to life imprisonment. He then quickly disposed of the J. J. McNamara case.

"Mr. McNamara," the judge began, "you have heard the court's remarks to your brother, and in no small degree, sir, they undoubtedly apply to you."

He then sentenced J. J. to fifteen years in San Quentin for his part in the bombing of the Llewellyn Iron Works. The court was then adjourned and the brothers led away, as one *Los Angeles Times* reporter put it, "sullen, shaking, half defiant, and half shrinking."

That afternoon Judge Bordwell issued a statement to the press that barely saw the light of day. He was clearly angry about Lincoln Steffens's article claiming that he had brought about the plea bargain and that he had met with Bordwell in order to persuade him to join in the settlement. Bordwell described Steffens's claims as being "without justification in fact."

In an unprecedented off-the-bench condemnation, Bordwell went on: "I wish also to denounce the claim of that gentleman, and of other persons for him, that the change of the pleas in these cases from not guilty to guilty was due to his efforts, as groundless and untrue. . . . There is no ground for any claim that he induced the prosecution to come to an agreement in the matter. The District Attorney acted entirely without regard to Mr. Steffens and on lines decided upon before the latter appeared on the scene.

"As to the defense, the public can rely on it that the developments last week as to bribery and attempted bribery of jurors were the efficient causes of the change of pleas which suddenly brought these cases to an end."

Returning to his chambers, Bordwell had one final matter to address— a letter he had received from a father who had deserted his family a lifetime ago. The precise contents of the letter in which John A. McNamara pleaded for clemency for his two sons are unknown, but Bordwell's reply is filed among his personal papers at Stanford University. "I can well understand how you feel," he wrote. "Your sons were and are in a very sad situation, and I pity them from the bottom of my heart. . . . I had a plain duty to perform, and sorrow or emotions of any kind which I might feel for the boys must not be at all considered. It was an awful crime that each of these boys had committed and commensurate punishment was demanded by the law. Again, I assure you of my deep sympathy for you in these hours of sorrow." There is no indication that the two brothers were ever made aware of the correspondence between their father and the judge.

Meanwhile, the December 5 morning newspapers were reporting Darrow's greatest fears—that Bert Franklin was cooperating with the district attorney. One *Times* story even reported that "Franklin may confess," and that Robert Bain's wife, Dora, already had. The convening of a grand jury on the bribery charges was a foregone conclusion; an indictment of Clarence Darrow for the attempted corruption of at least three jurors seemed inevitable.

On his way to the county jail, Clarence Darrow announced to reporters that he had fought his last case.

Outside the courtroom, Job Harriman was in the midst of a spectacular electoral defeat, with thousands of registered voters abandoning the McNamara defense attorney who had spent the last few months trumpeting the innocence of his clients. Never before in California history had an election become so interwoven with the progress and outcome of a criminal case. Still, Harriman held on to the slim hope that he would ultimately prevail. This, after all, would be the first time in California history in which women were allowed to vote. With Harriman standing not only as the "McNamara candidate" but also as the "suffrage candidate," the strong turnout of staunchly liberal women voters, he thought, might still save the day.

Well before the count was complete, the business leaders of Los Angeles sensed the warm premonition of victory. Everyone had assumed Harriman would lose, but few had guessed he would lose by a landslide—34,000 votes.

"The red flag is dead," the *Los Angeles Times* rejoiced editorially. "Long live the Stars and Stripes." And then, on New Year's Day: "Boycotting, picketing, assaulting and dynamiting are at an end.... Industrial freedom reigns supreme."

Lincoln Steffens saw it differently. Seemingly setting aside his brotherly love philosophy, he wrote: "The hate of old feuds, the rancor, personal spite and the small side generally of a small city were all turned up here today [amid] the utter rout of the Socialist party and the final disposition of the McNamara cases."

Chapter 43

Christmas 1911 was as cheerless a holiday as Clarence Darrow had ever spent. The McNamara trial aborted, the radical writers, including the Field sisters, who had swooped into town from all over the country, filed perfunctory articles and fled, leaving Darrow in an almost palpable gloom. Only Ruby remained at his side, and she did the best she could to lift his spirits. She put up a small Christmas tree and invited in friends for a turkey dinner. She accepted an invitation to the couple to go horseback riding in the hills behind Tujunga Canyon. Ruby would say later that as Darrow rode an old white horse and took in the beauty of the locale, his spirits were at least momentarily lifted.

He felt certain that he could not escape indictment and arrest for attempted jury tampering and subornation. He recognized that when that happened he would need the aid of the best lawyer in the city. When on January 22 he received a summons to appear before the grand jury, he consulted with his friends, who unanimously recommended Earl Rogers, a man he had casually met only once at a celebrity watering hole in downtown Los Angeles.

Still, Darrow wanted to see Rogers in action for himself. The problem was that Rogers at that moment was involved in a contested-will case in Hanford, some two hundred miles north of Los Angeles in the San Joaquin Valley, reachable only via the Central Pacific Railway (whose treasurer the town was named for). Darrow and Ruby threw some clothes into a bag and left the following day for Hanford. After arriving and settling into a small hotel, they made their way to the courthouse.

The door quietly opened and the bailiff led the hulking figure of Clarence Darrow and his tiny wife to a seat in the back row. Ruby sat "perched," recalled Adela Rogers, sitting like "a sparrow expecting war."

Rogers was in the midst of what he did best, slowly pacing behind the counsel table as he cross-examined a witness. Rogers's assistant, the young attorney Jerry Giesler, sat next to the seventeen-year-old Adela near the front of the courtroom. She felt a pinch on her arm. Looking up at Giesler, she surreptitiously followed his eyes to the celebrity attorney at the back of the room. The couple looked dour. Darrow's suit was rumpled, Ruby's white gloves plainly darned, her dress careworn in what Adela Rogers would describe as "an excessive display of poverty."

"Darrow doesn't like him," Jerry Giesler whispered to Adela.

"Neither does his wife," she whispered in response.

In fact, Ruby would later remark that Earl Rogers was "nothing but an actor." Darrow, however, understood that he was in a fight for his life, and that this man in the well-tailored suit with his gift for performance might be what it took to save him. Certainly he had no more witnesses and evidence to bolster his case than he did the McNamaras'.

And Rogers was something to behold, especially in this little town. The contrast between the two lawyers was pronounced. Darrow sat looking downright disheveled at the back of the courtroom. He had lost considerable weight, and his suit looked two sizes too large. His hair fell over his forehead and looked as if he had not combed it in days. Beard stubble was apparent.

Rogers, on the other hand, as strikingly handsome as any leading actor of his day, wore a cutaway coat with braided edges, a shirt with a bat-winged collar, boutonniere, spats. His black hair was parted in the middle and was well trimmed. He radiated elegance and magnetism in the courtroom.

Besides, as United Press reporter Hugh Baillie, who covered both Rogers and Darrow, once wrote: "Darrow was as much an actor as Rogers, and as skilled at putting across a point by the use of his personality. But he always seemed to have scored his point by pure logical argument, and you had to watch him carefully to see that he was acting. Rogers's acting was obvious and flamboyant. He generated electricity. Often, his theatrics overwhelmed the point he might be making with them—but even more often, the Rogers act made jurors forget whatever points the prosecution had tried to hammer home."

Philosophically and politically the two were at opposite ends. Darrow had built his reputation by defending the poor, and his friends were union leaders, Socialists, and assorted radical thinkers. Rogers had built his reputation defending the rich, usually those involved in vice cases. And, of course, he had been enlisted by the city at the beginning of the hunt that eventually ensnared Darrow's recent clients, the McNamaras.

The Darrows watched Rogers intently for three days, and on Saturday, January 27, hired him.

On Monday morning, January 29, Fredericks appeared before the grand jury with Bert Franklin in tow. Fredericks had negotiated a plea bargain with Franklin in which the Darrow investigator had agreed to pay a $4,000 fine and testify against his former boss. That afternoon, after learning that he had been indicted on two counts of jury bribing, Darrow, accompanied by Earl Rogers, appeared in court, was arrested on the charge of attempting to bribe George Lockwood, and was later freed on $20,000 bail.

As he left the building, newspaper reporters, who continued to admire him, if for no other reason than that he usually provided them with good copy, crowded around Darrow.

"I was expecting to be indicted, and I am prepared for it," he told them. "All I will say in regard to the indictment is this: I have repeatedly said I knew nothing about any attempts to bribe or influence a juror. I repeat that steadily. I confidently hope and expect to be acquitted."

Now that Darrow had been indicted, he became an even bigger celebrity than he had been during the McNamara trial, and the fact that none other than Earl Rogers, the very attorney who had been employed to track down the bombing terrorists, now stood at his side made the story irresistible. The odd coupling lifted Rogers's celebrity status as well.

"Selecting me to defend the nation's acknowledged premier criminal lawyer will eventually place me in Darrow's class," Rogers told his daughter.

Especially now. His alcoholism had sometimes become so incapacitating that he would often disappear for days after a bender and then enter the 1912 equivalent of rehab—in the form of Turkish baths, steam rooms, and saunas. He would then magically reappear, looking rested, refreshed—dapper, as usual—and ready to take up where he had left off. And yet as impressive as his recuperative powers seemed to be, decades of alcohol abuse were catching up with him. "I've been slipping somewhat," he admitted to a number of friends that winter. "I need Darrow almost as much as he needs me."

As the trial date approached, the pressure on Darrow became even more intense than it had been when he was representing the McNamaras. As his depression took hold, he refused to eat. He seemed to be shrinking inside his clothes. To Ruby's great exasperation, he also began to drink. His physician appealed to him to stop; Earl Rogers urged otherwise. "Oh, let him alone, Doc," the devoted alcoholic interrupted. "The liquor is good for him at a time like this."

From the beginning Clarence and Ruby feared that the trial could be financially ruinous. Darrow was receiving no help whatsoever from the AF of L for the cost of his defense. This time there would be no inflated legal staff, no band of investigators to scrutinize the jury pool. By and large it would be Darrow and Rogers who would handle what was an eminently complicated case.

Presiding over the court would be Judge George Hutton, a young, kindhearted Christian Scientist who seemed starstruck by the sight of two of America's foremost criminal attorneys sitting before him.

Finally, on May 15, 1912, Darrow's trial got under way in the Hall of Justice. It would become one of the most turbulent trials in the history of American jurisprudence, one that would receive unprecedented news coverage.

Three other lawyers assisted Darrow and Rogers: Harry Dehm, Horace Appel, and Jerry Giesler. Dehm had recently joined Rogers's law firm as a full-fledged partner but was occupied with other business for the firm and played little role in the trial. Appel was an eccentric Mexican Jew with a heavy accent, an often unkempt appearance, and a fiery disposition.

At one point during the McNamara trial, his behavior so angered Judge Bordwell that he clapped him in jail overnight. At Darrow's own trial, during the cross-examination of John Harrington, Darrow's chief detective during the McNamara case, Rogers noticed that Harrington refused to look at Darrow. "'Tell him to look you in the eyes," Rogers whispered to Darrow. DA Fredericks overheard the remark, leaped to his feet, and accused Darrow of attempting to hypnotize the witness. In response, Appel shouted, "I say that heepnotism is not recognized in a court of law! Anyway, I object to the questions wheech are being interpolated here from time to time by the deestrict attorney! They are eemproper. They are eerrelevant and eemmaterial, never asked in a court of justice before!" The exchange was greeted by a roar of laughter from the courtroom spectators, causing Judge Hutton to call a five-minute recess. At another point, Appel so infuriated Fredericks that the DA picked up an inkwell and threw it at him. Rogers, trying to block it, received a cut on his hand.

Although chewing gum in a courtroom would be viewed as disrespectful and censurable by a judge today, such was not the case in 1911, when trials could sometimes become rollicking affairs. J. B. McNamara had chomped on gum every day in court—but so too did Deputy DA Joe Ford, and at one point during the Darrow trial Appel infuriated Ford when he snidely remarked, "I'm seeck and tired of these gum-chewin' objections."

The twenty-five-year-old Giesler, who had been a law clerk for Rogers, had just passed the bar but was still looking up legal precedent for his boss. Darrow became aware of him after he and Rogers asked Giesler to look up a point of law and he returned with a forty-page-long brief. They were impressed and decided to bring him on as an attorney of record in the trial.

Giesler, who would go on to become one of the most famous criminal defense attorneys of the twentieth century, was overwhelmed. "Never," he would write in his autobiography, "have I had another thrill to equal what I felt on being allowed to be a member of such a team. There I was, just a kid, and the two men I idolized most were treating me as an equal. My eyes smarted. I couldn't talk. I couldn't even thank them."

Although their professional and private lives were diametrically opposed, Darrow and Rogers themselves actually got along, at least in the beginning. Unlike Darrow, Rogers felt confident of their chances in court. Perhaps most propitious was the fact that they had together concocted something of a reasonable defense, one that had the ring of truth: Why would Clarence Darrow, the chief counsel in the McNamara trial, participate in the bribing of a juror when a settlement had already been reached with the prosecution? Reasonable doubt, it seemed to both Rogers and Darrow, was self-evident.

Unfortunately, the prosecution had a small battalion of witnesses who were prepared to testify that Darrow had been the architect of an elaborate strategy to corrupt up to six jurors in order to prevail in a case that he knew he could not otherwise win. The bribery of the jurors, Fredericks and Ford would claim, was a hedge. Indeed, they would argue, Darrow had expected the case to go to trial—right up until the moment he was caught at the scene of the bribe. On December 5, 1911, Bordwell had claimed in open court that there had been no "settlement," and that the fifteen-year sentence he had imposed on J. J. McNamara was rather stiff for someone who had no criminal record and who was not personally involved in the commission of the crime (planting the dynamite at the Llewellyn Iron Works). The prosecutors' evidence indicated that Darrow had come to the scene of the bribery at Third and Los Angeles Streets on November 28, 1911, to warn Franklin that he was being trailed by the district attorney's detectives.

Newspapers from Chicago, New York, Washington—even from the capitals of Europe—assigned reporters to the trial. Telegraph wires were installed in the courtroom, and as reporters wrote out their copy on lined yellow pads, they handed it to a Morse man who tapped it out to their copy desks. In some instances they simply whispered their reports to the press telegraphers, whose hands were enclosed in a soundproof box that held the transmitting key. Two of the press seats were occupied by Lincoln Steffens and Fremont Older.

Earl Rogers was in fighting form from the time the jury-selection process began, but Darrow seemed as if he were gazing into the abyss. Rogers's daughter Adela was also struck by his morose behavior: "Darrow somehow imparted to the whole cast and proceedings a wildly emotional, breast-beating, bleating, gloom and wretchedness." She also witnessed his dramatic weight loss, how "his clothes hung looser and looser. None of us had ever seen anything like it before."

Ruby possessed the same gloomy disposition but managed to elicit sympathy, even admiration, from journalists, as she came to court each day wearing her darned white gloves, a gown of a thin, dark material, and a large-brimmed sailor hat with a green ribbon. She seemed always to have a comforting word for her haggard husband during the recesses of each day's courtroom melee—always patting his hand, always remaining composed while one witness after another paraded to the witness stand to accuse him of felony corruption.

On the other hand, Rogers put on a courtroom performance that even the *Los Angeles Times*'s reporter found spellbinding. "Rogers cross-examined brilliantly," he wrote in one article. "He used sarcasm, satire, innuendo, and raillery in such a way as to greatly embarrass the witness."

When prosecutor Fredericks objected to the needling, Rogers roared back, "I am showing up a perjurer."

Judge Hutton was outraged. "Do you insist on your right to call this witness a perjurer?" he asked.

Rogers replied that he had nothing to take back.

"Mr. Rogers," the judge said, "such conduct is contempt of this court. You cannot address a witness in any such language. It is the duty of every court to protect witnesses. I am exceedingly reluctant to take any action, but I cannot let this pass."

Rogers spent the night in jail.

On July 29 Darrow took the stand for the first time, submitting to four days of withering cross-examination from Fredericks and Ford.

"I had no more trouble about answering every question put to me than I would have had in reciting the multiplication table . . ." he would later write. "I felt as much at ease and as indifferent over my fate as I would have been standing comfortably at a harmless fireside surrounded by loving friends."

It wasn't quite true. On several occasions Darrow had to filibuster his way through Ford's questioning, particularly when it came to conversations he had had with Franklin as to what all the thousands of dollars he was turning over to him would be used for, if not for bribing jurors.

Eventually, outside of court, Darrow and Rogers began to argue bitterly, at first over the client's payments to his chief counsel, which were almost always late. Their final melee erupted as they prepared to rest their case, and this time it had to do with who would make the closing argument. Rogers didn't think Darrow, considering his tortured emotional state, was capable of making a moving plea. But if Darrow knew anything, it was how to make a moving plea. He felt outraged that Rogers felt otherwise. Besides, delivering the final remarks to the jury had been part of their original agreement when he offered Rogers the job. And it was his life that was on the line.

Moreover, Olaf Tveitmoe and Anton Johannsen had urged him to do so, and to bring in the argument of labor, the argument that hadn't been made in the aborted McNamara trial. Darrow thought such a plea would be particularly effective and would serve to mend fences with his disillusioned laborite friends. After doggedly objecting for most of the evening, Rogers finally relented. He would address the jury first, then Appel, then Darrow. It was a decision for which countless workingmen and women, union activists—and even students of law—would be grateful for generations to come. His plea would be for something far more than his own liberty, far more than a plea for greater economic and political equality in American life. Even Darrow's greatest critics would recognize it as a plea for the ages.

Early the following morning a throng of thousands came to the courthouse to hear America's greatest pleader plead for his freedom. The scene turned unruly as the crowd tried to squeeze through the doors to see what everyone realized would be history in the making. According to the *Chicago Daily Tribune,* whose reporters were carefully covering the story about its notorious hometown resident at the center of the storm, two men and seven women fainted, men's clothes were "torn from their backs" as they tried to gain entrance. A riot call was sent out, whereupon "the police charged the mob and swept it back." Then the doors to the courtroom, which was jammed with people, were locked.

On the morning of August 14, 1912, Clarence Darrow slowly rose from his seat behind the defense table, sank his hands into his coat pockets, and began in a steady, warm voice.

"Gentlemen of the jury, I am a stranger in a strange land, two thousand miles away from home and friends. . . . However, I don't feel that I am alone, for I have a faithful band working with me, a band as faithful as was ever gotten together." In this way Darrow acknowledged the steadfast team of gifted attorneys behind him.

As his oration got under way, it was clearly proving a catharsis for the tall, withered attorney. Without notes, reciting extemporaneously from lines he had strung together in his mind, Darrow spoke for the next day and a half, all the while attempting to drive home his contention that he was not being prosecuted for bribery but for being an effective counsel for the cause of labor.

"I have committed one crime," Darrow went on, "which is like the crime against the Holy Ghost, which cannot be forgiven. I have stood for the weak and the poor. I have stood for the men who toil. And therefore I have stood against the enemies of the poor."

"He wept each handkerchief into a sodden ball," Adela Rogers St. John would later write derisively, "cast it from him, and Ruby Darrow supplied another, which soon suffered a like fate. At last he began to wipe away the floods on his sleeves, they clung as though he'd plunged them into a rain barrel."

But the stirring effect he was having on the jury was slowly becoming evident, as several of the men began to weep openly. And those who did not sat thoroughly entranced. The surging Victorian cadence of Darrow's oratory gradually assumed the tenor of a sermon, throbbing with moral indignation, relentless in its appeal to the workingmen of the jury: "O, you wild, insane members of the steel trust and erector's association! O, you mad hounds of detectives who are willing to do your master's will! O, you district attorneys! You know not what you do.

"Let me say that if you can succeed in placing me behind prison walls, within the gray dim walls of San Quentin, there will breed a silence more ominous and eloquent than any word that my poor lips could ever frame."

But the further afield Darrow went in tying his circumstances to those of the cause of labor and, in effect, in putting his accusers on trial, the more dismayed Rogers grew. In Rogers's opinion, Darrow needed to drive home his defense that he had no reason to bribe the jurors, since the case was already settled, and that if someone had paid Franklin to do so, it wasn't him. By turning his tearful plea into a political platform, he needlessly risked alienating this jury, whose neighbors might have been killed or injured by his former clients. At one point during Darrow's closing argument, Rogers slipped out of the courtroom altogether. Noticing her father's absence, Adela went looking and found him in an empty witness room, brooding.

"He will get himself convicted yet," Rogers scowled. "Where does he think he is, in Indianapolis? I warned him. That jury was ready to acquit him. If he doesn't stop this wailing-wall weeping-willow blubber and snivel—that's not a speech, it's a lament."

"I know my life and I know what I have done," Darrow concluded on the second day of closing arguments. "It has not been perfect. It has been human. . . .

"I know of thousands of workingmen who are praying for my success—those who believe in me and are looking to this jury to vindicate me and my name. Gentlemen, I thank you."

And with that, Darrow turned away from the jury box, shuffled behind the defense counsel's table where Rogers, Appel, and Giesler sat, and slumped into his chair.

A long moment of silence descended over the courtroom. Then Fredericks rose, and in a closing argument as detached and bitter as Darrow's had been emotional and imploring, accused Darrow of twenty-two separate crimes during his work for the McNamara defense. Fredericks's most effective moments came when he attacked Darrow's alibi. "I don't care what they had agreed to about [the plea bargain]," he said, "they had to play out the Lockwood string. Of course, you can well imagine an ordinary man would wonder why the defense was trying to compromise on the one hand and to reach jurors on the other, but it was all part of the plan to free the two McNamaras."

Two days later the case of The People against Clarence Darrow was slated to go to the jury. By now Judge Hutton was ill and anxious for the mayhem of the trial to end, to remove himself from the raw emotions of the courtroom. In his instructions to the jurors, he gave the defense a shot in the arm when he observed that it was not "the duty of the defendant to prove who, if anyone, furnished the money to Franklin for the purpose of bribing the juror."

At precisely 9:20 a.m. on August 16, 1912, the bailiff gave his signal, and the jury rose from the box to begin deliberations.

Nearly everyone remained seated. The jury could be expected to be out for hours, even days, and yet no one was leaving the courtroom. Darrow sat next to his wife, clutching her hand until her knuckles bruised. Rogers, Appel, and Giesler surrounded Darrow, their heads bowed, while across the room Fredericks and Ford conversed with uncharacteristic levity behind the prosecution's table.

Just thirty-four minutes later a buzzer sounded. The crowd looked about, puzzled. It had come from the room where the jury was deliberating.

"What does it mean?" Ruby asked Darrow.

"Maybe they want some instructions," Darrow said.

Within seconds the twelve men, led by jury foreman M. R. Williams, were filing through the still-packed courtroom, returning to the jury box. A few of the men appeared to be smiling as they passed the defense table, others were not. Judge Hutton took his seat and asked of Foreman Williams, "Your pleasure?"

"A verdict," Williams replied.

"Read it," Hutton said.

No one was quite prepared for what followed, for it occurred so abruptly.

"Not guilty!" Williams nearly shouted.

The courtroom erupted.

"Men and women were hysterical," one newsman reported. "Several jurymen shouted," as Judge Hutton "made no attempt to quell the rejoicing."

According to a *Tribune* reporter, Darrow jumped to his feet, turned and took Ruby into his arms, and "for several minutes stood thus while friends and sympathizers crowded about them, showering congratulations."

Letting go of his wife, Darrow rushed to the jury box where the twelve men surrounded him, many taking the former defendant into their arms, three of them weeping. Many in the crowd then fought their way clear of the bailiff and charged the jury box, where they nearly overwhelmed Darrow's towering figure. Judge Hutton himself made his way through his courtroom-turned-madhouse to grasp Darrow's hands and tell him, "Hundreds of thousands of hallelujahs will go up from as many throats when they hear of this."

So it seemed amid the euphoria of the moment that at long last Darrow's bitter troubles in the city of Los Angeles were over. But just outside the courtroom DA Fredericks was making a speech that would bring a new degree of torment to Darrow's life.

"Certainly we will try the Bain case," Fredericks was telling a flock of reporters surrounding him in the hallway. "It is a much stronger case than this and with different circumstances. We have reason to believe we will secure a conviction."

❦

On October 1, 1912, two years to the day following the *Times* bombing, forty officials of the AF of L, including Frank Ryan, Herbert Hockin, Eugene Clancy, and Olaf Tveitmoe went on trial in Indianapolis accused of conspiring to violate federal law by aiding in the illegal transportation of dynamite and nitroglycerin on passenger trains traveling between states. Ortie McManigal had been the principal witness against them. There were thirty-nine convictions.

By the time Darrow's second trial opened in November, relations between Darrow and Rogers had deteriorated to the point that they rarely spoke to one another. The issue had little to do with courtroom strategy and everything to do with money. Darrow wasn't paying Rogers, and Rogers would make his displeasure known by simply not showing up in the courtroom. Noticing Rogers's absence from the courtroom for several days, Hugh Baillie of the United Press wire service phoned him at his home to ask why he was staying away.

"Well, Baillie," he replied, "I tried to give myself an enema yesterday and by mistake I used Sapolio [a harsh cleansing agent] instead of soap. I'm very sore and I won't be able to come back to court until I'm able to walk without it hurting so damn much." Baillie commented in his autobiography: "It was the perfect answer: It didn't tell me anything I could use, and it virtually prevented me from guessing at his real reasons. You could trust Rogers to have an excuse nobody had ever used before."

The result was that Darrow acted as his own lawyer for most of the second trial. Giesler and Appel assisted and cross-examined some of the lesser witnesses, but Darrow was now in full command. It was as if the result of the first trial had fortified him. He wanted the jury to know that he had previously been tried on a similar charge and had been found not guilty. In his opening argument, he declared, "If a tribe of savages had compelled a man to run the gauntlet once, they would have been satisfied and would not have compelled him to run it the second time."

There was a significant problem, however. Darrow was without his keystone defense. He could no longer argue as he had in the first trial that there was no need to bribe Lockwood since a settlement had already been reached. The bribery of Bain had occurred on October 6, 1911, a full month before the initiation of any talk of a settlement.

But Darrow once again operated on the theory that a strong offense is the best defense and repeatedly accused the prosecution of persecuting him because he was a prominent representative of the working man.

Rogers would return to the courtroom at odd intervals. He was present for the testimony of Darrow himself, wasting no opportunity to challenge the prosecution's line of questioning and drawing the jury's attention away from the accusations in the indictment. On one occasion, Deputy DA Ford was in the midst of questioning Darrow about the number of agents he had planted in the prosecution's offices during the McNamara trial. Darrow replied that he had none in the prosecution's but several in Burns's offices.

"I protest against this line of questions," Rogers shouted. "Ford, who is counsel for Burns, is trying to get information from this witness for his own private use." An uproar arose in the courtroom. Judge William Conley glowered at Rogers. The charge appeared reprehensible. The deputy DA a lawyer for Burns?

Ford fired back. "Mr Rogers, you lie when you insinuate these questions are intended to draw information as to alleged traitors in Burns's office."

Rogers now drew himself up. There was no hint of ill health or weakness about him now. He shouted at Ford: "I charge you with being counsel for Burns and that you are now seeking to elicit information for your client. I have been a sick man for weeks but no one shall call me a liar. I challenge you to meet me outside the courtroom."

The courtroom roared; the newspaper telegraph operators tapped their transmitting keys furiously. The judge banged his gavel for order, then adjourned the session.

Once the courtroom was cleared, he scowled at Rogers, telling him that his remarks were a serious breach of legal ethics. Ford, he said, had every right to call him a liar if he was not a counsel for Burns.

"I do not administer light punishment, nor do I expect that my admonitions are to be disregarded," he said. He was prepared to send Rogers to jail for at least ten days.

"I am perfectly willing to apologize," Rogers said at last.

"I take back my remarks," Ford responded.

But Judge Conley was not about to be dissuaded. Rogers's accusation that the prosecutor was in the employ of Burns was utterly reprehensible and tarnished the dignity of his courtroom, he remarked.

Ford now spoke up. Sheepishly he admitted that he currently represented Burns in his efforts to collect reward money in the McNamara case.

The judge was stunned. For the record he remarked, "In view of the statements of counsel I shall take no action at this time."

(Rogers was likely aware of Ford's representation of Burns because he too was seeking a piece of the reward money for producing the original witnesses and evidence that led to the McNamaras' conviction.)

Rogers's frequent absence from court in the second trial now put Darrow in the position of having to confront Bert Franklin directly. It was one thing for Rogers to cross-examine him about his claims that Darrow had given him the bribery money; it was another for Darrow to do so. At one point Franklin recalled being in Darrow's office when Darrow phoned a person named Job and asked him to bring him a large amount of cash. When Darrow began asking Franklin what he might have overheard during the conversation, the detective replied, "You remember, Mr. Darrow, you were on the other side of the wide table. I paid no attention to what you said."

At another point, when Darrow accused Franklin of receiving the money from someone else and putting the blame on him in order to make points with the district attorney in his plea bargain, Franklin noted that during the entire time he worked for Rogers, "you had every confidence in me."

In the end Darrow once again delivered the final argument to the jury, and this time, perhaps emboldened by his knowledge that his oratory in the first trial had saved the day, he delivered a closing address that seemed to include remarks that he had intended to deliver at the close of J. B. McNamara's trial.

"If no other voice shall be raised for J. B. McNamara, then let mine," he said. "The boy was not personally interested in putting dynamite in the alleyway of the Times Building. He didn't do it for himself but for humanity. He knew he could never get any fame or praise for his work. He thought he was doing good to the poor. . . . You can't settle the conflict between capital and labor by hanging men by the necks until they are dead or by putting them behind prison bars."

But that was what his accusers now wanted to do to him, he implied.

"I knew the chances I was taking when I defended the weak and lowly. But if I stop now I would have my reward. I could have made money and a different kind of fame. But I would not change places with my pursuers."

The fact that the state insisted on trying him twice and presenting virtually the same evidence and witnesses each time was proof enough he said, that "this is persecution, not a prosecution. . . . Had I been a robber or a defaulting bank cashier, I would not have been subjected to what has been given me. I have been acquitted. Why should I be tried again? Because I have dared to oppose the mighty in the defense of the weak. They have kept me here because the great forces of evil wanted me here.

"They have given Franklin immunity; they have let go every other criminal, but they want me. . . ."

Time and again, Darrow returned to the McNamara case.

"I am sorry for the McNamaras. I want them better understood. The placing of the dynamite was not the crime of the century. It was not even a crime. I want the poor boys brought back to society. They never morally committed murder. The explosion would not have even destroyed the printing presses save for the burning of the ink barrels. It was an accident. Under the laws of God the poor boys were not guilty."

But this time the jurors did not seem so receptive to Darrow's oratory as the ones in the Lockwood case. This time they deliberated more than forty hours before returning to court on March 8 to perform the usual ritual.

"Mr. Foreman, have you arrived at a verdict?" the judge intoned.

"No, Your Honor, and I am sure we can never get together," the foreman replied.

They were impossibly deadlocked, with eight jurors determined to convict, four holding out for acquittal.

"Such being the case, gentlemen, there appears to be no reason for keeping you any longer. . . . You have certainly held out longer than any jury in this county."

This time there were no hurrahs, no slaps on the back, no celebrations. Unlike Judge Hutton, Judge Conley did not descend from the bench and warmly congratulate the Great Defender on the defense of himself. Reporters pressed around Darrow and Ford, asking when a retrial could be expected. Darrow asked that he be retried the following week. Joe Ford insisted that would be impossible, and besides he had had enough of the case. If it was to be retried, another prosecutor would have to handle it, he said. Outside the courtroom, reporters found a juror willing to talk on condition of anonymity. He maintained that Darrow's defense of the McNamaras in his closing remarks had turned several jurors, including himself, against him.

A third trial was set on the court calendar for March 31. But in the days that followed, Darrow quietly cut a deal with Fredericks. He agreed to leave the state of California and never return in exchange for the charges against him being dropped. Fredericks, too, was thoroughly weary of the case.

The Great Defender had won a Pyrrhic victory, however. He had managed to save himself from prison in spite of the fact that even many of his most devout supporters thought him guilty. But his career and his reputation were in shambles. Even his great courtroom victories of the past on behalf of the working man were now regarded as suspect. He would now fade into obscurity for more than a decade, not to emerge again until 1924, when he would become the attorney in two historical cases that had nothing to do with labor or the working man. The Leopold and Loeb trial would involve two young and rich thrill killers; the Scopes trial the following year would involve a teacher who was accused of teaching evolution. They would become the two most famous cases of his career. And, like the McNamara case, they would result in the conviction of his clients. But they would be remembered. The Crime of the Century would not.

Chapter 44

In the shadow of the studio that produced *Citizen Kane* lies the cemetery where the real-life—indeed bigger than life—publisher, General Harrison Gray Otis, lies buried. In a vast family plot at what is now called Hollywood Forever Cemetery stands a hodgepodge of monuments bearing the names of generations of Otises and Chandlers and, most impressive of all, a veritable sepulcher displaying a plaque with the names of twenty "martyred men." It is topped with a bronze eagle, not unlike the one that once stood watch at the Los Angeles Times Building on October 1, 1910, and that refused to budge from its perch even as most of the rest of the structure crumbled beneath it.

Below the monument are buried most of the victims of the bombing, many of whom had been injured beyond recognition. When it was placed here a century ago, it was intended as an eternal reminder of the most horrendous crime ever committed in the history of Los Angeles.

The *Times* bombing remains that today and is only exceeded in its devastation and deadliness in peacetime US history by the Oklahoma City bombing in 1995 and the 9/11 attacks six years later. Nonetheless, history texts today now all but ignore that deadly event. It is as if it were merely a shameful embarrassment, as if politics, pride, and vanity had conspired to erase the foremost event of that time, a time not unlike our own, when righteous men, polarized to the extreme, waged undeclared war against one another, each side waving the banner of liberty and freedom.

There may be those today who regard the bombing as symbolic of the era, perhaps even as a prelude to the Bolshevik uprising. It was not. Many who are vaguely aware of the McNamaras think of them as anarchists.

They were not, as one of America's most prominent anarchists, Emma Goldman, would later observe.

"The McNamara brothers," she wrote, "were good Roman Catholics and members of the conservative American Federation of Labor. Perhaps they would have been the first to resent the charge of anarchy, since they knew nothing of our ideas and were unaware of their relation to the struggle of the workers."

J. J. McNamara, the mastermind of the bombing plot and the man who conceived an elaborate plan to burn down the entire city, did indeed consider himself a union man first, a good Democrat second. (J. B. McNamara did not embrace communism until well after he was behind bars, where he denounced Samuel Gompers and the union movement.) By and large the American public reacted with revulsion toward the bombings and felt ashamed that they had been duped into believing in the McNamaras' innocence. The claim that they were framed was to its generation what the claim that Iraq possessed weapons of mass destruction was to our own. Calculated disinformation—agitprop.

In the end, American workers turned out to be the chief victims—not just those who were killed in the bombing but also those who saw the movement toward unionization and better working conditions grind to a halt, not to revive until the Roosevelt years—a generation and a Great Depression ahead. When it did, no one wanted to revisit the McNamara case. It is as if those same workers, aware of the impact of the crimes perpetrated by many of their leaders in the first decade of the twentieth century, conspired to bury those events in the dark recesses of history.

Today the monument in Hollywood Forever Cemetery stands as a testimonial to Santayana's admonition that "Those who cannot remember the past are condemned to repeat it."

What the past century ought to have taught us is that the slow march of rational men will sooner or later win lasting social victories and that those won by violent means have generally proved to be transitory at best and counterproductive at worst. Who could have foreseen the sudden collapse of the Soviet Union—without a shot being fired—a generation ago or the peaceful development of a thriving market economy in Vietnam?

And, by the same token, is there anyone who still believes that the invasion of Iraq did not create more chaos and misery than ever existed under Saddam's dictatorship?

It is ironic that if there is any hero of this tale, it is Ortie McManigal, the man responsible for carrying out a relentless campaign of industrial sabotage unlike any other in history but who nevertheless had the courage in the end to say, "No more!" The man who recognized that the militant madness that had whipped up around him would, like a howling hurricane, eventually take more innocent lives.

McManigal might well have nodded in agreement with Theodore Roosevelt's assessment of the McNamara case. Reacting to those "foolish sentimentalists" who urged that the brothers be regarded with sympathy because they were struggling in a war on behalf of their class, the former president pointed out that all of their victims had been "laboring people."

"Murder," Roosevelt said succinctly, "is murder."

Epilogue

In March 1913 Clarence and Ruby Darrow finally packed up their belongings and prepared to leave L.A., the city in which they had known only misery. After nearly two years, they were returning to Chicago. One afternoon before leaving, Darrow was walking down Broadway with Earl Rogers and his young assistant, Jerry Giesler, when he spotted a tailor shop. "Come in here, Jerry," he said. They walked in and Darrow bought Giesler an overcoat. "That's the only fee I received for working in his two trials," Giesler would later write, "but the photograph I have of myself standing between Mr. Darrow and Mr. Rogers is worth far more to me than any fee."

Before heading to Chicago, Darrow and Ruby stopped first in San Francisco and went by car to San Quentin prison in nearby San Rafael. Darrow had hoped to bid a final goodbye to his former clients, the McNamaras, but the warden refused his visitation request.

Darrow had quietly managed to come away with most of the money he had received from the AF of L, but his reputation for being a bit money hungry would grow. Shortly after his return to Chicago, he expanded his criminal law practice. After winning a difficult case, his grateful client asked, "How can I ever show my appreciation, Mr. Darrow?" Darrow's response was classic capitalism: "Ever since the Phoenicians invented money, there has been only one answer to that question."

Paul Jordan Smith, who served as literary editor of the *Los Angeles Times* for twenty-five years, recalled in a 1969 interview that as an idealistic youth, he once met Darrow, whom he had long admired. "We all knew you could not be guilty of bribery," he recalled remarking at the time, to which, to his surprise, Darrow replied, "When you're up against a bunch of crooks you will have to play their game. Why shouldn't I?"

Ortie McManigal spent but a year in jail, much of that time traveling to Indianapolis and San Francisco to testify in the trials of union officials. Shortly after his release he shaved off his mustache to avoid being recognized by the many unionists who would have taken great pleasure in killing him. He became the principal witness in the trials of Caplan, Schmidt, and the San Francisco and Indianapolis union leaders. In November 1913 he was released "for his health" and soon found himself "adrift as a friendless cork on the sea of life." A *Los Angeles Times* reporter, visiting him at his "little bungalow" in Los Angeles in 1916, discovered that he was living there with his wife and children. The sight of them, he wrote, "occasioned some surprise as it was generally known that Mrs. McManigal deserted her husband following his confession." A photographer snapped their picture. (Ortie, for good reason, remained camera-shy.) The picture was captioned: "Dynamiter's Family His Own Again." A slight book that he wrote about his experiences sold well, and he invested some of the money in property in Honduras and lived there for a time, beginning in 1916. William Burns later wrote that he had assigned McManigal to an overseas position. To enhance his disguise, he gained a great deal of weight, "looking as fat as the proverbial stuffed pig," one journalist reported. He changed his name to W. E. Mack, and for twelve years, beginning in 1932, served as a watchman at the Los Angeles Hall of Records, a building he had once been assigned to blow up.

John Fredericks would attempt to parlay the acclaim he had received in the McNamara-Darrow cases into higher political office by running for governor of California. In 1914 he received the Republican Party's nomination but went on to lose to the reform-minded and General Otis–hating incumbent, Hiram Johnson, who had switched from the Republican to the Progressive Party. Losing didn't keep Fredericks down, as he went on to become a US congressman from California's Tenth District, serving two terms.

Job Harriman ran for mayor of Los Angeles again in 1913 and this time lost by a mere eight hundred votes. Frustrated, he and several partners went on to purchase two thousand acres of land near Big Rock Creek, California, and founded a utopian society based on Socialist models and ideals that attracted nearly one thousand residents. Five years later he founded another in Leesville, Louisiana. Tuberculosis, however, forced him to return to Southern California, where he died in 1925.

Lincoln Steffens would never completely overcome the ridicule heaped upon him in the aftermath of his claims about settling the McNamara case. In 1919 he paid a visit to the Soviet Union and returned to make his famous pronouncement about communism and the future. But his infatuation with the Soviets wouldn't last, and by the early 1930s he had become disillusioned with Stalin as well. He published his memoir, *The Autobiography of Lincoln Steffens*, in 1931, which became an enormous best seller and modern-day classic.

In the aftermath of the trials, General Otis retreated further from the daily operation of his newspaper, while his son-in-law marshaled the family business. With the outbreak of the Great War, Otis actually advocated isolationism until the United States joined the allies in 1917, at which point the General's jingoistic instincts took over. Later that year, on July 30, the old man's heart failed him. He was buried in his uniform. His *Los Angeles Times* would become a media empire, the newspaper alone generating a circulation in excess of 1.5 million at its peak, his grandsons and great-grandsons, Norman and Otis Chandler, becoming newspaper titans of unprecedented influence. His cherished home, The Bivouac, was donated to the county and became the Otis Art Institute.

In 1912 Olaf A. Tveitmoe and Eugene Clancy were convicted by an Indianapolis court of conspiracy in the *Los Angeles Times* bombing, and both were sentenced to six years at Leavenworth, where they would join Frank Ryan. Thirty-five of fifty-four labor codefendants were also convicted and given sentences ranging from one to six years. Tveitmoe's sentence, however, was overturned on appeal, and he returned to San Francisco as a hero to his vastly diminished membership in the Building Trades Council. He died on March 19, 1923, at age fifty-eight.

William J. Burns would go on to see fame and fortune, becoming the first director of the federal government's new Bureau of

Investigation, which was later enhanced by his successor, J. Edgar Hoover, to become the Federal Bureau of Investigation. He served in the post for only three years, until 1924, when he began earning a small fortune writing "true detective" stories for the New York newspapers and national magazines. After his retirement, he continued writing until his death in April 1932 in Sarasota, Florida. His firm is now the Burns International Security Services, and is the largest private security firm in America.

In July 1914 William J. Burns learned of a bomb that had gone off and killed three anarchists in New York City. The bomb was reported to have been "made of the same material and in the same fashion as the one which blew up the Los Angeles Times Building." Similar bombs had been detonated at St. Patrick's Cathedral and outside the Church of St. Alfonsus in New York City. In the ensuing investigation, Burns put under surveillance a man who was believed to be an associate of the men who had died. Moreover, he was said to have had "a bad eye." On February 13, 1915, Burns and New York City Police Captain Deevey arrested him at a small flat on Manhattan's west side. His name, he admitted to Burns, was Matthew Schmidt. He was now thirty-four years old and working as a mechanic.

Five days later William Burns's son Sherman approached a small shack on Bainbridge Island on Puget Sound. David Caplan was in bed when Burns and his fellow detectives pounded on the door.

"Hello, David," Sherman said as he entered the cabin.

"I know who you are," Caplan replied, rising from his bed. "I am ready to go back to Los Angeles and face the music."

Caplan then dressed and was promptly hauled off to Port Orchard, and then to L.A.. In the two-room shack made of forest wood, Sherman Burns found a few guns, volumes of Caplan's beloved Tolstoy, and of course a small arsenal of dynamite.

Caplan was convicted of manslaughter for complicity in the dynamiting of the Times Building and was sentenced to ten years at San Quentin, where he served seven. Matthew Schmidt was sentenced to life there but would serve twenty-two years.

J. J. McNamara would be released from San Quentin after serving a little over nine years. Upon his release he was taken back into the arms of his old union in Indianapolis. It was as if he had never left. He was soon charged with blackmail for threatening the destruction of the local Elks Club Building under construction if the builders did not employ union ironworkers. He again landed in prison. After his release he was found to have embezzled $200 from union coffers, whereupon he lost his principal means of employment. For what remained of his life, the young, promising, handsome secretary-treasurer of the Bridge and Structural Iron Workers' union would become a drifter.

His brother's life in prison, on the other hand, seemed to take on a sense of purpose. J. B. McNamara became a hero to the most radical Socialists and Communists worldwide, as he announced his allegiance to the Soviet Union and prolifically expounded on his belief in communism from his San Quentin Prison cell. In a letter dated February 10, 1924, he wrote to a friend, "You and [J. J.] should not consider me. The movement comes first." In the same letter, he remarked, "I was sorry to see Lenin go .... He was honest and sincere." He ridiculed Samuel Gompers for being "too far removed from the rank and file."

When Clarence Darrow's autobiography, *The Story of My Life*, was published in 1932, J. B. wrote a letter of endorsement to the publisher, Charles Scribners Sons, that expressed his feelings for his former attorney: "If the Gods were to destroy civilization, and decided on saving those who lived Christian lives according to the precepts handed down by the 'Creator,' they could be removed to safety with a Ford, in one trip. Darrow would be one of them, and the rear seat would be empty." Eight years later, in 1940, J. B. was diagnosed with cancer and taken to a San Francisco hospital where he was treated. The fight, however, was hopeless.

"I've come back home to San Quentin to die," he told the warden. As he approached his sixtieth birthday, the n'er-do-well from Indianapolis, the man who had killed twenty men, joined his victims on March 8, 1941. J. J. would follow him just two months later, on May 9, 1941, in Butte, Montana.

During his career Earl Rogers represented seventy-seven men accused of murder, losing only three times—an astonishing record. The

Times bombing had transformed him. The man who had lurched away from the smoldering building denouncing "the murderous fiends, the paranoiac assassins," told the jury at the conclusion of Darrow's first trial: "When all men in this country get their rights, when all have work, when all are equal there will be no dynamiting . . . but so long as there are hungry babes while others are living on the fat of the land, there will be violence." But by the time the second Darrow trial ended, his life was dissolving in the bottom of a highball glass. His wife divorced him but not before attempting to have him committed to a state mental hospital, a move that he protested in court. At the Norwalk, California, hospital he ran into Horace Appel, who had gone off the deep end and had delusions that he was one of the wealthiest men in the world. "Every morning," he would later recall, "Horace used to bring me a check for a million dollars. The real reason that I left there was because I found out that his bank account was slightly overdrawn." Shortly after his discharge, he would tell Adela, "I don't want to live long enough for them to say, 'There goes poor old Earl Rogers.'"

Within a few years he would drink himself to death.

The daughter would strike out on her own path, becoming the legendary Adela Rogers St. Johns, editor of the *Los Angeles Herald,* living a long life at the center of history and telling wonderful tales about her experiences, some of which she recounted in Warren Beatty's 1981 film *Reds.* She would die in 1988 at the age of ninety-four.

Rogers's devoted assistant, Jerry Giesler, would become more famous than his mentor, coming to represent theater mogul Alexander Pantages and actor Errol Flynn, who had been charged with statutory rape. He would defend Robert Mitchum against charges of possession of marijuana, Charlie Chaplin against violation of the Mann Act, and gangster Bugsy Siegel against murder charges. By the time of his death, his would be a household name as Hollywood's premier celebrity attorney.

Giesler never forgot the pyrotechnic Earl Rogers, and he would help see to it that no one else did either. He, along with Adela, would keep alive the stories of the man they loved, stories that would eventually reach the ear and pen of an attorney-turned-writer, Erle Stanley Gardner. A decade after Rogers's death, Gardner would bring him back, bigger than real life, as Perry Mason.

In the end it was the alcoholic attorney who seemed to have come closest to grasping what the bombing of the Los Angeles Times Building and its furious aftermath had been all about. Rogers had seen the tragedy from many points of view—as a prosecutor, a defender, a victim—and occupied the lonely ground of a moderate in this drama of extremes.

Joe Scott would become one of the best-loved citizens of Los Angeles and would eventually place Herbert Hoover's name in nomination for reelection at the 1932 Republican National Convention, but the *Times* would forever regard him as a turncoat, and Otis would attack him relentlessly. In 1913 Scott sued Otis and the *Times* for libel in three separate instances, winning judgments of nearly $70,000 (about $1.3 million today).

The *Pastime* boat would once again be linked to wrongdoing. It was sold to new owners, who also thought it would ideally conceal their illicit cargo. It was eventually confiscated by federal authorities, and its crew were convicted of using it to smuggle Chinese coolies.

The *Times* itself thrived under three generations of Chandlers throughout most of the twentieth century, but the Chandler dynasty ended when Otis Chandler stepped down in 1980. In 2000 it was acquired by Chicago's Tribune Corp., and in what was later referred to as "the deal from hell," a group headed by investor Sam Zell acquired Tribune in 2007 in an $8.5 billion leveraged buyout that loaded the company with such crushing debt that it collapsed into bankruptcy two years later. With hundreds of journalists jettisoned in recent years to cut costs, the *Times* is barely a shadow of its former self.

And lest they be forgot, these are the names of those who died in the bombing of the *Los Angeles Times* on October 1, 1910:

Churchill Harvey-Elder, assistant city editor

Wesley Reaves, private secretary to Harry Chandler

Harry L. Craus, assistant telegraph editor

R. L. Sawyer, telegraph operator

John Howard, compositor

J. C. Galiher, Linotype operator

Grant Moore, machinist

Edward Wasson, corrector

Elmer Frink, Linotype operator

Eugene Caroen, Linotype operator

Frank Underwood, compositor

Fred Llewellyn, Linotype operator

Charles Haggerty, pressman

Charles Gulliver, compositor

Carl Sallada, Linotype operator

Howard Courdaway, floor walker

Don E. Johnson, Linotype operator

Harry L. Flynn, Linotype operator

W. G. Tunstall, Linotype operator

Ernest A. Jordan, Linotype operator

(The apparent remains of one or two others were found in the wreckage of the building but were never identified.)

At the dedication of the monument to them at Hollywood Cemetery, the Rev. Robert J. Burdette concluded his eulogy by saying:

"Fragrant with honor be their names forever. Green as the palms that will wave above them in Hollywood be their memories. Everlasting peace to the lives that toiled and suffered. God's will, His righteous will, His will of justice—be done!"

ENDNOTES

1   When he eventually took over the *Los Angeles Times,* he gave orders to his staff that Santa Barbara was to be regarded as outside the newspaper's coverage area and that if mentioned at all, it was to be as an undesirable location. For example, they were never to report that an earthquake had occurred in Los Angeles. Earthquakes were bad for business. Instead reporters for the paper were to write that the earthquakes had originated in Santa Barbara.

2   When he arrived at Herbert Hockin's office in Chicago the next day, he was greeted with a volley of vituperation. Hockin clutched in his hand a newspaper account of an explosion that had wrecked a railroad bridge in Mount Vernon, Indiana.

"You will not be paid," Hockin told him. "You were directed to go to Mount Vernon, Illinois, not Mount Vernon, Indiana, and you have taken it upon yourself to blow up a bridge."

McManigal waited for a break in Hockin's rant, then told him that he knew nothing about the bridge in Indiana, that he had gone to Mount Vernon, Illinois, as assigned, and had pulled off the job on schedule.

A few days later he returned to Hockin's office and showed him a newspaper clipping about the results of his job in Mount Vernon, Illinois. Hockin offered no apology, merely informing McManigal that he had since learned that the Mount Vernon, Indiana, job had been pulled off by striking coal miners. (The Iron Workers were not the only ones attempting to cripple recalcitrant businesses.)

3   This name is sometimes also spelled Tvietmoe.

4   As secretary-treasurer of the California Building Trades Union, Tveitmoe was a charter member of the Asian Exclusion League founded in San Francisco in 1905 to protect the jobs of white workers through the exclusion of Asian immigrants and Asian Americans not only from labor unions but also from the workplace in general. In *Organized Labor,* a publication that he edited, Tvietmoe warned: "The almond-eyed Mongolian is watching for his opportunity, waiting to assassinate you and your children with one of his many maladies." San Francisco, he asserted, must cease being "an asylum for these Silurian ghosts."

Indeed, nonwhites were often unable to find work in anything but the most menial jobs in union cities like San Francisco, New York, and Chicago. They were barred from membership in virtually all the unions there. Many of them, Asians from the North, African Americans from the South, and Mexicans from the Southwest, therefore migrated to cities such as Los Angeles, where the open shop prevailed. Indeed, businesses in Los Angeles, including the *Times,* encouraged the migration partly as a means of keeping white workers in their place. Black-owned newspapers helped put out the word. Jefferson Lewis Edmonds's Los Angeles Liberator let it be known that blacks "will find no race problem in Los Angeles, only prosperity." "This is the city after all," wrote Frederick Madison Roberts in *The New Age*.

5   The Home Colony would eventually break up in 1919, unable to cope with a schism over the issue of nude swimming, or what came to be called "the battle between nudes and prudes."

6   At the same time, across the country, 75,000 members of the Lady Garment Workers Union went on strike in New York to protest against sweatshop conditions there. The massive strike—unprecedented in America at the time—made headlines everywhere. Not a word about it was published in the *Times*.

7   Hotel records would later show that they kept their rooms until September 28, always carried the keys to their rooms with them, did not eat meals at the hotel, and did not sleep in their rooms on the nights of September 20, 22, and 23.

8   McNamara and Caplan had assumed the names of two mine owners who were then warring with the Western Federation of Miners at their mines in Goldfield, California.

9   Heading the bill at the Pantages was that "renowned expert of fistic art, Robert Fitzsimmons." Johnson made it clear that he was more impressed with the ex-heavyweight champ's talk about his formidable fights and the "fistic art" in general than he was with Mrs. Fitzsimmons, who also appeared on the stage and sang some turn-of-the-century melodies in a vain attempt to impart some "class" to her pugilistic husband. (Part of the champ's onstage spiel: "I never did like prize fighting. I just liked the money. Now things are in a bad way with a Negro whipping the finest kind of a white man and everybody is mad. As sure as you live, there was a 'nigger in the woodpile' in the Jeffries-Johnson fight, and it is the business of the sporting public to find out who he is.")

    Drama critic Johnson had apparently paid little attention to another songbird well down the list on the Pantages bill, one Sophie Tucker, who was billed as "The Twentieth Century Singer; New York's Latest Noise in Vaudeville." In her later years she would be billed as "The Last of the Red Hot Mamas" and become a veritable entertainment institution. Nor would Johnson have had the occasion to mention the fifth act on the bill at the Orpheum, one Al Jolson, "Late Star of Dockstader's Minstrels," the country's leading minstrel organization. Jolson would one day speak the first words in a sound movie, *The Jazz Singer*, but at this time not even a silent movie had ever been filmed in its entirety in Los Angeles.

10   Sawyer was regarded as one of the top telegraph operators on the West Coast for his ability to translate quickly and accurately the dot-and-dash Morse code into alphanumeric characters. Auto racing was a new and bloody affair that, in its infancy, was capturing the imagination of the American public. This year's contest on the Long Island Motor Parkway would be emblematic of all the reasons why: A crash would kill four spectators; twenty-four would be injured. A quarter million people

would gather along the route where race cars reached the unheard-of top speed of 102 miles per hour and averaged 65. Ordinary automobiles, by contrast, traveled at about the same speed as horse-drawn carriages. Nationwide, lynchings still outnumbered automobile deaths.

11 The telephone number in Burns's original account was redacted. Named telephone prefixes were always spelled with the first two letters capitalized, to indicate that they were the only ones to be dialed.

12 Indeed, US Supreme Court Justice Joseph McKenna had observed in a similar case, "The foundation of extradition between the states is that the accused should be a fugitive from justice from the demanding state, and he may challenge the fact by habeas corpus immediately upon his arrest. If he refute the fact he cannot be removed."

13 There is probably nothing sinister in the line about Jim and Eral "working at bumpers." The *Dictionary of American Slang* gives no definition of the word "bumper," which would appear to rule out the possibility that the men were engaged in any criminal activity (like "bumping off" people). They were probably just making automobile or carriage bumpers. The letter is reproduced in its entirety here because it serves as a fascinating insight into the character of J. B. McNamara—that he saved this barely literate note for nearly two years. Evidently, a friendly message like this was, for J. B., something to treasure.

14 Several years earlier, an item in *Bridgemen's* said in part: "While Section 27 of the international constitution provides that the secretary-treasurer shall make a monthly report of all money received and expended and publish same in the official journal, it is the opinion of the executive board that it would be well to omit at least a portion of this report during our strike against the American Bridge and other companies. This being our opinion, the secretary-treasurer is hereby instructed to omit publication of expenditures and recapitulations until further instructions are given." Nevertheless, McNamara, in his train interview, told the *Examiner* reporter, "All expenditures must be officially sanctioned and accounts audited."

15 He was carrying another burden. His wife had died of acute peritonitis a few days earlier, leaving him to arrange for the care of their three small children.

16 The documents even contained records of money paid out to blackmailers who threatened to expose the dynamite plot. In one, J. J. McNamara wrote about plans to kill an ex-girlfriend who was blackmailing him.

Bibliography

Books

Adamic, Louis, *Dynamite: The Story of Class Violence in America*, Peter Smith Publisher Inc., 1963.

Babcock, Gwendolyn Garland, *The Ancestry of Harry Chandler* (online).

Baillie, Hugh, *High Tension: The Recollections of Hugh Baillie*, Harper Bros., 1959.

Bonelli, William G., *Billion Dollar Blackjack: The Story of Corruption and the* Los Angeles Times, Civic Research Press, 1954.

Burns, William J., *The Masked War*, George F. Doran Company, 1913 (also "My Greatest Cases – No. 10: Solving the *Los Angeles Times* Holocaust," *True Detective Magazine*, October 1931).

Carr, Harry, *Los Angeles, City of Dreams*, Appleton-Century, 1935.

Caughey, John and LaRee, *Los Angeles, Biography of a City*, University of California Press, 1976.

Cowan, Geoffrey, *The People v. Clarence Darrow*, Times Books/Random House, 1993.

Darrow, Clarence, *Attorney for the Damned*, Simon and Schuster, 1957.

-- *The Story of My Life*, Charles Scribner's Sons, 1904.

Giesler, Jerry, *The Jerry Giesler Story*, Simon and Schuster, 1960.

Goldman, Emma, *Living My Life*, Alfred A. Knopf, 1931.

Gottlieb, Robert, and Irene Wolt, *Thinking Big: The Story of the* Los Angeles Times, G. P. Putnam's Sons, 1977.

Haywood, William D., *The Autobiography of William D. Haywood*, International Publishers, 1929.

Hunter, Robert, *Violence and the Labor Movement*, Macmillan, 1914.

McDougal, Dennis, *Privileged Son*, Perseus Press, 2001.

McManigal, Ortie, *The National Dynamite Plot*, The Neal Company, 1913.

McWilliams, Carey, *Southern California: An Island on the Land*, Peregrine Smith Books, 1983.

Robinson, W. W., *Bombs and Bribery*, Unknown Publisher and Date.

St. Johns, Adela Rogers, *Final Verdict*, Doubleday & Company, 1962.

Starr, Kevin, *Inventing the Dream*, Oxford University Press, 1985.

Steffens, Lincoln, *The Autobiography of Lincoln Steffens*, Harcourt, Brace and Company, 1936.

Stimson, Grace Heilman, *Rise of the Labor Movement in Los Angeles*, University of California Press, 1955.

Stone, Irving, *Clarence Darrow for the Defense,* Doubleday, Doran & Company, 1941
(also assorted research papers, letters, and interview notes for this book at the
University of California, Berkeley).
Wood, Charles Erskine Scott, *Earthly Discourse,* Vanguard Press, 1937.

Newspapers and Periodicals
Appeal to Reason, 1909–1912
The Bridgemen's Magazine, 1909–1910
Chicago Examiner, 1910–1911
Chicago Tribune, 1910–1911
Indianapolis Star, 1910–1911
Los Angeles Examiner, 1910–1913
Los Angeles Herald, 1910–1913
Los Angeles Record, 1909–1911
Los Angeles Times, 1894–1914
New York Times, 1910–1913
San Francisco Chronicle, 1910–1911
San Francisco Examiner, 1910–1911

Interviews
Norman Chandler, 1964
Oscar Lawler, 1964
Adela Rogers St. Johns, 1965

E-mail Correspondence
Harry Chandler, 2009

Other
The McNamara Papers, University of Cincinnati

Index

ABOUT THE AUTHOR

Lew Irwin has had a hand in nearly every facet of the news media. His career in journalism began in high school at the *Los Angeles Times,* where he researched a sports trivia column. While still an undergraduate at USC, he tried his hand at news announcing and in 1955 began hosting *News Today,* a nationally syndicated radio program whose regular contributors included Eleanor Roosevelt, Randolph Churchill, and the legendary commentator H. V. Kaltenborn.

Two years later he became the first anchor/reporter at KABC-TV, where his investigative reports earned him numerous awards and the praise of national figures such as poet Carl Sandburg, who wrote, "I could make a case that he is one of the greatest reporters in America today." For the next fifteen years, Irwin's was a familiar face and voice in Southern California as he anchored television news programs or directed the news operations of leading radio stations, always adding his hallmark—a flair for humor and for pointing out the extraordinary. In 1968 he produced and hosted *The Credibility Gap* on Los Angeles radio station KRLA, which integrated topical satire and music with the news. *Time* and *Newsweek* wrote full-page articles about it, and it was featured in a long segment on the *CBS Evening News* with Walter Cronkite.

Following that, Irwin produced and hosted more than a half dozen syndicated radio series, including, from 1972 to 1985, *Earth News Radio,* which launched independent, bartered syndicated radio.

Since 1992 he has been the publisher/editor of the online *Studio Briefing,* a daily digest focusing on the events and issues affecting the entertainment industry. In 1995 he wrote *SINATRA: The Pictorial Biography.*